RETHINKING THE HOLLYWOOD TEEN MOVIE

RETHINKING THE HOLLYWOOD TEEN MOVIE

Gender, Genre and Identity

Frances Smith

EDINBURGH
University Press

Edinburgh University Press is one of the leading university presses in the UK. We publish academic books and journals in our selected subject areas across the humanities and social sciences, combining cutting-edge scholarship with high editorial and production values to produce academic works of lasting importance. For more information visit our website: edinburghuniversitypress.com

© Frances Smith, 2017

Edinburgh University Press Ltd
The Tun – Holyrood Road
12 (2f) Jackson's Entry
Edinburgh EH8 8PJ

Typeset in 10/12.5pt Sabon by
Servis Filmsetting Ltd, Stockport, Cheshire

A CIP record for this book is available from the British Library

ISBN 978 1 4744 1309 1 (hardback)
ISBN 978 1 4744 1310 7 (webready PDF)
ISBN 978 1 4744 1311 4 (epub)

The right of Frances Smith to be identified as author of this work has been asserted in accordance with the Copyright, Designs and Patents Act 1988 and the Copyright and Related Rights Regulations 2003 (SI No. 2498).

CONTENTS

List of Figures	vi
Acknowledgements	viii
1. Introduction	1
2. Rethinking the Teen Movie	7
3. Acting Up: Performing Masculine Delinquency in the Teen Movie	21
4. Making Over: Gender and Class at the High School Prom	64
5. Looking Back: Nostalgia, Postfeminism and the Teen Movie	105
6. Becoming Other: The Posthuman and the Teen Movie	146
7. Conclusion: Not Another Teen Movie?	185
Bibliography	192
Filmography	203
Index	209

FIGURES

3.1	Jim (James Dean) is first seen lying drunk in the street	27
3.2	Jim (James Dean) deceives Plato (Sal Mineo)	36
3.3	Danny (John Travolta) is granted a star entrance in *Grease*	40
3.4	Danny (John Travolta) and Sandy (Olivia Newton-John) arrive at the dance competition	46
3.5	J.D. (Christian Slater) watches the bullying unfold	57
4.1	A subculture: Andie (Molly Ringwald), Duckie (Jon Cryer) and Iona (Annie Potts)	73
4.2	Andie (Molly Ringwald) makes her dress	77
4.3	Andie (Molly Ringwald) tentatively enters the prom venue	78
4.4	Zack (Freddie Prinze Jr) notices his picture	83
4.5	Zack (Freddie Prinze Jr) is surprised by Laney's (Rachel Leigh Cooke) appearance after her makeover	86
4.6	Cady (Lindsay Lohan) meets the Plastics (Rachel McAdams, Lacey Chabert, Amanda Seyfried) for the first time	94
4.7	Cady (Lindsay Lohan) is crowned Spring Fling Queen	100
5.1	Mel's Drive-In	112
5.2	John (Paul Le Mat) and his yellow Ford Deuce	114
5.3	The Wolfman as myth	120
5.4	The Wolfman in reality	120
5.5	Baby (Jennifer Grey) is held over the audience at the conclusion of *Dirty Dancing*	131
5.6	Olive (Emma Stone) creates a spectacle of sexuality	137

5.7	Olive (Emma Stone) and Todd (Penn Badgley) re-create moments from Eighties teen movies	141
6.1	Peter Parker (Tobey Maguire) is positioned outside the high school community	154
6.2	Spider-Man (Tobey Maguire) and Mary-Jane (Kirsten Dunst) kiss	159
6.3	Bella (Kristen Stewart) swiftly finds friends at Forks High School	164
6.4	Bella's (Kristen Stewart) entrance recalls the makeover scenes of *She's All That*	171
6.5	Teen with a movie camera	174
6.6	Andrew (Dane DeHaan) is filmed by onlookers	181

ACKNOWLEDGEMENTS

This book started out life as a PhD thesis undertaken at the University of Warwick's department of Film and Television Studies. I have to thank Catherine Constable and Rachel Moseley for so diligently training me in the art of critical theory and textual analysis. At Edinburgh University Press, I thank Gillian Leslie and Richard Strachan for wholeheartedly supporting the project from the outset. The book's manuscript was read by Timothy Shary, and it has been improved immeasurably as a result of his insights. I'm also grateful to the anonymous readers, who provided valuable suggestions at the proposal stage. This book was written while at University College London's Writing Lab. Here, I thank all the tutors for your enthusiasm and conversations – you spark ideas more often than you know. Finally, for their constant support and encouragement, I thank my family; my parents, David, and George. And of course, the wonderful Mr Metcalf, for always being there.

1. INTRODUCTION

A telling incident occurs near the beginning of *She's All That* (Robert Iscove, 1999), a reworking of *Pygmalion* that was typical of the highly allusive cycle of teen movies in the late 1990s. The film introduces us to Zack Siler (Freddie Prinze Jr), who is not only the class president and captain of the football team, but also an A-grade student with a probable Ivy League future. To no great surprise, he later adds Prom King to these accolades. It is in this context that we view the character walking into school and spotting a photo portrait of himself which bears the caption, 'Zack Siler: Student Body President 1999'. Seemingly instinctively, he quickly moves his features into the smile and pose seen in the photograph. Although Zack is characterised by confidence and success, this brief moment reveals that this is an identity that has not emerged by chance, but is the result of continuous, repeated labour. He must work to assume the idealised figure crystallised in his photo, demonstrating that this is not an identity that Zack feels he has fully realised. The construction of teenage identities, witnessed through such moments of becoming and contestation, is the particular focus of this book on the Hollywood teen movie.

The sustained examination of the construction of identity differs from existing scholarship on the genre. Timothy Shary has provided a comprehensive overview of the Hollywood teen movie, and has delineated many of its sub-genres and shorter-lived cycles. In turn, Thomas Doherty supplies historical context, viewing the marked increase in the youth demographic in the 1950s as the impetus for Hollywood henceforth targeting the arsenal of its marketing efforts principally towards teenagers. Elsewhere, Catherine Driscoll has taken the discussion beyond Hollywood, to argue that the teen film is a transnational construct that embraces many other film-making contexts. Still others have entered the fray, with teen-oriented television and the role of music and subcultures now well-trodden avenues for academic endeavour.[1] Each of these scholars has demonstrated that the teen movie, and that put forward by Hollywood in particular, is a fruitful avenue for scholarship.

Yet clear consistencies remain. Shary sees what he terms the 'youth movie' as one that provides a representation of real American teenagers (2014: 1–2). Furthermore, Robin Wood argues that the teen movie of the 1990s, which he observes to be a particularly productive period in the genre's history, provides an indication of 'how young people would like things to be' (Wood 2003: 311). It is in this way, as a sociocultural artefact that reveals something about contemporary youth culture, that the Hollywood teen movie is predominantly seen to be of interest. Driscoll agrees, dismissing the aesthetic of the teen movie in favour of the sociological insights that might be gleaned from its study. As such, the aesthetic and narrative structures of the genre have been effectively sidelined. This book's stated ambition is to rethink the Hollywood teen movie. As I will demonstrate, it is the perspective – that the teen movie has little of aesthetic or narrative interest to detain us – that principally requires rethinking.

Part of the critical dismissal of the genre's aesthetic and narrative concerns can be traced to the teen movie's frequent designation as 'trash'. While brisk business at the box office and repeat viewings alike suggest that the films succeed at least in entertaining their audiences, there remains a sense that such works should not be the subject of sustained critical attention. Nonetheless, arguing in favour of studying the Hollywood teen movie, Adrian Martin proposes that their being popular and entertaining is sufficient to make them worthy of scrutiny (2009: 15). This argument has been so comprehensively taken on board that studies of popular culture now raise few eyebrows beyond some of the stuffier constituents of the popular press. Echoing George Mallory's assertion in relation to the considerably tougher task of climbing Everest, one can study the teen movie simply 'because it's there'.[2] It's certainly true that several examples of the teen genre are indeed derivative, with little to trouble traditional arbiters of quality. However, I suggest that this does not mean these films are somehow unworthy of close textual analysis. Attentiveness to the complex – often ambivalent – processes of identity construction within the teen movie require a keen eye for the particular uses of filmic elements – of *mise-en-scène*, of camerawork, and editing patterns, for instance – as well as areas that have previously been considered, such as the use of costume and soundtrack.

Martin supplies a further rationale for studying the genre, which has not been nearly so widely taken up. The teen movie, he argues, facilitates the exploration of liminality, 'the heightened moment of suspension between two conditions' (Martin 2009: 8). Held between the more stable constructs of childhood and adulthood, adolescence is an exemplar of the in-between state. This book aims to address the construction of liminality in the Hollywood teen movie. Jane Feuer notes in passing that the genre consists principally in a 'sexual coming of age narrative' (1993: 125), and this is how I also understand the teen movie's underpinning structure. As a result, I am especially attentive to the films' construction of gender as the key axis through which a move into adult identity is negotiated. A substantial proportion of Hollywood teen movies end in an idealised heterosexual romance. But attention to individual performance gestures, to the film's generic frame and to still other aesthetic elements often reveal the ambiguity that remains in many examples of such a seemingly uncomplicated, heteronormative conclusion.

Further to close textual analysis, this book's sustained examination of the construction of liminality is assisted by the use of critical theory. This ambition to theorise the identities in the teen movie is a clear departure from existing work on the genre. For some, the use of theory to examine film – and especially popular film – will be an unnecessary exercise in lily-gilding, which can only detract from close attention to the films themselves. However, these theories have not been arbitrarily selected. The book follows the chronological development of the genre, and with it, the theories and axes of identity gradually develop in complexity through each chapter. Thus, while 'Acting Up' is concerned with the construction of gender, 'Making Over' also takes in class, while 'Looking Back' reworks these ideas with a consideration of the construction of nostalgia. Lastly, theories of the posthuman support an analysis of recent teen movies whose characters encounter, and often become, something other than human. Critical theory supports, rather than masks, a close attention to the detail of these films.

In a further distinction from previous scholarship, this book aims not to create a comprehensive history of the Hollywood teen movie, but to provide an in-depth analysis of selected examples of the genre. A question might be posed here as to why the case studies need necessarily be plucked only from Hollywood cinema. To be sure, films about the lives of teenagers have been, and continue to be, produced in a number of other national and production contexts.[3] We might think in this regard of works such as *Mustang* (Deniz Gamze Ergüven, 2015) and *Bande des Filles* (Céline Sciamma, 2015), respectively Turkish and French releases, which secured widespread critical acclaim. Driscoll is particularly clear that teen film is a transnational phenomenon that embraces British and Japanese releases, *Bend it Like Beckham* (Gurinder Chadha, 2002) and *Akira* (Katsuhiro Otomo, 1988) as much as it does *The Breakfast Club* (John Hughes, 1985) and *Clueless* (Amy Heckerling, 1995) (Driscoll 2011). However, as will become clear in the following chapter, it is in Hollywood that the conventions of the teen movie were forged, and that ideas of adolescence were cemented in the popular imaginary.

Hollywood cinema, to be sure, is the dominant force in the global film industry. Its overwhelming influence is such that it has given rise to concerns that its supremacy will surely lead to the establishment of a global, American monoculture. Roz Kaveney's observations of the influence of Hollywood cinema in Britain demonstrate such a fear. For her, Hollywood has colonised the lives of British teenagers to such an extent that they now expect to conclude their school years at a prom and to vie for positions like 'Homecoming Queen' and 'Student Body President', which, prior to their popularisation through teen movies, were largely unknown to these shores (Kaveney 2006: 2). It is arguably as a result of the dominance of Hollywood that other cinemas have provided constructions of adolescence precisely as an alternative to the weight of these globally distributed, idealised narratives of American teendom. Despite the clear dominance of Hollywood, there are a number of well-known teen movies that have not been subject to extended critical scrutiny.[4] Consequently, it will be important to question the critical consensus that can build up around a film.

It should be acknowledged that examining Hollywood cinema as the default mode of the teen movie entails some replication of its flaws. In recent years, the popular and academic media have converged in their recognition that Hollywood is problematically lacking in diversity, particularly when it comes to the representation of people of colour. Even to cast a black actor as a stormtrooper – a fictional entity – as John Boyega was in one recent iteration of *Star Wars* (J. J. Abrams, 2015), is to court a vicious backlash from a frantically bigoted online commentariat.[5] The Hollywood teen movie is similarly conservative in its continued portrayal of predominantly white, able-bodied, middle-class characters. Only in *Chronicle* (Josh Trank, 2012), the most recent film examined in the book, is the class president played by a black actor, Michael B. Jordan (and even then, he is the first character to be killed). Recognising that the construction of adolescence in the Hollywood teen movie is a narrow one, this book also mentions in passing examples from elsewhere that help to provide a fuller picture.

This book has two principal aims: firstly, I focus on the construction of identity in the Hollywood teen movie, with the understanding that adolescence itself is a liminal construct in which identities emerge, morph and finally consolidate into adulthood. This is achieved through close textual analyses of significant examples of the genre, which are informed by key theoretical perspectives. It is through these means that the book's second aim will be achieved, namely to reposition the Hollywood teen movie as one with a particular narrative and aesthetic, as well as one that has value as a sociological artefact. As a result, the book secondarily aims to provide an alternative history of a genre that has previously been so well delineated into cycles and subgenres.

Accordingly, following a critical and historical overview of the genre, this book examines the construction of gender in the light of Judith Butler's conceptualisation of gender as performative. Butler does not directly address the question of adolescence, yet her contention that gender is constructed through a 'stylised repetition of acts' (Butler 1990: 185) chimes with the ephemerality and liminality of teenage gender identity, and adolescence more generally. What is more, Butler's theorisation of gender as 'never fully finalised' precisely parallels the heightened moment of becoming that constitutes adolescence.

Titled 'Acting Up', the chapter on juvenile delinquency is concerned with the star performances of three actors who play male rebel characters, the teen movie's most widely known archetype. Butler argues that there exists a discursive compulsion to cite particular gender norms. Yet even the juvenile delinquent, who supposedly flouts the rules, remains bound by gendered norms of behaviour. Indeed, their rebellion can itself be cast as a norm of youthful masculinity. Examination of the individual star performances of James Dean in *Rebel Without a Cause* (Nicholas Ray, 1955), John Travolta in *Grease* (Randal Kleiser, 1978) and Christian Slater in *Heathers* (Michael Lehmann, 1989) promises to dissect the particular performance gestures that constitute rebel masculinity. While these male rebels purport to eschew the norms of masculinity, these characters must grapple with their realisation that even rebellion itself is bound by particular rules.

The book progresses in a loosely chronological order, such that the following chapter begins with *Pretty in Pink* (Howard Deutch, 1986), one of the films with which teen movie pioneer John Hughes was associated, and a star vehicle for its principal player, Molly Ringwald. Building on the previous chapter, these analyses consider how social class inflects the construction of gender in Ringwald's film, as well as in *She's All That* and *Mean Girls* (Mark Waters, 2006). In all three of these films, the high school, and most particularly the high school prom, provide the denouement of the film's narratives. As will become apparent, the prom is a primary locus of gender and class expectations and is the subject of much concern on the part of the main characters and their peers alike. Titled 'Making Over', this chapter also examines the centrality of the makeover, a transformation concerned with the processes through which girls become a viable subject of the gender and class norms upheld by the prom.

Teen movies that have a relationship with the past are addressed in the following chapter. As Shary notes, all teen movies can be regarded as looking back into the past in a sense, since they are made by adults, who perhaps call on their own experiences for inspiration (Shary 2014: 2). Teenagers typically lack the means or experience necessary to direct or produce a mainstream teen movie themselves, such that all teen movies can be regarded as therefore inflected to a greater or lesser degree with a reflection of the director's own adolescence. Although one of this chapter's case studies, *American Graffiti* (George Lucas, 1973), is regarded as the paradigmatic nostalgia film, this chapter will demonstrate that the nostalgia of such films is not the straightforward, rose-tinted gaze into history with which the term is most commonly associated. In turn, *Dirty Dancing* (Emile Ardolino, 1987) mediates its representation of the early 1960s with a dance narrative and soundtrack that is tied to the late 1980s, while *Easy A* (Will Gluck, 2010) is a highly allusionist text whose protagonist desires a return to the gender mores of the 1980s teen movie.

The book's final chapter considers encounters with the Other in the teen movie. These films are analysed in the context of theoretical work on the posthuman, which provides a critical perspective on the tacit anthropocentrism that governs the assumptions of the previous chapters. *Spider-Man* (Sam Raimi, 2002) provides the chapter's first case study, allowing for an exploration of the construction of a character whose physicality has taken on that of a spider. In *Twilight* (Catherine Hardwicke, 2008) we see an encounter between a human and a vampire that provides an alternative perspective on human identity, desire and attractiveness. Through analysis of the film's audiences, too, we see how the teenage girl is herself constructed as something other than human. Finally, *Chronicle* sees the film apparatus merge with the subjectivity of its main character. The chapter titles themselves indicate that the book, the teenager, inhabits the present continuous, held at the point of becoming. Thus, moments of acting up, of making over, looking back and finally, becoming Other are considered in order to bring into focus the Hollywood teen movie as a sustained examination of the construction of identity.

Notes

1. We might think here of Ross and Stein (2008); Tropiano (2006); Kaveney (2006); Dennis (2006) and Woods (2016).
2. From an interview, 'Climbing Mount Everest is work for Supermen', *The New York Times* (18 March 1923); on being asked why he wanted to climb Mount Everest: 'Why did you want to climb Mount Everest?' [. . .] 'Because it's there.'
3. For a thorough discussion of some of the teen movies that have been made elsewhere, see Shary and Seibel (2007).
4. One such example is *Grease* (Randal Kleiser, 1978). Stephen Tropiano has published a book on the film (2011) which acknowledges some of the film's complexities. However, it is better conceived as a commemoration of the film than a close analysis.
5. See Wyatt (2014).

2. RETHINKING THE TEEN MOVIE

There have always been teenagers. But it was only in 1904 that American psychologist G. Stanley Hall's ground-breaking publication, *Adolescence: its Psychology and its Relations to Physiology, Anthropology, Sex, Crime and Education*, established the existence of a hitherto undocumented period of 'storm and stress' between childhood and adulthood (Hall 1904: 2). As the case studies in later chapters will demonstrate, it is this sense of liminality that motivates my interest in the construction of identity found in the Hollywood teen movie. Here, I address both the evolution of the on-screen teenager in Hollywood cinema and, in tandem, the various ways in which film scholars have conceived the teen movie as a genre. With this understanding of how the field has developed over time, I explain how this book aims to rethink the Hollywood teen movie.

Hall's conception of adolescence as a distinct developmental phase quickly gained ground, and was a key tenet of the movement calling for an end to child labour.[1] As Shary points out, for most teenagers in 1904 the time between childhood and adulthood was minimal, with the majority of Americans entering the labour market at 14 years of age (Shary 2002a: 3). It is therefore clear that the extended period of transition towards adulthood that Hall envisaged – he conceived adolescence as taking place between the ages of fourteen and twenty-four – was an unfeasible luxury out of the grasp of most people. Radical changes in the structure of social life would therefore be required if adolescence was to be recognised as a clear life stage; not least a compulsory, universal high school education.

One such seismic shift in the cultural landscape was the invention of cinema. Published in 1904, Hall's conception of adolescence as a specific phase of life is roughly coincident with the technological and cultural developments that encouraged the development of cinema as it is experienced today. By the 1920s, when cinemas peppered large American cities, gatherings of teenagers in these venues increased the visibility and understanding of adolescents as a definable group. While Shary ascribes greater importance to the growth of the multiplex in the 1970s as a site of teen congregation, Driscoll maintains that these earlier examples of teen gatherings were at least as significant, both in increasing the currency of Hall's work, and later, in developing films that cater to their tastes (2011: 13). Illustrating the interconnectedness of the teenager and the cinema by the mid-1920s, Driscoll refers to an article in *Photoplay* in which producer J. P. Schulberg describes the film industry as 'adolescent', given its potential, lack of formalisation, and, indeed, appeal to teenage audiences (Schulberg in Driscoll 2011: 5). Arguably, Hollywood cinema and adolescence as a sociocultural category possess a shared history, in which one contributes to the vitality of the other.

While the cinema has long provided a site of teenage congregation, the notion of a genre that specifically accommodates adolescent tastes is a relatively recent one. Such market stratification would have been antithetical to the proclivities of the Hollywood studios during the classical era, which typically courted as wide a range of audiences as possible (see Doherty 2002). For her part, Driscoll argues that for a film to be considered a teen movie, it must be primarily intended for an audience of teenagers. Indeed, she states that 'the teen film is determined most of all by its audience' (Driscoll 2011: 1). As a result, although the 1940s saw a spate of hugely popular teenage stars, not least Mickey Rooney, Judy Garland and Deanna Durbin, their 'wholesomeness, hard work and perseverance' signalled their appeal to an adult audience (Shary 2005: 8). In Driscoll's view, then, the presence of teenagers in a film is no guarantee that that film is a teen movie; rather, it is said to be defined by those characters' intended relationship with their audience.

By the 1950s, the demographic swell of teenagers would grow harder for studios to ignore.[2] Nonetheless, Thomas Doherty describes Hollywood's continued reluctance to engage in market research, with studio heads preferring to trust their instinctive feel for the market. To illustrate, the president of Columbia Pictures, Harry Cohn, reportedly delegated the matter to his behind, which, he claimed, would squirm during the screening of a likely flop (Doherty 2002: 49). The question of who was the audience for such films was not considered, since the answer – everyone – appeared to be obvious (Doherty 2002: 49). Yet the American teenager did not entirely pass Hollywood by. In contrast to their predecessors, this particular generation of teenagers possessed a strong sense of identity *as teenagers*, which was further encouraged by other forms of popular culture such as rock and roll music (Doherty 2002: 14). Such a strong sense of group identity, which often manifested itself in opposition to the older generation, facilitated the portrayal of teenagers in the popular media as delinquent tearaways, surely destined to fritter away American values and unprecedented economic prosperity. Teenagers, then, were not only a vitally lucrative cinema-going audience but also a sensational, spectacular threat to the dominant order, which could be exploited for commercial gain.

These two distinct opportunities – as a significant cinema-going audience and a source of moral panic – aligned in films depicting juvenile delinquency. Hollywood studios were assisted in this endeavour by the Supreme Court's 'Miracle Decision', which, in 1952, applied First Amendment rights to the motion picture.[3] Accordingly, studios were now able to depict hitherto forbidden content such as 'the sexuality of minors, crime and drug use' (Biltereyst 2007: 9). Significantly, Daniel Biltereyst argues that 1950s juvenile delinquency films such as *The Wild One* (László Benedek, 1953), *Blackboard Jungle* (Richard Brooks, 1955) and *Rebel Without a Cause* were intended as cautionary tales for wary, watchful parents, and as a general lament on the dramatic transformation in social values that teenagers were perceived to embody (Biltereyst 2007: 9). Certainly juvenile delinquency had been portrayed in Hollywood prior to the 1950s, particularly in the social problem films of the 1930s and 1940s. Those films depicted errant youth as the product of poverty and poor education. In contrast, the 1950s juvenile delinquent might be found in any ordinary suburban home, a fear encapsulated by the very title of *Knock on Any Door* (Nicholas Ray, 1949). While juvenile delinquency had previously been the product of destitution, the 1950s conceived the male rebel figure as the fruit of pampered, suburban prosperity.

Amanda Ann Klein's consideration of the 1950s juvenile delinquency films as a distinct cycle observes that studios had a tendency to cloak their salacious depictions of teenagers in the guise of public duty (2011: 103). Accordingly, *The Wild One* opens with the following call to arms: 'This is a shocking story. It could never take place in most towns – but it did in this one. This is a public challenge not to let it happen again.' Other appeals to parental vigilance are found within the films themselves. Driving to the Griffith Planetarium near the conclusion of *Rebel Without a Cause*, Jim's mother looks directly into the camera, ruminating that 'You read about things like this happening to other families, but you never dream it could happen to yours.' The intended audience for such films is clearly an adult one, as the films appear to cast a disdainful perspective on teenage behaviour.

Despite these indicators of the films' adult appeal, Doherty observes that these films somehow found favour with the era's teenagers (Doherty 2002: 57). Indeed, a Gilbert Youth Research Report from 1956 found that *Blackboard Jungle* was high school students' favourite film, and James Dean their actor of choice. Despite their overt adult address, then, the films evidently held some appeal for teenagers that escaped the stern warnings described above. Almost certainly, the film was intended for an audience of concerned adults, rather than their adolescent offspring. Yet its discovery by millions of teenagers, and their adoration of its star, James Dean, cannot be dismissed as an accident of history. I therefore argue that the film merits inclusion here as a teen movie.

The complex positioning and address of films like *Rebel Without a Cause* demonstrates the problems of defining the teen movies as a genre whose films intentionally target teen viewers. What is more, Doherty contends that ever since the 1950s, the American film industry in general has juvenilised, such that the majority of Hollywood releases now target a primarily teenage audience (Doherty 2002: 1). His thesis is corroborated by Wheeler Winston-Dixon's assessment of Hollywood in the 1990s (2000), and by still more recent scholars and critics of contemporary cinema who bemoan the dominance of the vitally lucrative PG13/12A-rated film.[4] Consequently, although Driscoll is surely correct that youth appeal is an important aspect in determining whether a film can be regarded as a teen movie, the near-ubiquitous targeting of this audience means that it cannot be the genre's sole identifying criterion. Alternative narrative or stylistic identifiers are needed to classify the teen movie as a genre in its own right.

Both Shary and Doherty agree in identifying *Rock Around the Clock* (Fred Sears, 1956) as the first film to be marketed to teens at the exclusion of their elders (Doherty 2002: 55; Shary 2005: 30). Indicating the influence of the juvenile delinquency film, *Rock Around the Clock* took up Bill Haley and the Comets' song of the same name, which had previously been used in the opening and closing scenes of *Blackboard Jungle* and was widely suspected to be a key element of the film's teen appeal (Doherty 2002: 57). Shot within a month on a shoestring budget, and featuring the rock and roll music favoured by youth audiences, Sears's film established the blueprint for a number of films specifically targeting teenagers in the 1950s and 1960s.

Established in 1954, American International Pictures spied an opportunity to produce other films that adhered to the formula established by *Rock Around the Clock*. The studio worked in short bursts of low-budget film cycles, among them the Rock Film, the Hot Rod Film, the Teen Horror and the Beach Film. Klein's discussion of the differences between the film cycle and the film genre is instructive here. The film genre, Klein argues, is characterised by repetition of key images and themes.[5] In contrast, the film cycle is defined by the more pragmatic considerations of how those images and themes are used. That is, the film cycle lives or dies by its immediate financial viability, and the currency of public discourses that surround it (Klein 2011: 4). In short, while a genre provides an enduring template for a series of films across an extended period, a cycle is intended to tap into what is doubtless a short-lived trend. Consequently, the cycle consists of concentrated bursts of films released over a short period of time. Film cycles rarely endure longer than five years, and must change to adapt to audiences' changing tastes and jaded palates.

The prioritisation of commercial rather than artistic ambition has characterised not only the teen movie, but academic perceptions of the genre. Certainly, the aggressive targeting of the teen audience from the mid-1950s onwards leads Doherty to designate the teen movie as a type of exploitation film (Doherty 2002: 2) – that is, to quote *Variety* journalist Hy Hollinger, a type of low-budget film 'based on controversial or timely subjects that made newspaper headlines ... engineered to appeal to "uncontrolled" juveniles and "undesirables"' (Hollinger 1956 in Doherty 2002: 9). What is at stake in Hollinger's designation of the exploitation film is a thinly veiled sneer at the youth audience's uncultivated tastes, the objects of which would be disparaged by more sophisticated cinema-goers. Any film containing the requisite teenage trends, be they hot rods or rock and roll music, would be guaranteed a sympathetic airing regardless of its 'quality', whose judgement remained in the eyes of a discerning few. Doherty concedes that subjects other than teenagers have featured in exploitation films.[6] Yet the teenage audience remains at least a secondary, if not the primary, intended audience in all cases (Doherty 2002: 9). Since the teen audience was so often targeted by studios like American International Pictures, the teen movie became predominantly associated with the designation of 'exploitation film'.

As will shortly become apparent, the teen movie has since developed beyond its origins as a low-budget exploitation genre. Yet its stain and concurrent associations of disregard for characterisation, innovation or style has had consequences for the teen movie being considered as an object worthy of critical analysis. Despite the critical as well as commercial success of the teen movie in the 1990s, Wood argues that the genre reveals 'how young people would like things to be' (Wood 2003: 311). Driscoll's more recent work echoes Wood's arguments, maintaining that 'teen film is generally thought more interesting for what it says about youth than for any aesthetic innovations' (Driscoll 2011: 2). Both scholars' assessment of the genre as interesting purely as a sociocultural artefact rather than an example of art is arguably founded in the teen movie's aspirations not only to entertain its audience, but also to make commercially profitable films. As such, for Wood, the genre bears the stench of capitalist enterprise, rather than that of the artist's bourgeois ego (2003: 209). This criticism could be meted out to any number of popular genres whose narratives are more formulaic than innovative. Yet it is perhaps because the teen movie coalesced into a genre in the period after the demise of the studio system, and primarily for economic ends at that, that such criticism has stuck particularly for the teen movie.

As a consequence of the teen movie's origins in exploitation, moral panic and commercial savvy, two interrelated critical consensuses have developed around the genre: the use of teen movies as sociocultural evidence of contemporary teenage life, as outlined above (Driscoll, Wood), and secondarily, a focus on how youths have been represented in fictional accounts of their lives (Considine; Shary). This latter tendency, which I will shortly describe more fully, is explained by the perceived vulnerability of the youth audience. Certainly, the perception of the teenage audience as artless naïfs without the discerning sensibilities of their more erudite elders is central to critics who deem the teen movie to lack stylistic merit.

Adult concern for the susceptibility of youths to the mass media is nothing new. Even Hall, writing years before the advent of the violent computer games and social media that now dominate discussions of the effect of media on the young, identified the mass media as a potential cause for concern. 'Inflamed with flash literature and "penny dreadfuls"', Hall argued, suggestible teens might be incited to commit a crime (Hall 1904: 361). For Driscoll, Hall's work on adolescence was key to the establishment of the highly conservative Hays Code in 1926, one of whose aims was to limit the exposure of children and teenagers to adult themes (Driscoll 2011: 6). Unease concerning the influence of the media on the young continues to this day, as studies increasingly call for the application of higher rating classifications for films that feature characters smoking (see Sargant, Tanski and Stoolmiller 2012). As such, teenagers continue to be constructed as the vulnerable objects of adult regulation and concern.

The first book-length study of teenagers in film, David Considine's *Cinema of Adolescence*, appears to draw on such discourses concerning the protection of teenagers and the need to regulate the images they see. Published in 1985, Considine deserves praise for providing such a wide-ranging account of an area that had hitherto received only limited attention. However, his approach is characterised by the belief that cinema functions like a mirror, which has the ability either to reflect or to distort reality. As a result, Considine is interested primarily in how the real, everyday goings-on of contemporary adolescence are represented on screen (Considine 1985: 9). More problematically, there is a clear moral undercurrent to Considine's work, as he describes as 'lamentable' those films that do not represent teenagers in a positive light (Considine 1985: 273). Taking up – if only implicitly – Hall's reading of adolescence as a time of particular susceptibility, Considine suggests that the distorted representation of teenagers found in many a film is a missed opportunity to impart a more positive, truthful message (Considine 1985: 273). He does not therefore consider what might lie at the heart of these films' appeal to teenagers, nor does he consider the stylistic elements that constitute them.

Timothy Shary's *Generation Multiplex*, published in 2002 and revised in 2014, builds on the foundations established by Considine. Shary's work is unarguably the most significant in demonstrating the potential of studying the teen movie, and, with its author having 'viewed and analysed hundreds of films', *Generation Multiplex* can reasonably claim to be one of the most comprehensive works on the subject (Shary 2002a: 11). In an important contrast to Considine, who considered the representation of teenagers in films across a number of genres, Shary argues that what he calls the 'youth movie' should itself be conceptualised as a genre (Shary 2002a 11). Noting the difficulty of ascribing the status of genre based on subject matter, theme or narrative form, Shary opts instead for the seemingly simple designation that the youth movie consists in 'films where youth appear' and are positioned in lead roles (Shary 2002a: 17). In making only limited reference to the intended audience of these films, Shary's emphasis is distinguished from the commercially minded limitations of the approach advocated by both Doherty and Driscoll.

If Shary's description of the youth movie as one that predominantly features youths is a relatively straightforward one, the question of who counts as a 'youth' is less certain. In this Shary defers to the Library of Congress's *Moving Image Genre: Form Guide*, in which films featuring characters up to and including twelve years old, such as *Stand by Me* (Rob Reiner, 1987), were designated as 'children's films'. At the other end of the spectrum, young adults portrayed in a university environment, or, as in the case of *St. Elmo's Fire* (Joel Schumacher, 1985), set in the fraught period that follows university graduation, are deemed to be 'College Films'. Shary makes the decision to include films featuring twelve-year-old characters, since this is the age at which American children enter middle school, thereby bringing them into contact with the world of teenagers, and makes twenty his loosely defined upper age limit.[7]

Driscoll's afterword for the new edition of *Generation Multiplex* observes that *Pitch Perfect* (Jason Moore, 2012) is not considered to be within the book's remit, since it features characters attending university (Driscoll in Shary 2014: 305). Nonetheless, as she acknowledges, this is a film that was dubbed a teen movie in the popular press and was extremely popular with the teen audience (see Richards 2012). For Driscoll, what is at stake here is the way in which notions of adolescence have bled out into other, adult forms of media, an argument that accords with her suggestion that the teenage audience is the most significant aspect in delineating what constitutes the teen movie. However, I argue that the intuitive positioning of *Pitch Perfect* as a teen movie is consistent with the genre's focus elsewhere on the characters' striving for identity and autonomy within a framework of parental control. In *Pitch Perfect*, Beca (Anna Kendrick) rather improbably attends an institution at which her father (John Benjamin Hickey) is the Dean. Much of the film consists in Beca reconciling her ambitions to become a DJ with her father's desire that she complete a university education. As such, the film can be seen to echo other, high school-set teen movies, in which teenagers' urges for independence clash with their immaturity, most obviously displayed in the perennial trope of the party staged at the parental home (Bailey and Hay 2006: 222). So in some cases, films featuring college-age characters can be regarded as teen movies, although the majority, such as Richard Linklater's recent *Everybody Wants Some!!* (2016) would not be.

Shary's work is undeniably ambitious in its aims and achievements. However, his principal aim, 'to determine how recent generations of young people have been represented in American cinema', endorses Considine's concern for the representation of youth on screen at the expense of an analysis of film style or aesthetic (Shary 2002a: 11). In contrast to Doherty's work, which argues that the American teenager is privileged as the audience for most Hollywood films, Shary perceives youth as a marginalised minority. As Shary astutely observes, teenagers are the only demographic without the capacity to produce and disseminate films from their own perspective into the mainstream (Shary 2002a: 2). Teens must therefore tolerate whatever representations of adolescence adults see fit to produce. Accordingly, he positions *Generation Multiplex* alongside Molly Haskell's *From Reverence to Rape* and Thomas Cripps's *Slow Fade to Black*, which respectively analysed the cinematic representation of women and African Americans as marginalised groups (Shary 2002a: 12). It is perhaps this concern for upholding the interests of youth that leads Shary to deploy a number of value judgements on whether films portray youth in a positive or a negative light, thereby obfuscating other insights that might have emerged from more nuanced analysis of the films themselves.[8]

While there are areas where we differ, I agree with Shary's assessment that the 1980s was the decade in which the teen movie calcified into a coherent genre. For Shary, the emergence of the multiplex cinema and the shopping mall as sites of teen congregation present the key impetus for what he describes as an 'explosion' in the number of teen movies during that decade (Shary 2002a: 6). Conversely, Adrian Martin contends that the 1970s, not a period with which the teen movie has much been associated, saw the release of three films that contain within them the seeds for the emergence of the 1980s teen movie: *American Graffiti*, *Animal House* (John Landis, 1978) and *Saturday Night Fever* (John Badham, 1977).[9] Examining the influence of *American Graffiti*, Martin argues that the film is notable for its use of music in creating a youth-oriented sonic space, and for its portrayal of private life as public spectacle (Martin 2009: 9). Of course, as will be discussed more fully in Chapter 5, Lucas's film has principally been associated with the 1970s nostalgia boom, which looked back to the supposedly more innocent 1950s and 1960s (Grainge 2000: 28). While many critics, not least Fredric Jameson, have derided the film's apparent conservatism (Jameson 1984; 1991), Martin is attentive to the youthful address of this outside example of Hollywood's new wave.

Martin's second example, the crass *Animal House*, has influenced a number of films featuring similarly low comedy, such as *Porky's* (Bob Clark, 1982), *Fast Times at Ridgemont High* (Amy Heckerling, 1982) and, more recently, *American Pie* (Paul Weitz, Chris Weitz, 1999) and *Superbad* (Greg Mottola, 2007). Gross-out comedy has certainly proved to have an enduring appeal, such that it is now a mainstay of Hollywood comedy whose audience is intended to extend beyond the teen market, such as *The Hangover* (Todd Phillips, 2009) and even *Bridesmaids* (Paul Feig, 2012).

Finally, *Saturday Night Fever* portrayed the gritty, urban adolescence of its protagonist, Tony Manero (John Travolta), whose mastery of the dancefloor enables his temporary escape from his otherwise tiresome Brooklyn existence. The film's distinctive Bee Gees soundtrack and Travolta's dance-led performance would, alongside the debut of MTV in 1981, influence a number of teen dance musicals in the 1980s. The impact of aesthetics derived from the music video is readily apparent in a wave of films such as *Flashdance* (Adrian Lyne, 1983) and *Footloose* (Herbert Ross, 1984), which often spawned music videos of their own. These films incorporated a specifically recorded soundtrack and well-choreographed dance sequences, without the diegetic singing that is typically held to be a key determinant of the musical genre.[10] Kay Dickinson goes further, arguing that MTV has actually shaped the aesthetic style of the teen movie itself, describing the accelerated pace of shots and rhythmic editing styles which, she argues, are traceable to the music video (Dickinson 2001: 6). While no longer as prevalent as they were in the 1980s, the recent success of the *High School Musical* (2006–8) and *Pitch Perfect* (2012; 2015; 2017) films suggests the continued appeal of musical forms in the teen movie.

Despite the continued influence of the Hollywood film musical on the teen movie, it is the films that John Hughes wrote, produced or directed between 1984 and 1987 that are central not only to the success of the teen movie in the 1980s, but to the development of the genre as a whole. As Shary rightly argues, 'no other director has so profoundly affected the way that young people are shown in films' (2005: 72). For Ann De Vaney, the appeal of Hughes's work can be attributed to his ability to formalise specific sets of visual and behavioural codes to denote different character types and social cliques within the high school (De Vaney 2002: 203). These codes could then be transferred from film to film by the use of a particular turn of phrase or item of clothing that had become invested with a particular trope. The most enduring of Hughes's films, and a paradigmatic example of the phenomenon De Vaney describes, is undoubtedly *The Breakfast Club*, which presents five key character types – 'the brain, the princess, the athlete, the basket-case, and the criminal' – which still retain their currency.

Following the proliferation of teen movies in the 1980s, the early 1990s saw a sharp drop in their numbers, before the genre resurged at the end of the decade. Now that the teen movie's longevity precludes its classification as a cycle, the 1990s also saw a change in its conceptualisation as a distinct genre. Indeed, Adrian Martin takes up Rick Altman's approach, which proposes that film genre is comprised of a combination of semantic and syntactic elements. The semantic consists of a genre's 'common traits, attitudes, characteristics, shots and locations' (Altman 1987c: 34). In turn, a film genre's syntactic level refers rather more vaguely to 'certain constitutive relationships' that structure those building blocks (Altman 1987c: 34). The teen movie's semantic level, Martin argues, refers to 'the prom, cheerleaders, snatched conversations at the school locker, the shopping mall and the juvenile delinquent gang' (Martin 1994: 66). However, Martin argues that the teen movie's syntax is always derived from elsewhere, observing the teen-oriented musicals, horror films and romantic comedies, which expressly borrow their narratives from more established forms. The wave of teen-oriented literary adaptations in the late 1990s of works such as *Emma* (*Clueless*) and *The Taming of the Shrew* (*Ten Things I Hate About You*, Gil Junger 1999) did much to reinforce Altman's contention that the teen movie was one that consisted in a productive tension between a rich semantic and derivative syntactic level.

In contrast, Jane Feuer argues that the 'sexual coming of age narrative' has emerged since the 1980s as a syntax that is particular to the teen movie (Feuer 1993: 125). Driscoll agrees, citing coming-of-age plots that centre on graduation from high school and characters losing their virginity (Driscoll 2011: 2). Certainly, these 1990s literary adaptations show a propensity for film-makers to derive their narratives from elsewhere. However, their adaptation for a teen audience brings to the fore the coming-of-age narratives that remain an undercurrent in their source texts. It is in this way that Howard Davis suggests that the high school, the setting to which these texts are so often transposed, provides an apt reflection of the ritualised and self-contained environments represented in the original works (Davis 2006: 55). These adaptations thus provide the opportunity to explore the continuities, such as the prom as a representation of marriage, as well as the evident differences in tone and content.

The 1990s also saw significant changes in the representation of the teenage girl on screen. Winona Ryder's unintentionally murderous protagonist in *Heathers* (Michael Lehmann, 1989) paved the way for representations of a figure that Shary and Kimberley Roberts have respectively termed the Tough Girl and the Angry Girl, whose presence was felt by the mid-1990s (Shary 2005: 93; Roberts 2002: 217). Films such as *Foxfire* (Annette Hayward-Carter, 1996), *Girls Town* (Jim McKay, 1996) and *Freeway* (Matthew Bright, 1995) depicted teenage girls either alone, or in small groups, as fundamentally and justifiably angry at the rest of the world. Both Roberts and Shary suggest that these films were a self-contained cycle, explained by girls' fragile positioning among the ever-shifting tectonic plates of feminism and postfeminism.

In the latter part of the 1990s and early 2000s, the Angry Girl made way for the *Mean Girls* who were so well realised in Mark Waters's film (2004). Although both the Angry Girl and the Mean Girl are defined by their 'unfeminine' aggression, it is the manner in which that hostility is expressed that distinguishes the two. The Angry Girl films depict their characters physically attacking their antagonists, as Vanessa Lutz (Reese Witherspoon) does with such gusto in *Freeway*. In contrast, *Mean Girls* sees the rich-girl clique dubbed 'The Plastics' place Cady (Lindsay Lohan) in situations designed to humiliate her. Such is the protocol of 'girl world', a refined social sphere in which status is highly prized.

For Jessica Ringrose, the move from Angry Girl to Mean Girl reflects the popularisation of postfeminist discourses (Ringrose 2006: 406). In this, Ringrose takes up Angela McRobbie's definition of the term, wherein feminism is said to be 'taken into account' such that it is perceived as no longer needed (McRobbie 2004: 205). Postfeminist discourses, Ringrose argues, claim that girls are as able as boys to display aggression, yet also stipulate that it must occur in gender-specific forms.[11] As such, physical violence might be expected of an aggressive boy, while girls are said to express aggression through psychological manipulation of their peers (Ringrose 2006: 406). Consequently, Ringrose argues that the Mean Girl archetype serves to contain acceptable behaviours of girlhood such that violent girls come to be viewed as doubly pathological, as not only violating the norms of femininity but of social life as well (Ringrose 2006: 407). The expression of aggression and its mediation through postfeminist discourses of gender and class will be explored in the final case study of Chapter 4.

Despite the postfeminist prohibitions on female violence, it is noticeable that one of the most predominant trends apparent in teen cinema today is the strong, physically capable girl, as seen in both *The Hunger Games* (2012–15) and *Divergent* (2014–) franchises.[12] Certainly, as these films are set in alternative, dystopian worlds, their characters have ample reason to hone their fighting skills. They must also be viewed, though, in the light of the ambivalent characterisation of Bella Swan (Kristen Stewart) of the *Twilight* films (2008–12). As will be demonstrated in Chapter 6, Bella is certainly a determined individual. However, she is also one whose coming of age must inevitably result in death, owing to her romance with vampire Edward (Robert Pattinson). Nevertheless, *Twilight* presents an important precursor, since the films' commercial success demonstrated the box-office potential of a franchise headed up by a female character. The heroines of *The Hunger Games* and *Divergent*, by contrast, are the figureheads of revolutionary movements as well as being handy with weapons. Beyond Hollywood, we might also consider indie drama *Hard Candy* (David Slade, 2005) as well as Céline Sciamma's *Bande des Filles* (2014) and *Mustang*, whose narratives also explore the rebellion and containment of teenage girls. It seems clear that these girls provide a vehicle through which discourses of sexuality and rebellion are explored on screen.

Examining the history of the teen movie and its analysis by film scholars has revealed two principal approaches to the genre; those who, like Shary, argue that the dominant presence of teenage characters determines whether a film can be classed as a teen movie, and those who, like Doherty, consider an intended teenage audience to be more significant. Both schools of thought nonetheless share a conceptualisation of the teenager that the films feature, or to whom they are said to appeal. However, muddying these otherwise (relatively) clear waters, Martin asserts that the 'teen' of the teen movie refers not necessarily to a teenager per se, but to one who possesses a 'youth sensibility' (Martin 1994: 66). That is, Martin observes Robert Benayoun's list of qualities denoting youth: 'naïveté, ideation, humour, erotomania and a sense of injustice' (Benayoun, quoted in Martin 1994: 66). Driscoll, too, takes up Martin's reading of youth as a sensibility rather than a biological age, arguing that 'not every film with the conventional content about teenagers is a teen film, and some films not literally about teenagers are' (Driscoll 2011: 2). This would certainly account for the adult address of 2015's *The Diary of a Teenage Girl* (Marielle Heller, 2015) and the juvenile tone of *The 40-Year-Old Virgin* (Judd Apatow, 2005), which, despite featuring middle-aged characters, is centred on the sex quest narrative common to the teen movie.

That Apatow's film may be regarded as a teen film, while another work that is centred on a teenager may escape the designation, is indicative of the dangers in this general conceptualisation of the youth audience. Given the importance of teenagers as a cinema-going, or at least, in the age of streaming, film-watching, audience to all mainstream releases, an approach that centres on the teen audience alone will be insufficiently discriminating. For his part, Shary's determination of the age at which characters are or are not considered youths in his typology is suitably rigorous, and he does delineate various strands that have contributed to the genre over time. Yet his sense of any overriding syntax in the genre as a whole remains somewhat sketchily conceived.

In contrast, taking up the sexual coming-of-age narrative as the primary determiner of what constitutes the Hollywood teen movie, my aim is to direct attention away from the commercial circumstances that surround the film's release, and instead to reorient our gaze to the construction of identity that such films depict. This is not to say that sexual (in)experience determines the genre's structures, but rather that the focus should be on the physical and psychological processes of becoming. As such, I aim to restore the focus on 'storm and stress' – on the sense of liminality – that Hall identified in 1904 as defining the adolescent experience. This is not to say that I jettison entirely the hard-won insights of other scholars. Indeed, I follow Shary and Considine in their delimitation of the teen movie as featuring characters between twelve and twenty years of age (Shary 2002a: 17). Reflecting the work of Doherty and Driscoll, too, I consider only films marketed with the teen audience in mind.

Nonetheless, turning my attention to the construction of identity, and, in particular, the depiction of adolescence as a heightened moment of becoming, necessitates a new approach to the teen movie. As has been apparent, the principal approach to the genre has been a sociocultural, and secondarily, a historical one. Much of this has been predicated on the understanding that the films have little artistic merit to detain the busy film scholar. In contrast, this book engages in close textual analyses of particular examples of the teen movie. Certainly, an understanding of the circumstances surrounding a particular release can only be useful. Yet I want to draw attention to the films' textual detail; to individual performance gestures, camera position, the use of costume and a host of other attributes that inform the construction of identity on screen. My intention is to examine the teen movie as a film, rather than as a reflection of a phenomenon that might be better observed elsewhere.

In a further contrast to the approach that has characterised much previous scholarship on the teen movie, this book is not intended as a spotters' guide to the genre. Rather, it provides in-depth analysis of only a few key case studies. Certainly there is an argument, which Martin briefly airs, that the choice of a few supposedly exceptional texts obscures the general landscape of the genre (Martin 2009). However, the case studies I have selected are not only key to the development of the teen movie – as readers will observe, many of the films I identify here as especially influential turn up in later chapters – but also embody a particular tendency in the genre at the time of their release. Thus, the chapters follow a loosely chronological order wherein trends in the teen movie can be observed, as well as the particular construction of identity in question. The book functions secondarily as a history of the teen movie.

A further key difference from previous scholarship is the integration of critical theory into the analysis. For some, I realise, this can only get in the way of the 'real' business of analysing the films and the circumstances that produced them. Yet in her sustained argument in favour of film theory, broadly defined, Catherine Constable maintains that the application of theory to film necessarily engages in a type of feedback loop, as the textual examples may not only instantiate, but also suggest the limits of a particular approach (Constable 2005: 22). The teen movie is thus not characterised as a passive object that gratefully submits to the validation supplied by 'high theory'. Rather, the examples provided by the genre are active participants in a collaborative effort; the theories elucidate the construction of identity within the genre, while textual analysis of the films themselves promises to complicate and expand on the theories that inform their analysis. Considering the construction of gender and class, and even the shaky relationship between teenagers and the human condition itself, this book aims to think anew the construction of identity in the teen movie.

Notes

1. Arnett and Cravens note that 25,000 copies were sold at the time of publication, a huge number for a two-volume work totalling over 1,300 pages (2006: 165).
2. In addition to the widely documented post-war baby boom, Doherty observes that the number of five to nine-year-olds grew by 24 per cent between 1940 and 1950, leading to a marked increase in the teenage population during the 1950s (2002: 34–5).
3. The First Amendment stipulates the right to freedom of speech as follows: 'Congress shall make no law respecting an establishment of religion, or prohibiting the free exercise thereof; or abridging the freedom of speech, or of the press; or the right of the people peaceably to assemble, and to petition the Government for a redress of grievances.'
4. American International Pictures drew up what has been described as the 'Peter Pan syndrome' syllogism to describe the intended audience for its films, as follows: 'A younger child will watch anything an older child will watch. An older child will not watch anything a younger child will watch. A girl will watch anything a boy will watch. A boy will not watch anything a girl will watch. So to catch your greatest audience, you zero in on the 19-year-old male' (Betrock 1986: 103; in Shary 2005: 42).
5. Klein draws on Rick Altman's 1987 work on the semantic and syntactic aspects of genre here.
6. We might think of the 'Blaxploitation' film cycle of the early 1970s in this regard.
7. Notably 12–20 is also the delimitation observed by Considine.
8. Shary identifies films as 'positive' and 'negative' on various occasions in the first edition of *Generation Multiplex* (2002a). See for instance p. 78; p. 140; p. 162.
9. Barbara Brickman (2012) goes further, arguing that the 1970s have been unduly dismissed as a nadir in the production of teen movies. Her book *New American Teenagers* calls for a reconsideration of 1970s youth culture.
10. See Jane Feuer's discussion of *Dirty Dancing* and its complex positioning as a musical, 'Is *Dirty Dancing* a Musical and Why Should it Matter?' (2013).
11. In this way, Ringrose echoes Rosalind Gill's emphasis on the re-emergence of binarised gender roles in postfeminist culture (2005).
12. It should be noted here that the fourth film in the *Divergent* series (*Ascendant*, Lee Toland Krieger, 2017) will be a TV movie without a theatrical release, perhaps suggesting that this cycle is waning.

3. ACTING UP: PERFORMING MASCULINE DELINQUENCY IN THE TEEN MOVIE

James Dean's fatal car crash on 30 September 1955 ensured the actor's swift canonisation as an icon of youth rebellion. This chapter examines Dean's performance in *Rebel Without a Cause*, in addition to those of John Travolta in *Grease* (Randal Kleiser, 1978) and Christian Slater in *Heathers* (Michael Lehmann, 1989). James Dean, to be sure, was a star. Will Scheibel observes the quasi-idolatry in which he was held even among his fellow performers, Sal Mineo and Natalie Wood, not to speak of the legions of fans whose acres of correspondence required Warner Brothers to create a dedicated mail service (Scheibel 2014: 178). Fascinated by the intense identifications that such magnetic performers cultivate with their audiences, Richard Dyer identifies the star as a complex nexus of texts, ideologies and desires (Dyer 1979). His seminal work continues to provide a touchstone for scholars working in star studies, and testifies to the enduring ideological and textual basis for stardom. Since then, a new and related field of celebrity studies has taken account of the extraneous labour in which film stars are now routinely obliged to engage (as well, of course, as those for whom fame itself is a vocation).[1]

The art of performance provides the backdrop, but rarely the focus, of these related areas of study. The study of stars, and latterly of celebrities, has tended to view the star in aggregate across time, in accordance with Dyer's readings. In contrast, James Naremore (1998) and Andrew Klevan (2005) have argued that an analysis of film performance requires a 'minute-by-minute' assessment of the individual gestures that performers bring to bear in any given film (Klevan 2005: 28). Despite more recent work by Virginia Wexman (2004),

Cynthia Baron and Sharon Carnicke (2008), and Donna Peberdy (2011), which all combine performance studies with complex analyses of stardom, studies of acting and film performance lag considerably behind star studies.

Increased attention to stars and celebrities in both academic and popular literature attests to the difficulties in finding the vocabulary to disentangle the individual contribution of the performer from other aspects of the film's signifying frame. It is perhaps for this reason that discussion of acting and performance in the popular media is generally limited to the ever-growing window, roughly between November and February, and culminating in the Oscars ceremony, known as 'awards season'. Such accolades typically praise an actor's bodily labour, or indeed an accurate impersonation of a well-known figure, suggesting that judges are persuaded by the apparent measurability of these types of performance.[2] While the ability of such awards to recognise quality is much contested,[3] the focus on obvious physical transformations not only obscures the merits of more subtle performances but also demonstrates the central difficulty in analysing performance, namely how we might isolate the performer's contribution from other aspects of the film.

Dyer proposes a solution, arguing that performance consists in '*how* the action/function is done, *how* the lines are said' (Dyer 1979: 151, my emphasis). However, Peberdy's assessment of the current state of performance studies and their relation to constructions of masculinity questions whether delineating these aspects is really as clear-cut as Dyer claims (2011: 35). The 'how' elements on which Dyer centres can be affected by technology, direction and cinematography, over which most actors have limited control, as much as they are the results of their performance (Peberdy 2011: 35). She therefore proposes that performance must be understood in a mutually interactive relationship between the selection and combination of shots, direction and other filmic elements. Adding to Dyer's proposition, Peberdy argues that performance must be considered in conjunction with, rather than at a remove from, other elements of cinematography and *mise-en-scène*.

Turning to juvenile delinquency in particular, these are performances that are characterised by displays of emotional distress, perhaps best illustrated by Jim Stark's anguished wail to his parents that 'you're tearing me apart!' Yet, as the case studies show, the delinquent will equally often display a shrugging indifference to the events he experiences. The many levels of performances generated by this particular character type, where an overt assertion of aggression may well mask an acute vulnerability, pose particular difficulties for performance analysis. Evidently, any performer only has at their disposal their own outward gestures and expressions to convey their character's anxieties, and it is only these gestures that can then be assessed for their emotional weight. Aspects of the film's photography can certainly help: a close-up directs the audience to examine an actor's face for traces of the character's inner emotional life. Nonetheless, that actor requires an understanding of emotionality, and crucially, of what physical actions or gestures best convey psychological distress on screen.

Lee Strasberg's Actors Studio, which came to prominence in the 1950s, aimed to combat the equation of performance with superficial 'actorly' gestures. Based in New York, Strasberg was influenced by Constantin Stanislavsky's quest for naturalistic acting that was wholly expunged of artifice. To achieve this end with his own acolytes, Strasberg coined an idiosyncratic battery of dramatic exercises – known enigmatically as the Method – designed to elicit an actor's emotional memory, in order to suggest a character's interior life. Recalling a particularly resonant experience from their past, the actor was able automatically to express the emotions required of the scene, by the force of the memory itself (Strasberg 1987: 43). Actors working in the Method came to be known for their mumbled, inarticulate speech and erratic physical actions, the calling card of Montgomery Clift, Marlon Brando and James Dean. Although the true extent of Strasberg's work with the famous names with whom he is associated remains questionable,[4] this acting style, and the thinking behind it, remains widely associated with these 'new' star identities of the 1950s.

That actors trained in the Method can be identified by particular gestures complicates its pretence to convey natural emotion. Rather, attention to the four material sites for the production of acting signs: the facial, the gestural, the corporeal and the vocal (King 1985: 136), provide a more instructive rubric for the examination of film performance. Indeed, these are the parameters that Klevan emphasises when he argues that it is the individual gestures a performer brings to bear which should inform performance analysis (2005: 58). Consequently, while noting the tradition to which a particular performance is said to belong, this chapter will ascribe greater importance to the analysis of bodily gestures themselves.

The focus on individual bodily gestures as the locus of performance analysis finds echoes in the work of Judith Butler, whose theorisation of gender provides the principal framework for this chapter. As many critics who have attempted to compile an overview of her work have noted with chagrin, Butler's work continues to develop in dizzyingly diverse areas, making a summary of her ideas particularly challenging.[5] She remains principally known for *Gender Trouble* (1990) and its follow-up *Bodies that Matter* (1993), both of which theorise the construction of gender. However, later works, most recently exemplified by *Precarious Life* (2006) and *Frames of War* (2010), are overtly political and question who counts as human in the global war on terror. What emerges throughout her oeuvre, though, is the particularly American ambition to 'maximise the possibilities for liveability' (Butler 2004: 31); that is, to ensure that all subjects are included in the (still-contested) category of the human. This chapter focuses only on Butler's theorisation of gender, as detailed in three of her best-known works: *Gender Trouble*, *Bodies that Matter* and, more recently, *Undoing Gender*. As I will demonstrate, examining these films in this context exposes the performance and performativity in manifestations of teen masculinity and its attendant rebellions.

Butler's key contribution to gender theory has been her contention that gender is a performative construct. Gender, then, should be understood as 'set of repeated acts, within a highly rigid, regulatory frame that congeal over time to produce the appearance of substance, of a natural sort of being' (Butler 1990: 45). This central definition of performativity is a complex one that requires some unpacking to explicate its relevance for the examination of performance in the teen movie. In the first instance, Butler understands gender as a 'set of repeated acts' (Butler 1990: 45), a choice of language that brings into play a theatrical frame of reference. Yet what Butler refers to here is not performance as an actor might conceive it, but the series of everyday, mundane actions that sustain a coherent expression of gender identity, which include, but are not limited to, gesture, posture, voice and clothing. Significantly, Butler emphasises that these actions are repeated. Indeed, she argues that what is intended by these actions is an approximation of a gendered ideal that can never, in any event, fully be instantiated (Butler 1990: 191). The subject is therefore trapped in a perpetual moment of becoming whose end point can never be realised, a state that recalls the liminality of adolescence. Butler's theorisation of gender consequently provides an apt framework through which to examine the on-screen construction of teenage masculinity through film performance.

These repeated acts, Butler claims, occur in a 'highly rigid regulatory frame' (1990: 45). It is for this reason that, despite the wide range of possibilities accorded by varying configurations of sex, sexual practice, desire and gender, only those who are female, heterosexual and feminine can count as culturally intelligible women. In turn, culturally intelligible men – those who are male, heterosexual and masculine – are figured as their opposite-sexed counterparts. Butler describes the regulatory regime that demands coherence along these lines as the 'heterosexual matrix' (Butler 1990: 30). In *Gender Trouble* she observes the fate of the intersexed Herculine Babin, whose ambiguous anatomy, appearance and sexual practices challenged the heterosexual matrix (Butler 1990: 32–3).[6] For Butler, the discursive refusal to acknowledge the seeming incoherence of Babin's gender identity indicates that all gender is a series of attributes arbitrarily ordered in the service of heterosexual kinship.

Butler's theorisation of performativity ends with the assertion that it is the '*appearance* of substance' that is denoted by the repetition of gendered acts over time (Butler 1990: 45; my emphasis). In this, she takes up the work of language theorist J. L. Austin, whose *How to Do Things with Words* defines the performative utterance as one wherein 'in saying what we do, we perform the action' (Austin 1962a: 65). Supplying the highly ritualistic example of the wedding ceremony, in which an authorised individual states, 'I now pronounce you man and wife', Austin notes that this person is not reporting on the marriage, but in fact bringing it into being (Austin 1962b: 67). Similarly, the gendered acts that Butler discusses should not be understood to be the outward manifestations of a gendered being. Rather, the gender of the subject is constituted solely of these repeated acts, which create the impression of a lasting identity, rather than an aggregation of numerous snapshots. Butler's account of gender therefore radically undermines the ontology and stability of gender as a locus of identity.

Given the present context of film performance, it is notable that Butler also considers how gender performativity is received by others, such that a process of recognition is always implicit in her account. Individuals whose morphology, gender and ethnicity falls outside the prevailing matrix of norms are categorised as unreal – the 'other against whom the human is made' (Butler 2004: 30). In this, she draws from Hegel's *Phenomenology of Spirit*, which claims both that subject and Other are engaged in a mutual process of offering and receiving recognition for one another, and that 'if we are not recognisable, then it is not possible to persist in one's own being' (Butler 2004: 31). It is the challenge presented by those currently perceived as unintelligible, but who nevertheless demand recognition as viable subjects, who present the most radical possibilities for change, since they demonstrate the need to expand the norms of intelligibility.

Butler's work on gender is particularly applicable to the study of film performance, as Cohan (1997) and Peberdy (2011) have observed. Her theorisation of gender is still more relevant to examining the on-screen construction of the juvenile delinquent. Butler's disaggregation of seemingly coherent gender identity into a series of 'acts, gestures and desire' (1990: 191) allows us to deconstruct the ways in which gender identity is presented on screen. In examining the juvenile delinquent in particular, we encounter an identity that is constructed in ambivalent relation to gender norms. Certainly, all the characters examined here are presented as heterosexual. Yet the construction of 'delinquent' identity suggests that the characters are understood to defy social norms. As the case studies demonstrate, although the juvenile delinquent figure is understood to rebel against dominant values, there are limits to the norms that may be legitimately flouted within this character type, and those limits have altered considerably over time.

This chapter examines the star performances of James Dean in *Rebel Without a Cause*, John Travolta in *Grease* and Christian Slater in *Heathers*. The historical span of these characters and performances attests to the longevity of this particular character type. For Shary, such films are a subgenre, the 'youth delinquency film', which is characterised by its portrayal of teen rebellion within a 'relatively typical cultural context' (2014: 83). It is therefore distinct from more recent film franchises like *The Hunger Games* (2012–15), whose protagonist leads a youth uprising in a dystopian future, albeit one that shares many resonances with contemporary American life. Despite a brief wave of female-led youth delinquency films, the subgenre remains a predominantly masculine one, with many films staging a preoccupation with the vicissitudes in becoming 'fully masculine'. Examining these performances of masculine rebellion in the light of Butler's theorisation of performativity promises to reveal the vulnerabilities in the construction of teen and hegemonic masculinity alike.

Rebel Without a Cause (Nicholas Ray, 1955)

James Dean haunts all subsequent manifestations of teen rebellion. Of Dean's small corpus of films, only *East of Eden* (Elia Kazan, 1955) was released while the actor was still alive. Consequently for Graham McCann, his 'presence projected an absence', since audiences watched Dean's performance in the knowledge of his prior death (McCann 1991: 164). McCann's remarks are reflected in contemporary reviews of *Rebel Without a Cause* (hereafter referred to simply as *Rebel*) and *Giant* (George Stevens, 1956), which lament '"a talent that might have reached the heights" [and] "the blazing up of a lost light"' in reference to the young star (reviews taken from Spoto 1996: 254–5). It appears that Dean's star burned brightest in the absence of the actor himself, since his death enabled audiences to project their own desires onto the blank canvas provided by the star.

Dean was marketed by Warner Brothers as an embodiment of rebellion, the trait for which the actor remains best known (Springer 2007: 27). Yet the star did not stand for any specific countercultural commitment, but for rebellion in a general sense, allowing Dean to appeal to millions, rather than provide the focal point for a niche interest group. With its lavish Warner Color, *Rebel* was conceived as a prestige picture, in contrast to the low-rent fare more often oriented towards teenagers. Instead, the film calls on the tropes of the family melodrama, most obviously seen when Jim's mother looks directly into the camera to declare, 'You read about things like this happening to other families, but you never dream it could happen to yours.' Although *Rebel* retains a sympathy with its teenage characters, this moment marks its acknowledgement of the threat to the dominant order posed by the juvenile delinquent. Indeed, it is the very suburban ordinariness of Dean's character, Jim Stark, which marks him as a particularly destabilising influence.

While Dean's status as an embodiment of rebellion is somewhat ill-defined, his gender identity was regarded as transgressive in a more specific sense. The changing nature of male star identities in the 1950s is widely documented (see for instance McCann 1991: 139; Naremore 1988: 195; Wexman 2004: 131;

Cohan 1997). In contrast to the on-screen virility embodied by the previous generation of stars, such as John Wayne or Clark Gable, Naremore situates Dean alongside Montgomery Clift and Marlon Brando, whose sexuality and ostensible inarticulacy signalled a new focus on the teen market (Naremore 1988: 195). Elsewhere, Springer points out that this new breed of star revealed the 'vulnerability and confusion' within elements of masculine identity, pointing to the status of masculinity as a construction (Springer 2007: 33). Significantly, these three figures, Dean prominently among them, portray their characters trying to come to terms with, and failing to embody, the roles associated with hegemonic masculinity. An analysis of the individual details of Dean's performance in the light of Butler's work promises to reveal the inconsistencies in the construction of masculinity.

'You're tearing me apart!' Fragmentation and the Failure of Gender Identification

I have argued that James Dean is indisputably a star. However, in *Rebel*, he is not accorded what Valerie Orpen describes as a typical star entrance. Orpen's close reading of film editing practices observes that the arrival of a film's star is typically 'delayed and fragmented', providing only brief, tantalising glimpses of the performer, before we see their body in its totality (Orpen 2003: 68). This technique, she argues, generates maximum expectation and anticipation for the audience, and bolsters the status of the star within the text (Orpen 2003: 68). In contrast, from the opening moments of the film, Dean's face and body are shown in full. What is more, the star is shown lying in the street, clearly drunk, among discarded debris, creating the impression of a low status at odds with his position of a promising star at one of the leading studios. This disparity is paralleled in the image's juxtaposition of class signifiers: while Jim

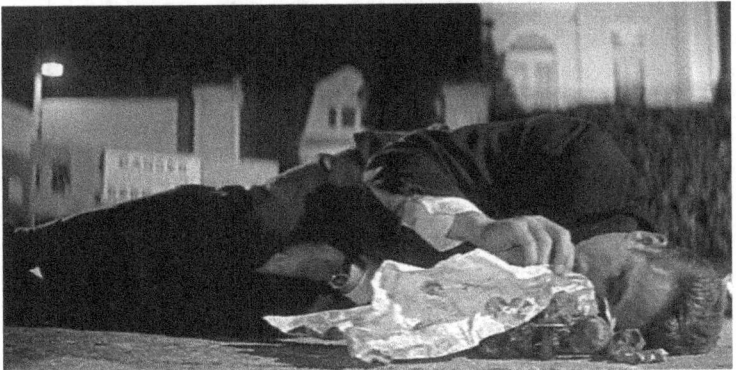

Figure 3.1   Jim (James Dean) is first seen lying drunk in the street.

lies in the gutter, the character's tweed jacket continues to convey middle-class respectability. The very beginning of *Rebel* anticipates a sense in which conventions of masculinity, and Jim's identity with it, are in a state of flux.

Dean's brief, opening performance demonstrates the liminality of Jim's gender identity. The character notices a toy monkey positioned in the screen's foreground. Grabbing it, Jim winds it up and briefly watches it move before quickly snatching it, clasping it within his hands and laying it back on the ground. Using a piece of waste paper and a leaf, he then constructs a semblance of a bed for the toy. Then, curling into a foetal position as much as his clothes will allow, Jim inches towards the toy on his side and gently pats it, as though soothing the toy to sleep. Although Naremore points out that 'no-one has proposed how we might recognise the Method on screen', Dean's erratic movements in this scene, rendered all the more so by his character's apparent drunkenness, appear to demonstrate the stylised gestures associated with this acting style (Naremore 1988: 197). These movements allow Dean to convey his character's positioning between different norms of masculinity: those associated with boyhood and those associated with manhood. Significantly, Jim is shown to be able to embody neither set of norms successfully. The toy no longer provides substantial amusement for the teenager, and he quickly tires of watching the monkey's awkward mechanical strut. Yet, being constructed of tin, it cannot be effectively nurtured either. The scene shows a character positioned between identities.

Butler's theorisation of recognition also provides an important context in which to view the following scene, in which Jim is taken to the police station for 'plain drunkenness'. In the film's opening scene he is shown to embody neither the norms of childhood nor adulthood, such that his is an identity in flux. The police, however, recognise such an identity as a 'juvenile delinquent', and have established a department – the juvenile division – to deal with such individuals. The police's treatment of Jim, and with him Judy (Natalie Wood) and Plato (Sal Mineo), speaks to Butler's claim that recognition under particularly restrictive norms can in fact prove detrimental to survival, and should therefore be resisted (Butler 2004: 34). Later in the film, it is the police's belief that they are able to recognise the traits of a supposed juvenile delinquent that causes the final tragedy.

The disjointed geography of the police station itself embodies the fragmentation and incoherence within Jim's own gender identity. Depth of field allows the audience to see both Plato sitting scowling with his guardian on the left side of the screen, and Judy immediately behind him in an adjacent interview room. The three teens' coincidental presence at the police station on the same night foretells their later friendship and invites comparisons between them. Judy's infractions, like those of Jim, stem from the liminality of her gender and sexual identity. While she wants affection from her father, and recognition of her vulnerability as a child, he has determined that she is a young adult woman, whose sexuality should be policed accordingly. Her positioning as a spectacular object of the heterosexual male gaze is indicated by her bold red attire, and further emphasised as Jim unabashedly turns his head to watch her as she walks into the interview room. It is not clear that Judy has committed any criminal offence. Rather, like Jim, she finds herself placed between two sets of gender norms that do not wholly fit her. In contrast, accused of having shot some puppies, Plato is constructed as a substantially more pathological figure than either Jim or Judy. Tellingly, he is accompanied only by his guardian, who laments to the police that his mother is frequently on business abroad, while his father is absent. Plato is a troubled figure who shows no remorse for his crime and refuses the offer of psychiatric help. In a theme that reverberates throughout *Rebel*, it is women's deviations from the norms of femininity that are presented as the cause of their sons' often violent infractions. All three teenagers find that they are positioned outside of the norms of childhood and adulthood, such that they must forge a sense of identity on their own terms.

The arrival of Jim's parents and grandmother at the police station contributes to further outbursts of volatile behaviour on his part. Finally reaching the teenager perched unnaturally on a shoe polish chair, the low camera position emphasises the absurdity of Jim's sudden increase in stature as he towers over his parents. Jim immediately focuses on his father, Frank (Jim Backus), and places him in the chair instead, providing the first example of Jim's attempt to 'restore' his father's authority within his seemingly feminised household. In an echo of Jim's ineffectual attempt to nurture the toy monkey, Frank is shown to be unable to protect his son from the punishments meted out by the police. As he proceeds to highlight Jim's formerly good behaviour and their recent arrival in the town, Jim imitates Frank's defence, drunkenly pleading with his father to 'tell 'em . . . tell 'em how we moved here and . . .' Read in the light of Butler's theorisation of citationality, according to which the norms being approximated are vulnerable at the moment of citation (Butler 1993: 108), we can see how Jim's mock earnestness undermines his father's attempt to assert himself. As such, Dean's performance in this scene draws attention both to the cultural norms at stake, which require Jim's father to make the case for his son, and to Frank's inability to live up to those expectations.

Arguably, *Rebel* is a conservative film that positions juvenile delinquency as the fault of women, who, like Stella Dallas, sought to be 'something else besides a mother'. Certainly, Frank is positioned as belittled by his wife, credited dismissively as 'Jim's Mom' in the film's script,[7] who in turn is undermined by Frank's mother (Virginia Brissac). A Freudian interpretation of the film, a school of thought that had been widely popularised in the USA by the mid-1950s (see Naremore 1998), supports this view. In 'Mourning and

Melancholia', Freud states that masculinity is consolidated through identification with the father following the loss of the mother as an object of desire (Freud 2005: 37). This, of course, is the resolution of the Oedipal conflict wherein the (male) child's identification with the father is motivated in large part by the fear of castration that he wields. Yet Frank does not possess such a threat. Alone with Ray (Edward Plett), Jim states his wish for his father to assert his physical dominance 'to knock Mom cold'. In turn, Frank's offer of the phallically symbolic cigars is firmly rejected by the police officer. A Freudian interpretation thus explains Jim's angst as the consequence of his phallicised mother and emasculated father.

In contrast to this conservative, psychoanalytic interpretation, I argue that the scene demonstrates the impossibility of instantiating idealised gender under the prevailing matrix of norms. Jim, Judy and Plato find that their identities lie between and among the understood frameworks of childhood and adulthood, and that the principal institution that recognises their liminality, the juvenile division of the police station, is a punitive one. Similarly, Frank's attempts to embody the norms of idealised, middle-class fatherhood are shown to be inadequate. Yet Jim's assertion that violence towards his mother would enable Frank to instantiate these norms can be seen implicitly to question whether normative fatherhood is one that ought to be idealised. For her part, Jim's mother's authoritative yet impotent position on the sidelines reveals the importance of exactly who is embodying those strict norms that Jim seems to admire so much.

'What do you do when you have to be a man?'

The film's opening scenes make it clear that Jim is preoccupied with the questions of what it means to instantiate the norms of masculinity. As he begins high school, this concern brings him into confrontation with Buzz (Corey Allen), whose status as a gang leader and Judy's boyfriend codes him as an idealised representation of teen masculinity. The animosity between Buzz and Jim begins at the Griffith Planetarium, an arena that will later provide the scene of the film's erasure of gendered ambiguity. Here too, the planetarium is a setting for the assertion of heterosexuality, as Buzz slowly crawls his hand across Judy's chest to pinch another companion's nose, remarking 'hey, I'm a crab!' (a *bon mot* that references a lecturer's identification of the crab-shaped Cancer constellation). The shot scale allows us to see Jim observing the interaction with interest from three rows behind. The positive reaction to Buzz's joke prompts Jim to imitate the gang leader, such that when the lecturer identifies a further constellation, for 'Taurus, the bull', Jim emits a loud 'moo' sound. In contrast to the appreciative laughter with which Buzz's comment was received, the characters respond to Jim's interjection with a mixture of scorn and incomprehension. While citing precisely the same norms of masculine behaviour as Buzz, there is a sharp contrast in the way in which the two jokes are welcomed by Buzz's gang. In this we can see a parallel between the gang's reaction, and Jim's perception of his parents; in both cases, it is not the norms of behaviour themselves that are idealised. Rather, the identity of the person who instantiates those norms is more significant.

Jim's seemingly friendly intervention appears to establish him as a threat to Buzz's status. However, Dean's performance makes it clear that violence is not the outcome he sought. Close-up shots of Jim show an expression contorted with anguish, demonstrating not only his reluctance to engage in a physical confrontation with Buzz, but also its inevitability. Despite neither party especially desiring a fight – it is Buzz's gang that are principally invested in this spectacle – there appear to be forces at play over which neither teen has any control. The evident disinclination of both characters speaks to Butler's contention that gender is a mandated, rather than willed, approximation of an ideal (see, for instance, Butler 1993: 95). That the pair are both caught up in the unwritten laws of masculinity is indicated by the prominence of the phallic knife in the foreground as Buzz and Jim circle one another. It is the promise of this impossible signifier that impels the fight between the pair.

Interrupted by a security guard who breaks up the fight, Buzz proposes that they resolve their dispute later that night at a 'Chickie Run'. Believing this to be an important masculine rite of passage, Jim consults his father for advice, asking the question with which this section began: 'what do you do when you have to be a man?' Tellingly, Frank's advice – that Jim would be better off not participating in such a dangerous ritual – follows the most vivid depiction of his own emasculation, when he ineptly struggles to clear a tray of food he has dropped before Carol notices it. Wearing a floral apron over his grey suit, Frank presents an absurd figure, prompting Jim to laugh uproariously at the spectacle. Butler asserts that drag can provide means of subverting heteronormativity by making apparent the ways in which gender identities are constructed in accordance with particular discursive norms (see 1990: 192; 1993: 208). Yet she also maintains that many mainstream manifestations of cross-dressing in fact work to uphold heteronormativity, by affirming one gender identity as 'true'.[8] Frank's evident inability to prepare and serve food – tasks often coded as feminine – cast this particular manifestation as a conservative one. While Jim's father rejects his son's assertion that participating in the Chickie Run is a 'matter of honour', the floral apron serves to undermine his authority in Jim's eyes.

As Jim rejects his father's prevarication and leaves the house to find Buzz and the gang, his change of allegiance is signified through costume. Jim quickly changes from the tweeds he has worn since the start of the film into the red jacket, white T-shirt and blue jeans that constitute something of a uniform for

Buzz and his gang. Initially this appears to be a moment of childish defiance for Jim, who gobbles down a chunk of cake and a bottle of milk as he leaves the family home by the back door. Yet the very conformity of his actions to a model of juvenile delinquency should not pass unacknowledged. The Chickie Run is a highly ritualised event that, contrary to the teens' claims of rebellion and machismo, in fact serves to demonstrate their 'boredom and conformity', as Jon Lewis observes (1992: 25). While ostensibly operating outside the law, then, the Chickie Run indicates the tenacity of norms that regulate gendered conduct.

Murray Pomerance discusses the Chickie Run as a masculine ritual, arguing that the event is intended to 'produce a circumstance where Jim can be added to the gang' (Pomerance 2005: 41). In this context, the Chickie Run should be understood not as a reassertion of dominance, but of initiation into the gang. Pomerance draws attention to the brief interaction that takes place between Buzz and Jim when the pair are alone, away from the crowds. It is only here that Jim can ask Buzz, 'why do we do this?' to which Buzz, shorn of his former swagger, can only bleakly respond, 'You gotta do something.' For Pomerance, their dialogue highlights the performance of masculinity required of the pair, without which 'social life would be unthinkable' (Pomerance 2005: 44). What Pomerance makes clear is the restrictiveness of the norms of masculinity to which Jim and Buzz are required to ascribe, which a Butlerian reading further reinforces. Further, Pomerance observes the social audience – the other teenagers – that mandate their conflict. Certainly, there is a sympathy between the two characters that is not otherwise apparent when they are in the presence of a larger group. This 'backstage moment' (2005:42) thereby reveals the power exerted by the gang members themselves over their nominal leaders, since Buzz is performing to their requirements rather than for his own needs.

The homosocial provides an important context with which to view the growing friendship between Buzz and Jim. Eve Kosofsky Sedgwick's famous examination of the literary love triangle argues that while the ostensible love object is the woman at the centre of the love triangle, the more important relationship is that which develops between the two men in question (Sedgwick 1985: 25). The woman merely serves as a conduit to the men's homosocial desires. In *Rebel*, Judy serves as the guarantor of Buzz's (and later, Jim's) heterosexuality, while also facilitating their ritual of male competition and bonding, clearly enjoying her role in giving the cue to 'hit the lights' and in doing so, begin the race. Both her change of loyalties and the similarity in the role she performs for the two characters are signalled when she sprinkles some dirt first into Buzz's hands, then into Jim's.

Plato's presence at the Chickie Run complicates the apparent heteronormativity of the scene. A number of cross-cuts between Buzz and Jim preparing for the event, and Judy and Plato discussing the newcomer, work to align Plato with the position of the love interest. Critical readings of *Rebel* make much of Sal Mineo's performance as Plato, whom the actor himself describes as the 'first gay teenager in film' (quoted in McCann 1991: 151). The strict Hays Code stipulated that Plato could not be expressly portrayed as homosexual. However, details of Mineo's performance, including his stolen glance at a glossy photo of Alan Ladd that he keeps in his locker, and the lingering gaze with which he regards Jim, indicate his sexuality. For his part, Jim's gender identity is complicated by his acceptance of Plato's as well as Judy's desiring gaze, further to extra-textual knowledge of Dean's own bisexuality.

Cross-cuts between Buzz and Jim see the characters watching one another to determine when would be the most opportune moment to jump from their respective cars. As the cars veer ever closer to the cliff edge, a cut from a close-up of Buzz to another of the handle of the car door reveals that the sleeve of his leather jacket is caught, such that he cannot open the door. Unaware of this development, Jim continues to watch Buzz, before finally diving out of the car just as Buzz's car, and Buzz within it, careers over the cliff edge. As the only remaining participant, Jim has technically won the race. However, his apparent victory is problematised by the rules Buzz had stipulated at the beginning of the race, which stated that the *first* one to dive would be the 'chicken'. Since Buzz never left the car, the film presents the possibility that it is he who is the winner of the Chickie Run and Jim, the 'chicken'. If that were so, then the scene can be read as demonstrating that only in death can a subject fully embody the norms of idealised masculinity – a grim assertion that chimes with Butler's theorisation of the impossibility of ever embodying idealised gender.

That idealised masculinity is instantiated only in death in *Rebel* has potent resonances with Dean's stardom, which, as previously discussed, is marked by tragedy and death as well as rebellious insouciance. In retrospect, the unintended similarities between Buzz and Dean are manifold: Buzz's apparent fearlessness constructs him as an embodiment of youthful rebellion. Similarly, accounts of Dean's fatal car crash present an audacious driver, with little regard for his own safety and misplaced faith in his driving skills. His passenger, Rolf Wütherich, reports that the star drove at the legal limit at his request, the implication being that Dean otherwise preferred to drive much faster (Spoto 1996: 248). On the day of the fatal collision Wütherich also reports that Dean accelerated towards the crossing, assuring him, 'that guy's gotta see us – he'll stop' (Spoto 1996: 248).[9] There is pathos in Butler's assertion that idealised gender is always impossible to embody, despite the discursive compulsion to cite a rigid formula of gender norms. Yet close attention to the editing and *mise-en-scène* of the Chickie Run complicates the apparently idealised masculinity of Buzz's pyrrhic victory. Indeed, Buzz did not remain in his car on account of his daring, but because he was trapped. As a consequence,

Rebel shows how mythic, fearless masculinity comes to be constructed in retrospect, and in so doing undermines its mystique.

Questioning the Family Unit

For Lewis, Jim's is a quest to re-establish the ideal of a family (Lewis 1992: 27). As a result, he argues, Jim's ostensible project of rebellion is somewhat disingenuous. Similarly, McCann argues that *Rebel* 'affirms' rather than undermines the family institution (McCann 1991: 31). The family unit is depicted as vulnerable throughout the film, most obviously in the scenes after Jim wins the Chickie Run and retreats to the mansion that Plato had pointed out earlier in the planetarium. The screen is momentarily filled with a succession of images of the pair's respective parents and Plato's guardian, anxiously clasping telephone handsets as they speak urgently. These images are linked by dissolves, providing the impression of several hours passing. The film's melodramatic heritage and substantial identification with the older generation is apparent here, as the film's soundtrack amplifies the emotional impact felt by the adults even as the action positions us with their offspring. Following these shots, the film cuts to an establishing shot of an abandoned house. Although the camera is level, the house's position on a hill makes it appear as though shot at an angle. Likewise, with its shutters falling off and in an obvious state of disrepair, the unlit house signifies disorder. The juxtaposition between the frantic parents and the dilapidated mansion suggests that the family unit itself is no longer fit for purpose – an impression that is emphasised by the sound of breaking glass heard off-screen, indicating further destruction taking place.

The arrival of Plato at the house precipitates the group's play on the norms of middle-class family life. Asking Jim and Judy what they think of his refuge inspires Jim to ape the norms of adult male respectability, as he asks Judy, 'Would you like to rent or are you looking to buy, dear?' Following Jim's lead, Plato and Judy assume the roles of estate agent and wife respectively, both adopting the same overtly stilted mannerisms. In these roles, both Jim and Judy make clear their disinterest in having children. Jim even states that he would 'drown them like puppies', a line that references Plato's deviance earlier in the film. Dean's performance of respectable masculinity recalls Mr Magoo, the visually impaired character voiced by Jim Backus, who plays Jim's father in *Rebel*. Dean's choice to imitate a character noted for his literal and figurative blindness as an embodiment of middle-class masculinity both demonstrates the character's lack of admiration for his father, and lampoons the myopia of the era's norms of respectability.

The normativity of the group's role-playing also calls to be read in terms of Butler's conception of the 'parodic inhabiting of conformity', which, she argues, undermines the discursive authority to which it ostensibly appeals

(Butler 1993: 122). That is, while appearing to embody gender norms in a way that upholds their validity, the very fervour with which one attempts to embody them paradoxically serves to undermine them. As the scene's estate agent, Plato emphasises the absurdity of the situation, giving a price of three million dollars a month to rent the house. Calling into question the gender and class norms of adult heteronormativity, the three characters are seen to undermine rather than re-affirm the validity of the family unit.

The playful atmosphere culminates in a wistful scene that further undermines the norms of the nuclear family. Here, Jim rests his head on Judy's lap, while Plato sits on the floor leaning on Jim in turn. For McCann, Lewis and Shary, this scene, and the characters' positioning, demonstrates their replication of domesticity, since Judy and Jim appear to occupy the roles of parents for Plato (McCann 1991; Lewis 1992; Shary 2005). When they abandon Plato, seemingly in dereliction of their parental duties, Jim and Judy paradoxically seem to play the role of his parents effectively. As Shary points out, their actions replicate those of Plato's own parents (Shary 2005: 27). This is not to say that the relationship between Plato, Jim and Judy is straightforwardly parental; the fond glances exchanged between Dean and Mineo suggest that the bond they share is more than a fatherly one. What is more, Plato's exaggerated claims of his real father, that he was a 'hero in the South China seas' demonstrate the extent to which his conceptions of a male role model are themselves fantasies.

Judy appears to endorse Jim's relationship with Plato when she muses on the ideal masculine love object. Looking up, away from Jim and the camera, she asks 'What kind of a person do you think a girl wants?' Jim's nonchalant response, 'A man?', illustrates that for him, the only obvious attribute required to be a woman's partner is masculinity. However, combining Dyer's ear for 'how a line is said' (Dyer 1979: 151) with Butler's work on gender enables Dean's hesitant, somewhat sarcastic delivery of the line to be read as questioning rather than reaffirming heteronormative expectation. Jim's apparent disinterest in Judy's heartfelt declarations of love opens a space for disrupting the scene's heteronormativity. For her, 'being Plato's friend when nobody else liked him' makes Jim not only strong, yet also 'gentle and sweet'. Judy's ideal of masculinity can be seen to reflect the new style of male star that came to prominence in the 1950s, of which Dean is a key example, who were portrayed as vulnerable and conflicted in contrast to the steadfast virility of the previous generation. Further, Judy's description of an ideal masculine love object as one who offers Plato friendship is distinctly ironic given the latter's obvious infatuation with Jim. As a consequence, Dean's hesitant, pensive performance complicates the scene's overt aim to cement the relationship between Jim and Judy.

The film's apparent endorsement of the queer potential between Jim and Plato is cut off in its concluding scenes, as Plato is killed and Jim is reintegrated into society. Mineo demonstrates characteristic awareness of the role his character plays in Jim's heterosexual coming of age: 'You can see [Plato] has the hots for James Dean . . . Ergo, [he] had to be bumped off, out of the way' (Mineo, quoted in McCann 1991: 151). The concluding scenes of *Rebel* call to be read as a containment to the ideological threats posed by both juvenile delinquency and nascent homosexuality.

Jim's performance of friendship when left alone in the planetarium with Plato provides a further example of the character's incoherent subjectivity. The soft, hesitant delivery of the plaintive 'I'm not going to hurt you or anything like that,' and the reassurance that he will not turn on the lights even as he fumbles in the dark for the switch, add to the sense of Jim's duplicity, despite his desire to be recognised for his masculine honour earlier in the film. However, this deception passes unnoticed by Plato, as he asks to know why Jim and Judy abandoned him at the mansion. Holding his arms around his chest, with his thumb in his mouth, as he looks up wide-eyed, Jim asks, 'Don't you trust me, Plato?' The pose, seen in Figure 3.2 below, constitutes a star moment for Dean, since it conveys his boyishness and vulnerability – the qualities for which he remains best known. It is significant that this star moment occurs only when Jim and Plato are alone, particularly given Judy's preference for a male partner who accepts and reciprocates Plato's affections. Temporarily protected from the authorities because Plato is armed, the planetarium becomes a safe space for the pair, even as Jim's removing the magazine from Plato's gun punctures their intimacy. Indicating the significance of this breach of trust, the action is shown in extreme close-up. Jim's actions here demonstrate that his character remains deeply conflicted; while he plays the role of Plato's protector, he also

Figure 3.2   Jim (James Dean) deceives Plato (Sal Mineo).

serves as an agent of the community who deprives his friend with the means to rebel against the authorities.

Jim's conflicting ambitions – to be Plato's friend, and to redeem himself in the eyes of the police – arguably help to bring about Plato's death at the hands of the police officer who believes him still to be armed. There are also significant consequences for Jim's reintegration into normative society. Dean crumples his body to the floor, indicating the acuity of Jim's grief for his friend. Attempting to comfort his son, Frank steels himself momentarily in acknowledgement of Jim's need for him to perform a stereotypically 'strong' version of masculinity, the impact of which is amplified by the camera's tilt as he rises to a standing position. Affirming his newly acquired power and control, Frank places his jacket over Jim's shoulders, echoing his son's gesture to Plato when the pair first meet at the police station. In contrast, a cut to a close-up of Jim's mother shows her watching the pair silently, indicating that she has relinquished her earlier dominant position. For George M. Wilson, Frank's gesture is a particularly revealing one, demonstrating that the red jacket of rebellion, now clothing Plato's body, is symbolically dead, while Jim, newly enveloped in his father's tweeds, is recuperated into ordinary adult society (Wilson 1983: 187). Jim's rebellion is thus cast as a brief phase, an essential and formative element of his coming of age.

The reassertion of the normative appears to be further consolidated as he introduces Judy to his parents. John Gibbs observes the physical resemblance between the two actors playing Jim's mother and Judy – Ann Doran and Natalie Wood, respectively – an echo that is emphasised by two medium shots, first of Jim and Judy, then of Frank and his wife (Gibbs 2002: 8). For Gibbs, these shots emphasise that despite the teens' former idealism, they will undoubtedly replicate the failures of Jim's parents (Gibbs 2002: 8). The concluding scenes of *Rebel* seem all too quick to brush over the extent of Jim's troubled behaviour at the beginning of the film. Indeed, the character's contradictory and erratic tendencies are hastily elided in this scene. While *Rebel* ends by seemingly upholding heterosexual norms, close reading of Dean's performance throughout the film reveals the fragile foundations on which those norms rest.

Grease (Randal Kleiser, 1978)

In contrast to the other two films analysed in this chapter, both of which have a contemporary setting, *Grease* looks back to an idealistic fantasy of 1950s adolescence, and in so doing draws from the conventions of the Hollywood film musical. For Lesley Speed, *Grease* is a revivalist text – that is, one that participates 'in a shared recognition and manipulation of signs with reference to a particular historical period' (Speed 2000: 23). Echoing Fred Davis's distinction between personal and public nostalgia (1979), Speed contrasts the collective recollection of popular culture from the past with what she believes to be the considerably more melancholic, individualised and subjective experience of nostalgia, which is concerned with mourning the past. In *Grease* there is nothing hinting at a sense of loss in the deployment of figures from 1950s pop culture, such as Elvis Presley, interspersed with the Bee Gees' distinctly 1970s soundscape. Rather, the mood is celebratory and in keeping with the film's generic heritage as a musical.

This case study focuses specifically on John Travolta's performance as the film's male lead, Danny Zuko. Travolta's role follows his Oscar-nominated performance in *Saturday Night Fever* (John Badham, 1977), which saw his character, Tony Manero, channel youthful masculine anomie through mastery of the dance floor. As the leader of the T-Birds gang in *Grease*, Danny is subject to many of the same norms of masculinity that were observed for Buzz in *Rebel*, and indeed for Tony in *Saturday Night Fever*. Like those characters, Danny must be the aggressive face of his group and initiate confrontation with rival gang the Scorpions. However, his embodiment of these norms is troubled by his romantic feelings for Sandy, with whom he shared a brief romance the previous summer. Close analysis of Travolta's performance as it develops over the course of *Grease* promises to reveal the tensions in maintaining these distinct masculine personae. Travolta's performances in *Grease* and *Saturday Night Fever* alike showcase the star's ability to embody his characters' conflicts through bodily movement. Even strutting down the street while listening to 'Staying Alive', in the opening scenes of *Saturday Night Fever*, the audience is given to understand the gaping chasm between Tony's aspirations, his self-perception, and the reality of his situation as an assistant in a Brooklyn hardware shop. As a result, Butler's theorisation of gender, which is attentive to the impact of gestures and movement, is particularly apposite for an analysis of Travolta's performance here.

Idealised Heterosexuality and the Dual-focus Narrative

Adapted from the 1971 Broadway show of the same name, *Grease* subscribes to the generic structures of the Hollywood film musical. For Rick Altman, these narrative structures consist principally in the 'dual focus narrative' (Altman 1987a: 42). That is, in contrast to the causal narrative common to the majority of Hollywood cinema, the film musical is constructed around a fundamental distinction between two protagonists of the opposite sex, whose difference from one another is reinforced by other, secondary characteristics such as nationality, class and values (Altman 1987a: 42).[10] The musical's narrative sees the eventual union of these two protagonists, and the values they embody, in marriage. Thus, the film musical can be seen to uphold the heterosexual relationship as an idealised union of opposites that complement and complete one another (Altman 1987b in Cohan 2002: 37).

All textual elements of the studio-era musical are intended to emphasise the diametric opposition between the male and female leads, as well as the inevitability of their union in marriage. The use of two-shots, parallel sets and duets, for instance, allow the spectator to perceive the eventual formation of the couple even if the two characters have not yet met, or the animosity between them seems insurmountable (Altman 1987b in Cohan 2002: 35–7). Significantly, Altman's reading of the film musical as heterosexist chimes with Butler's conceptualisation of the heterosexual matrix, in which the traits that constitute masculinity are constructed in opposition to those that denote femininity. This observation provides an important backdrop to the analysis of *Grease*.

The film's opening scenes portray the summer romance between Danny and Sandy, which occurs some weeks prior to the main narrative at Rydell High. This romance takes place at a geographically vague yet idyllic place referred to throughout only as 'the beach'. A slow montage of the pair kissing, holding hands and running down the beach is edited using dissolves, which provide the impression of temporal ellipses. The liberty and timelessness of these scenes corresponds to Altman's conception of a 'valley', a liminal space, away from the constraints of ordinary life, in which the protagonists are permitted to express a 'truer' idea of themselves (Altman 1987a: 86). As a result, our perception of the two characters is anchored as we see them here; as two romantic, clean-cut teenagers. Later on in the film, as Danny's other, less romantic social roles assert themselves, this knowledge secures the audience's faith in their compatibility.

The film's opening sequence indicates the status of *Grease* as pastiche in the mould of Dyer's theorisation of the term. That is, as a 'text that shows similarities with another, earlier text but with clear discrepancies and distortions' (Dyer 2007: 3). Noting the origins of 'pastiche' in the Italian *pasticcio*, Dyer argues that that the pastiche text may combine a number of otherwise disparate elements in a stylised imitation (Dyer 2007: 8). The scene's non-diegetic soundtrack, a choral rendition of 'Love is a Many-Splendored Thing' evokes the 1955 film and later soap opera of the same name. What's more, the scene's seaside location recalls American International Pictures' *Beach Party* series, which also portrayed the adventures and romances of so-called clean teens.[11] The many references to other romance narratives in this opening scene dispute Altman's claim that the 'valley' provides some respite from the logic of the dual-focus narrative. However, the hyperbole of the sequence, with the soundtrack's sweeping strings and the idealised perfection of the romance shown here, demonstrate the extent to which *Grease* sends up the elevated expectations such narratives evoke in their viewers.

Figure 3.3 Danny (John Travolta) is granted a star entrance in *Grease*.

Following the credit sequence, Danny is introduced a second time, at Rydell High. In the opening sequence at the beach, he is presented as Sandy's equal partner. However, at Rydell, Danny is accorded a star entrance, as a medium close-up of his smiling face fills the frame when he turns toward the camera, as seen in Figure 3.3 above. Changes in Danny's characterisation are also apparent in costume. Dressed in a tight white T-shirt, dark jeans and black leather jacket emblazoned with the name and insignia of the T-Birds, Danny's clothing is immediately recognisable as that of the juvenile delinquent, and is particularly evocative of Marlon Brando's role as Johnny Strabler in *The Wild One*. This costume is in marked contrast to the pastel shirts and jackets principally associated with the clean teen style of the Beach films, which Danny wore in the film's opening scenes. These changes of costume signal the many layers of Danny's construction of masculinity, and the number of gender 'scripts' that the character is attempting to fulfil.

Travolta's own star persona is also significant to this second introduction to Danny. When he is summoned by the other T-Birds, Kenickie (Jeff Conaway) and Sonny (Michael Tucci), Danny's mannered, rolling swagger comically recalls the similarly bouncing gait of Tony in *Saturday Night Fever*. Discussing his acting style, Travolta states that when preparing for a role, he first considers how the character might move, and how he would occupy a space (Reeves 1978: 62). Throughout *Grease*, Travolta uses his character's movement to signal his lack of ease with his multiple social roles, which he must learn to navigate. Since Travolta's star persona is bound up with his dancing skills, his movements and gestures are particularly significant to understanding his film performances. It will therefore be important to consider how Danny alters his physical mannerisms at various narrative junctures.

The film's first musical number, 'Summer Nights', co-opts filmic devices that Altman associates with the dual-focus narrative, and thus portrays the opposing traits embodied by Danny and Sandy. Both characters are shown in this sequence, yet neither is aware of the other's presence at Rydell, making their equal participation in the duet all the more prescient for their final union. In this sequence, the T-Birds assemble at the athletics track, while Sandy and the Pink Ladies take their positions at the school cafeteria. Thus, the male and female characters are shown to inhabit distinct spaces, reinforcing the differing attitudes between the two sexes along the lines that Altman (1987a) proposes.

At the athletics track, the T-Birds position themselves on the bleachers at the farthest point away from the track itself. In doing so, they acknowledge their place on the very margins of normative constructions of masculinity. In *Grease*, normative teen masculinity is embodied by the 'jockstraps', whose conventionality and slow wit are represented by their grey regulation varsity kits. The T-Birds, then, are constructed as a subculture – in opposition to, and at the margins of, the dominant mainstream (Hebdige 1979). Yet, as was observed at the Chickie Run in *Rebel*, the ostensibly delinquent gang is also bound by its own system of rules and expectations. Notably, the song's lyrics demonstrate that this system of rules is oriented around the performance of heterosexual masculinity. Danny's recent experience at the beach therefore casts him as the authority on sexual romance and by extension, the gang's de facto leader.

The call-response form of 'Summer Nights', where Danny and Sandy alternate their lines with interjections from other characters, calls attention to the comic disparity in their recollections of the previous summer. While Danny claims that 'we made out under the dock', Sandy only states that they 'stayed out 'til ten o'clock'. Similarly, Danny maintains that 'she got friendly down in the sand', whereas Sandy's beau merely 'got friendly, holding [her] hand'. The choreography of the scene, where the Pink Ladies and T-Birds pursue Sandy and Danny around their respective spaces, signals the extent to which the two characters may be providing a narrative that suits the requirements of their peer group. This is particularly the case for Sandy, who is new at Rydell, and whom Rizzo (Stockard Channing) suspects may not be a good fit for the Pink Ladies. However, the rhyming couplets and the centrality of the duet form indicate the compatibility between Danny and Sandy. Their contradictory accounts function as a proxy of heterosexuality as an idealised union of opposites.

As the film cuts with increasing rapidity between the T-Birds and the Pink Ladies, we are able to perceive the differences in the two groups' interest in this summer romance. While Danny's friends are solely concerned with his sexual conquest, the girls are more interested in Sandy's tale of lost romance. Reflecting Altman's dual-focus narrative, textual elements in the sequence reinforce the surface distinctions between the protagonists, while parallel sequences (and, indeed, the two characters' participation in the duet itself) foretell their eventual unity. Such differences are emphasised by the colour palette and costumes associated with each group. While Danny and his friends are clad largely in black, set off by the grey bleachers behind them, the girls are surrounded by pastel shades, with their full skirts providing a further contrast to the T-Birds' tight trousers. Reading these surface differences alongside Butler's and Altman's work on gender and the film musical respectively highlights the acute, binarised distinction between the film's construction of masculinity and femininity.

Rizzo provides a notable alternative to the dominant construction of femininity in the sequence. On the periphery for the first half of the song, a quick cut from Danny in medium shot shows Rizzo in the same shot scale lying on her side, and wearing a black dress. Her sexual pose and dark colour palette, with echoes of the T-Birds' costuming, provide a visual clue to her shared past with Danny. Further demonstrating her difference from the other girls, Rizzo rejects Sandy's romance narrative. To their repeated pleas to 'tell me more', Rizzo flatly responds 'cos he sounds like a drag', in a deep, monotone voice that sets her apart from the girlish timbres of Sandy and the chorus. Embodying aspects of the T-Birds' attitudes and costuming while heading up the Pink Ladies, Rizzo's characterisation can be seen to complicate the heterosexual binarism otherwise presented in the scene.

The two versions of Danny and Sandy's summer romance – one sexual, the other sweetly chaste – invite the audience to question which is likely to be the more accurate. Certainly, Sandy's account is entirely consistent with her presentation as naïve and innocent. When she initially meets the Pink Ladies, she does not catch the double entendre of Rizzo's toying 'How are things down under?' Sandy, they conclude, is 'too pure to be pink'. Sandy's innocence carries with it implications of honesty. If we determine that the romance was as sweet as Sandy describes, then we can also infer that Danny understands that his role as the leader of the T-Birds requires him to maintain an appearance of sexual promiscuity, and that he is willing and able to provide them with a narrative that fits this image. As I later demonstrate, when the two audiences for these competing visions of masculinity – as the T-Birds' leader, and as Sandy's partner – collide, Travolta's movements and gestures demonstrate the layering of these multiple identities in a single figure, disputing the apparent wholeness and integrity of gender (and of masculinity in particular).

Multiple Performances of Masculinity

As was demonstrated in the analysis of the 'Summer Nights' sequence, in *Grease* the T-Birds' use of space is particularly significant to the construction of masculinity. Taking place in the Rydell Auto Shop, the 'Greased Lightnin'' sequence shows the extent to which the eponymous car stands in for the T-Birds' collective embodiment of idealised masculinity. Following an encounter with the Scorpions, who deride Greased Lightnin' as a 'heap of junk', Danny inspires the gang to enhance their car through song. His lyrics expressly connect the prospect of remodelling the vehicle with enhanced sexual desirability for the group:

> With new pistons, plugs and shocks
> I can get off my rocks.
> You know that I ain't braggin'
> She's a real pussy wagon.
> Greased Lightnin'

Despite the overt heterosexuality of the choreography and lyrics, the group's easy collaboration recalls the homosocial aspects of the gang seen in *Rebel*. However, in *Grease* the characters are far more keenly aware of the fragile continuum between homosociality and homosexuality (Sedgwick 1985: 6). Following their later race against the Scorpions at Thunder Road, Kenickie and Danny briefly embrace, before both characters quickly realise their error and abruptly pull away. Butler's theorisation of a discursive prohibition on homosexuality elucidates the young men's movement between revelling in masculine bonding, and their otherwise overt heterosexuality. The 'Greased Lightnin'' sequence in particular lampoons the gang's aspirations for heterosexual desirability, while they remain uneasy about the evident affection they hold for one another.

The comic impossibility of the gang's vision for themselves is made clear when the drab garage, the T-Birds and the car itself are abruptly transformed. While the garage becomes a fantastical non-place in which all furnishings other than the car are whitewashed, the T-Birds acquire new, matching outfits that reflect the idealised cohesion they seek from membership of the gang. For its part, the car now features a transparent bonnet and a fresh paint job. That these changes take place during the song draws attention to the utopian structures of the musical genre. For Dyer, entertainment and the musical in particular offers 'the image of something better to escape into' (2002: 20). In other words, the utopia offered by the musical supplies a temporary response to society's ills and injustices; one that vanishes once the credits have rolled. In this case, the T-Birds' utopian vision of themselves corresponds with the idealised hegemonic masculinity which, as Butler theorises, always remains just out of reach.

The status of *Grease* as a revivalist musical, looking back to the past, is also significant here. Dyer notes a tendency for studio-era musicals to set narratives at the turn of the twentieth century, an era that represents in film, if not in actuality, a 'more free-and-easy stage in American development'

(Dyer 2002: 30). One key attribute of this carefree epoch is the prevalence of music, the source of which, Dyer proposes, is the folk communities for whom music was a part of everyday life (Dyer 2002: 30). In the case of *Grease*, it is scarcely credible that 1950s suburban California constituted a hub of instantaneous song and dance outside of the professional studio musical. However, the mobilisation of pop culture icons of the time, among them Elvis Presley in the Greased Lightnin' sequence, can be seen to call attention to the disparity between the growth of American rock and roll music in the 1950s and its substantial transformation by the late 1970s. The very American-ness of the pop culture referenced in *Grease* indicates the significance of the 1950s as a time of national – albeit inward-looking – cohesion.

The scene conveys the ludicrousness of the characters' associations between masculinity, heteronormative desirability and their car. One telling example occurs when Kenickie applies motor oil firstly to its correct location – the car's engine – before using it to style his hair. The choreography of the scene further emphasises the ridiculousness of the gang's aspirations, as they leap and thrust all over the car. The comedy of the scene calls to be read in the light of Butler's claims that the endless, and ultimately fruitless, attempts to instantiate idealised gender norms is an 'occasion for laughter' (Butler 1990: 178). Certainly, this scene conveys the absurdity of the T-Birds' hopes for the car in a way that serves ultimately to undermine the validity of those aspirations. As if to demonstrate the impossibility of their desires, the gang and their car are brought abruptly down to earth at the end of the song, when they find themselves back at the Rydell Auto Shop in their tatty overalls. The fantasy of idealised masculinity is thus shown to fail on screen.

Danny is able to create a compelling illusion of rebel masculinity with the T-Birds. However, at the gym, his attempts to embody normative masculinity are markedly less successful. Tellingly, while Danny's transformation into the ideal figure of subcultural masculinity is seemingly instant and achieved through song, his attempts to embody mainstream masculinity, here figured by Sandy's oafish boyfriend Tom (Lorenzo Lamas), is seen to require repeated efforts. At the gym, Danny's appearance is immediately incongruous. Following rapid cuts between medium shots of students on the gym horse and rings, the camera settles in a three-quarter shot from behind Danny to foreground his distinctive silhouette of greased hair, sunglasses, cigarette and black leather jacket – the antithesis of the grey Rydell High sports kit. The contrast in appearance and manner between Danny and the other students at the gym foregrounds Travolta's characteristic bouncing swagger after Coach Calhoun (Sid Caesar) tells him to change into appropriate gym clothes. While ostensibly an aggressive saunter, Danny's awkward sashay into the gym conversely indicates his unease in the environment, once again highlighting how the multiple spaces created by the school allow for the creation of multiple value systems.

On the basketball court, Danny is shown in medium-long shot standing at a slight distance from the other players. The space between Danny and his classmates shows how he has customised the sports kit, having rolled up the short sleeves of his T-shirt, restyled his hair and tucked a comb into the waistband of his shorts, creating a close approximation of the T-Birds' style. Despite Danny's apparent intention to become a romantic partner for Sandy, his appearance demonstrates the extent to which his role as the leader of the T-Birds leaks through the prescribed boundaries of the regulation attire, and in so doing, his reluctance to give up this position. Danny's T-Birds identity further manifests itself in excessive aggression, such that all the sports he attempts end in a physical altercation with another student. When handed the ball on the basketball court, he breaks through his opponents by waving a fist at the other players, while holding the ball in the other hand. When another player gains possession of the ball, Danny punches him in the stomach rather than attempt to out-manoeuvre him. The camera's distance from the action invites a comparison between Danny's gestures and those of the other players. Whereas the other students appear well-versed in the rules of sportsmanship – the codification of which also equates them with normative gender – Danny's aggression shows him as an embodiment of excessive masculinity. His attempts at basketball reinforce his positioning as a rebel, since a central tenet of the T-Birds' group identity is breaking school rules and mocking those who obey them.

The Dance Competition

Signposted from the very beginning of *Grease*, the National Bandstand dance competition is presented as a key event in the school calendar. The competition occupies over twenty minutes of screen time, indicating the significance of the event not only for the film's characters but also for John Travolta, whose dancing skills remain a signature element of his star persona. As if to emphasise the reference to his earlier performance in *Saturday Night Fever*, the wide lapels and unbuttoned shirt of Danny's black and pink ensemble, as seen in Figure 3.4, undoubtedly recall Tony Manero's fashion sense in the earlier film. This costume choice serves to remove Danny from the film's overall 1950s signifying economy, and reinforces Travolta's extraordinariness as the film's star.

Scenes at the dance competition provide key examples of Travolta's character negotiating social audiences and masculine roles through movement. In *Saturday Night Fever* Tony's inability to refuse his friends' expectations caused him to lose a potential relationship with Stephanie (Karen Lynn Gorney). In *Grease* too, when Danny's leadership of the T-Birds clashes with his role as Sandy's boyfriend, his negotiation of these roles occurs primarily through his abrupt changes in posture. Earlier in the film, Rizzo orchestrates Danny and

Figure 3.4   Danny (John Travolta) and Sandy (Olivia Newton-John) arrive at the dance competition.

Sandy's reunion, aiming to embarrass Danny and to disabuse Sandy of the wide-eyed romanticism she found so grating in the 'Summer Nights' sequence. At his first sight of Sandy, Danny's immediate grin conveys his unalloyed happiness at seeing Sandy again so unexpectedly. However, observing Kenickie's sharp stare as the T-Birds surround him, Danny rolls his head back on his neck, bounces his body slightly and changes the tone of his voice to a deeper timbre that attempts to convey nonchalance, and converses in casual platitudes that deny the depth of his feelings and alienate Sandy. Grinning and sniggering behind him, the T-Birds clearly approve of Danny's later performance, while Sandy is distinctly unimpressed and rejects it. The control exerted by the gang over its apparent leader corresponds to the power relations between Buzz and his gang in *Rebel*, demonstrating the paradoxical dependence of the ostensible leader on their followers to maintain their mastery.

The differing expectations of Sandy and the T-Birds also come into conflict at the dance competition itself. With Sandy at his side, Danny sings along with the love ballads heard at the dance. However, spying two of the T-Birds coming into earshot, he starts to screech out of tune, appearing to mock the romantic sentiments expressed in the songs. Travolta's performance can be seen to demonstrate the possibility of inhabiting disparate masculinities simultaneously, thereby disputing the coherence of masculinity as an identity category. Observing that Danny cannot fulfil the requirements of both audiences and realise his own romantic desires, *Grease* calls on him to embody only one of these identities.

At the dance competition, the 'game rules' stipulated by the principal demonstrate the prohibitions at stake at such an event. She states: 'All couples must be boy/girl, any couple tapped on the shoulder must leave the floor,' and finally that 'anyone displaying tasteless or vulgar movements will be disqualified'.

Further to the heteronormativity and chastity of these rules, their application necessitates the judgement of others, in this case that of vain TV personality Vince Fonteyn (Edd Byrnes). Frequent cuts between the principal's anxious expression and high-angle medium shots of the raucous students indicate her awareness of the potential for students to subvert the rules she has so carefully specified. Indeed, her words, and the lack of probability that these stipulations will be adhered to, is backed up by Butler's contention that the citation of the law sets in motion the potential for its subversion (Butler 1993: 95). That is, by so carefully stating what is not permissible behaviour at the dance, the principal has clearly laid out to the T-Birds and others like them what the parameters for rebellious behaviour might be. It is therefore no surprise when, later on, the T-Birds moon at the TV cameras to celebrate Danny's success.

For their part, Danny and Sandy's dance demonstrates the idealised compatibility associated with the Hollywood film musical's couple dance (Dyer 2002). Their easy co-ordination contrasts with the spectacle of the more ridiculous couples, where girls are dragged across the floor, couples rigidly count their steps and fights break out between the male students. Frequent cutaways to the growing crowd on the sidelines showing those whom Vince has removed from the competition serve as ellipses and demonstrate the difficulty of assuming the idealised teen coupledom advocated by the contest's stringent rules on both heterosexuality and sexual display. Dancing the hand jive, Danny and Sandy are shown facing the camera rather than each other, and in fact touch very little. The Frosty Palace waitresses cooing over how 'adorable' the pair look on TV confirm Danny and Sandy as the ideal, young heterosexual couple.

Danny's dancing style changes considerably when Sonny drags Sandy off the dance floor, to replace her with Cha Cha (Annette Charles), whose dark hair and Latino looks contrast her with Sandy's blonde, virginal pallor and girlish white dress. Danny is only mildly startled by this sudden change in partners, yet continues to dance with Cha Cha. Consistent with her reputation as the girl with the 'worst reputation', Cha Cha's dance with Danny takes on a considerably more sexual tone, as reaction shots of the principal's anxious expression indicate. As the music's tempo increases, Cha Cha and Danny use more of their bodies in the dance. Unlike the rapid, contained movements required by the hand-jive, this dance sees Cha Cha exuberantly passing through Danny's open legs, and she in turn raising her legs high over Danny's head. That Cha Cha is the partner of whom the T-Birds approve demonstrates the values they believe a female acolyte of theirs should possess. Notably, too, although it was Danny and Sandy who seemed to be upheld as the ideal couple, it is this later pair that in fact wins the dance competition overall. Unusually, it is the promiscuous mores of Danny and Cha-Cha which are upheld over Sandy's innocence and chastity.

Personality Dissolve at the Carnival

Grease concludes with a carnival that constitutes Rydell High's commencement and celebrates the students' completion of their high school education. In line with Altman's dual-focus narrative, the carnival provides the space for the idealised reconciliation of opposites, and in so doing, allows for the establishment of a new form of community (Altman 1987a: 86). Accordingly, 'You're the One that I Want', which cements the relationship between Danny and Sandy, is closely followed by 'We Go Together', a song that promises the enduring friendship between the film's cast of characters.

In Altman's model, the personality dissolve provides the narrative resolution in the Hollywood film musical (Altman 1987a: 86). The term refers to the final synthesis that takes place between the two opposite-sexed protagonists such that 'each partner must give up his/her own surface desires and become the other' (Altman 1987a:86). That this union takes place at a carnival, with that space's widely documented reversal of norms, is an important backdrop to the interpretation of Danny and Sandy's final union (see Mikhail Bakhtin 1941). Clues that the reunion is not to be taken entirely seriously are apparent in the *mise-en-scène*, firstly in the use of cardboard cut-outs through which characters put their heads to create amusing scenes. The shot of Jan (Jamie Donnelly) and Putzie (Kelly Ward) behind a cut-out of a man proposing to a woman both dressed in Victorian costume appears to foretell Danny and Sandy's likely future. However, the comically surreal cut-outs that follow call for an alternative explanation: Sonny is shown posing as a King Kong-like figure saving Marty, while Doody poses as a cowboy with a pug filling in for his shapely partner. These three shots can be seen to lampoon the heteronormative expectations of the Hollywood film musical's conclusion.

While many critics have focused solely on the visually arresting changes that Sandy undergoes at the end of *Grease* (see Speed 2002; Shary 2005; Driscoll 2011), those made by Danny in this scene should also be acknowledged. Sonny's call, 'There's Zuko!' echoes Danny's first appearance in the film. The quick pan, which mimics a character rapidly turning their head, shows Danny walking towards the group in medium shot wearing a Rydell High sports team jacket. As the camera spins around the group, reinforcing their cohesiveness, the other T-Birds pull at the jacket while Danny explains that he 'lettered in track' much to his friends' obvious dismay. The gym scenes showed Danny's inability completely to renounce the T-Birds identity. And here too his varsity jacket provides an addition to, rather than a substitute for, his usual black ensemble. The normative identity represented by the jacket can therefore be cast off at will, as he soon does upon sight of Sandy's transformation. Although the group's mockery indicates a sense of Danny's having 'dressed up', his selection for the school running team demonstrates the extent of his desire to become an ideal partner for Sandy, as much as his successful approximation of normative masculinity. The carnival's status as a place in which norms may be temporarily toppled is significant here: this is a space in which the glamorous, formerly promiscuous juvenile delinquent can be transformed into a loving and monogamous partner. Travolta's presentation here can thus be read as an idealised corrective to his earlier role in *Saturday Night Fever*, where Tony Manero was not able to make such a change.

For her part, following the T-Birds' triumph at Thunder Road, Sandy decides that it is time to say 'goodbye to Sandra Dee' and to enlist the services of the Pink Ladies to mould her into a more sexual image. Notably, Cha Cha appears to be something of a role model for Sandy's transformation, as the silhouette of the tight yellow Capri trousers and grey scoop-neck T-shirt worn by Cha Cha at Thunder Road are reflected in Sandy's off-shoulder black catsuit. In turn, Sandy's new perm echoes her rival's curly dark hair. Sandy has evidently transformed herself into an image that she believes will sustain Danny's attention, something that has become a focus of feminist criticism of *Grease*.[12]

Indicating Sandy's new status as sexually available, her arrival at the carnival is observed firstly by the T-Birds, who gaze open-mouthed and silently alert their friends to the spectacle. As the film cuts to allow the spectator the same view, non-diegetic music accompanies the camera's slow tilt up her body. Once settled on a medium close-up of Sandy's face, apart from her strong make-up and permed hair, we immediately notice that she is smoking, and has had her ears pierced – actions she had rejected earlier in the film. The effect of Sandy's image change on Danny is immediate, as he gazes at her in surprise and desire before quickly casting aside his varsity jacket. Sandy's transformation into a version of femininity acceptable to his gang effectively solves Danny's problem of wanting neither to lose her nor to renounce his position as leader of the T-Birds.

Butler's theorisation of gender allows for a reading that compromises the film's conclusion in a conventional personality dissolve. Although neither Danny's nor Sandy's makeovers are shown on screen, which might otherwise provide the illusion of instantaneous achievement, close attention to small, individual actions demonstrate the labour necessitated by their transformations. In Danny's case, his position on the running team will have required considerable, repeated effort, which is only obliquely referenced here. As for Sandy, her breathy 'Tell me about it, stud,' and her hasty glances to the Pink Ladies when unsure what to do with her cigarette can be seen to demonstrate Butler's contention that the approximation of idealised gender is never fully finalised (Butler 1990: 185). In demonstrating the effort in Sandy's new role, *Grease* makes clear that her performance of sexualised femininity is exactly that, and in consequence the innocence and morality that she has displayed throughout the film surely remain intact.

Sandy's performance continues into 'You're the One That I Want', in which she encourages Danny to pursue her playfully through the fun house while the pair affirm their desire for one another. Despite the certainty of the lyrics 'you're the one that I want', the fun house can be seen to demonstrate the instabilities in their union. With the couple following signs displaying the message 'wrong way' and dancing on the 'shake shack', which moves beneath their feet, the film seems keen to emphasise the fragility of their relationship. Nonetheless, *Grease* quickly moves from celebrating the relationship between Danny and Sandy to portraying their integration within a wider community, signalled as 'You're the One That I Want' switches to the euphoric refrains of 'We Go Together'. In accordance with Altman's dual-focus narrative, this closing song sees the dissolution of subcultural differences in favour of a united community in which the principal players are paired into opposite-sexed couples. Consequently, as discussed previously, the heterosexual couple is positioned as an idealised unit of social life.

Yet the hyperbole of the scene, with crowds of smiling characters rushing in to confirm their endorsement of the central couple, invites to question as to whether, like the opening scenes at the beach, this too might be pastiche. Certainly the lyrics of 'We Go Together' quickly descend into nonsense, as if to demonstrate that the easy conclusion offered by the film is an equally absurd proposition.[13] The combination of the slippages in Sandy's transformation, the carnival setting and the ecstatic onslaught of the film's closing sequences open up a space in which, contrary to the norms of the Hollywood film musical, the romance between Danny and Sandy might be a temporary one. This possibility is further suggested by the reappearance of the fantasy car from the 'Greased Lightnin'' sequence, in which the pair fly away into the sunset. Earlier, I argued that Altman's dual-focus narrative supports Butler's contention that a heterosexual matrix structures the construction of gender. In this closing scene, however, the forcefulness with which the reunion of Danny and Sandy is engineered, along with their friends' swift approval of the relationship, cannot mask the evident slippages that portray its contingency. The end of *Grease* is Danny's fantasy of being able to maintain his leadership of the T-Birds and have a relationship with Sandy, while the film makes clear throughout that such a bargain is impossible.

HEATHERS (MICHAEL LEHMANN, 1989)

Heathers is a considerably bleaker work than either *Rebel* or *Grease*. The latter presented a pastiche of the heteronormativity of the Hollywood film musical. In turn, the release of *Heathers* twelve years later followed a wave of films produced, written and sometimes directed by John Hughes that celebrated and idealised high school life. Hughes's works are of defining importance to the Hollywood teen movie, and will be discussed more fully in the following chapter. In *Heathers*, the murderous activities of the film's antagonist, J.D. (Christian Slater) serve both to puncture the pious bonhomie of Hughes's work and to question the extent of rebellion that is permissible in the teen genre. At this point in his career, Christian Slater was not yet regarded as a star. This case study nevertheless demonstrates that the actor's performance references a number of star identities, which in turn take in a number of different instantiations of rebel identity.

The 1980s brought with them a number of different models of youth rebellion. The 'harmless mischief' of *Ferris Bueller's Day Off* (John Hughes, 1986) and the 'dance rebellion' cycle typified by *Footloose* saw privileged teenagers testing authorities at home and school in a fairly wholesome fashion. In contrast, others depicted the youth rebel as a distinctly unsympathetic figure whose unthinking violence was shown in increasingly graphic detail. The controversial *River's Edge* (Tim Hunter, 1986), for instance, exposed the extent of suburban youth apathy as a nonplussed group of high school students, faced with the murder of one of their friends by another of their classmates, strive initially to protect the killer and only begrudgingly report the incident to the police. These different types of rebel figure convey not only the extent to which some kind of rebellion had become an expectation of teen cinema, but also the distinct types of behaviour permitted and considered rebellious in particular contexts.

In *Heathers*, Christian Slater's character, Jason Dean, abbreviated simply to 'J.D.', synthesises and satirises the generic conventions of youth delinquency on screen. As James McKelly observes, J.D. provides 'a synecdoche of the rebel genre as a whole' (McKelly 2005: 213), evoking not only juvenile delinquency in general but the posthumous star of *Rebel*, while the character's black costuming, itinerant lifestyle and large motorcycle recall Brando's character in *The Wild One*. As a consequence, J.D.'s plot to bomb the school in a nihilistic fantasy that promises to rid high schools everywhere of their ubiquitous social divisions can be seen both to expose the latent menace of previous representations of the teen rebel, and to question the limits of teen rebel identity.

Christian Slater, Jack Nicholson and Jason Dean

Unlike *Rebel* and *Grease*, whose central rebels were unquestionably the film's stars, *Heathers* sees an encounter with a teen rebel from the point of view of his love interest, Veronica (Winona Ryder), for whom J.D.'s nonchalance and verbal dexterity initially prove an attractive combination. This unusual narrative perspective is showcased in the film's opening dream sequence, in which Veronica is cruelly excluded from the Heathers' croquet game. Her humiliation is underscored when the ball is substituted for her head, at which Heather

Chandler (Kim Walker) takes a well-executed swing. Veronica's dream is easily deciphered: she fears rejection by the all-conquering trio comprised of Heather Chandler, Heather McNamara (Lisanne Falk) and Heather Duke (Shannon Doherty), and feels the precariousness of her position as the only girl in the clique not to be named Heather. She is, then, an 'insider' seeking escape, a position more akin to that of Danny Zuko than of Jim Stark, an outsider who sought affiliation with Buzz and Judy. It's worth noting here that Butler's work, which provides this chapter's theoretical underpinning, does not consider the subversive potential of mainstream, normative gender identities. Rather, she is attentive to the ways in which those on the margins of intelligibility can trouble the constitution of intelligibility itself. Yet, as this case study will demonstrate, normative identities also exist in a complex negotiation of idealised gender.

For his part, Slater's performance at the school cafeteria references the persona and performance style of Jack Nicholson, whose early roles, Dennis Bingham argues, portray him as a liminal figure who participates in, but is not fully part of, 1960s counterculture (Bingham 1994: 110). Consequently, Nicholson's characters can be said not only to recall the alienation from the mainstream evoked by Brando and Dean, but also a further marginalisation, as they find themselves out of step with the youth-dominated counterculture. To illustrate, in *Easy Rider* (Dennis Hopper, 1969), Nicholson's role as alcoholic lawyer George Hanson shows him participating in Wyatt (Peter Fonda) and Billy's (Dennis Hopper) journey to New Orleans, even as his age and profession prevent him from wholly embracing their biking subculture. I argue that Nicholson's positioning on the fringes of the action provides the source of his characters' unknowability and volatility, since they do not conform to an obvious, pre-existing type. Likewise in *Heathers*, J.D.'s dangerousness emerges at least in part because his actions evade easy categorisation.

Close attention to Nicholson's performance style reveals how the actor deploys his even, reedy voice, which in other circumstances might convey calm placidity, to communicate instead an impression of thinly concealed rage. The level of anger – and the effort of its suppression – are apparent in a famous scene in *Five Easy Pieces* (Bob Rafelson, 1970). Here Nicholson's character's request for a 'plain omelette, no potatoes – tomatoes instead – cup of coffee and toast' is delivered quietly, in a level tone. This order, though, goes against the diner's policies, which stipulate no side orders of toast and no substitutions, at which the character abruptly explodes in anger, and sweeps the crockery and glasses off the table. As Nicholson's stardom develops in later years, the star makes increasing use of facial movements, such that in *The Shining* (Stanley Kubrick, 1980), his wide flashing smile, arching eyebrows and wide, leering grin add to his impression of poorly concealed psychosis.

While Nicholson's characters find themselves distanced from those around them, Bingham suggests that the star's performance style itself creates a distancing effect between character, actor and audience. Despite Nicholson's training at the Actors Studio, which, as previously discussed, aims to create a sense of emotional depth and realism, Bingham argues that his performances highlight the artifice of the roles he portrays (Bingham 1994: 101). To illustrate, he cites a moment in *Batman* (Tim Burton, 1989) in which, as the Joker, Nicholson's eyes 'move deliberately and precisely . . . in facial expressions that describe rather than portray surprise and suspicion' (Bingham 1994: 103). In *Heathers*, Slater's evocation of Nicholson's mannerisms constructs him as a substantially more sinister star persona than Brando and Dean's misunderstood youths.

Slater deploys the full complement of Nicholson's performance gestures in the cafeteria scene where he meets Veronica for the first time. J.D. appears settled, fully aware and in control of his surroundings as he steadily observes the action unfolding around him. Sitting alone, accompanied only by another student sleeping near him, J.D.'s positioning in the far corner of the cafeteria underscores the character's positioning as an outsider. His clothing, too – an austere long black duster coat – further provides an impression of otherworldliness, apparently untouched by other students' more prosaic concerns. In contrast, Veronica, although positioned as part of 'the most powerful clique in the school' is shown to lack control, as she silently follows Heather Chandler and is reprimanded for her friendship with those deemed to be 'lesser', such as Martha (Carrie Lynn) and Betty (Renee Estevez). This contrast, and others that develop during the scene, highlight the constraints imposed by her apparently enviable position at the apex of high school popularity.

Shot/reverse shot editing, which conveys J.D. and Veronica's growing mutual interest, shows that his outsider status is an attractive one. In contrast, Martha provides a representation of a female outsider figure, a girl whose shyness and physical size makes her a social outcast and object of comedy. Like J.D., Martha sits alone at the far corner of the cafeteria. Thus, her near-identical positioning provides a commentary on the gendered construction of the rebel figure: whereas a male outsider figure can be cool, his female counterpart is deemed merely an embarrassment.[14] It is arguably Veronica's awareness of the 'unreality' of the female outsider – in Butler's terms, the possibility of no longer existing as a viable subject, and a threat that Heather Chandler obliquely invokes with some regularity – that compels Veronica to continue her friendship with the Heathers.

Further insight into the difference between the positioning of J.D. and Martha can be gleaned from Dick Pountain and David Robins's study of cool, the intangible currency of the (male) juvenile delinquent. Defined as 'a permanent state of private rebellion', the opposition represented by cool is not a collective, political response but is instead a stance of individual defiance, which lies behind a mask of ironic passivity (Pountain and Robins 2000: 19).

What is significant for this analysis is that Pountain and Robins expressly position cool as a particular type of embodiment, and as a 'mask', indicating that cool is a particular type of gendered bodily performance. Considering cool as a bodily style has important consequences for understanding how this stance is gendered, and for considering how it is only particular types of bodies – lean, youthful and masculine – that can be regarded as cool.

Slater's ironic passivity, along with his evocation of Nicholson's brand of distancing performance, combine to create an impression of J.D. as cool. Aiming to give this new student a 'good scare', Ram (Patrick Labyorteaux) and Kurt (Lance Fenton) reproach J.D. for his otherworldliness, coded here as homosexuality. To their homophobic diatribe, J.D.'s calm, evenly-delivered reply, 'They certainly have an open door policy for assholes though, don't they?' disconcerts the two jocks, not used to such displays of verbal fluency. J.D.'s cocked head and the carefully measured pace at which he delivers the line, recalls Nicholson's performance in *Five Easy Pieces*, where an initially calm response has an unexpectedly dramatic consequence. Here, though, J.D. pulls out a handgun and fires blanks at the two young men at close range. His retaliation is shocking not only because of its disproportionate force, but also because of its disruption to the audience's expectations of the teen rebel. Such violence overreaches the quietly oppositional force Pountain and Robins stipulate in their conceptualisation of cool, shifting instead to the psychotic. As will later be demonstrated, the disruption of cool is what ultimately comes to undermine J.D. at the film's conclusion.

Killing Heather Chandler

When J.D. and Veronica kill Heather Chandler, *Heathers* most clearly announces itself as at a remove from the teen rebel subgenre. What's more, the event can be regarded as a parallel to the Chickie Run first encountered in *Rebel*, in which Jim's participation confirms his rejection of his father's passivity and his desire to assimilate the ways of Buzz and his gang. In other words, for Jim, the Chickie Run is the moment at which his status as a juvenile delinquent is fully realised. Here too, Veronica's implied complicity with Heather Chandler's death implicates her in J.D.'s murderous plans.

The film's tendency for generic subversion is apparent when Veronica and J.D. plan how they might punish Heather Chandler for her callous treatment of Veronica at the college party earlier that evening. This party is a space that Heather Chandler feels privileged to attend, such that she is especially chagrined when Veronica shows her up by vomiting on another of the guests. She therefore promises Veronica that 'on Monday you're history'. When Veronica encounters J.D. at her home, the pair head into the garden, after which the camera pans slowly to discover underwear carelessly abandoned on a pair of croquet mallets, before alighting on Veronica and J.D., seemingly naked underneath a coat. Their discussion of Heather Chandler demonstrates J.D.'s complex blend of juvenile delinquency with Nicholson's adult, psychotic malevolence. When he comments that 'Heather Chandler is one bitch that deserves to die,' Veronica simply smiles, seemingly perceiving his statement as an example of teen hyperbole rather than a declaration of intent. This is perhaps a wilful denial on Veronica's part. J.D.'s statement tells her exactly his intentions towards her former friend. Nonetheless, interpreting him on the register of the youth rebel tradition allows Veronica to dismiss him as merely humorous. Consequently, although J.D. reveals his murderous potential early on, his generic positioning prevents others from recognising it, and allows his words to pass unremarked.

Although this is Veronica's family home, the nocturnal setting, camerawork and the upper-class associations of croquet itself provide strong recollections of the dilapidated mansion in *Rebel*. The close shot scale and the two teens' position within it evoke those of Jim and Judy in the earlier film, and the latter's musings about the ideal masculine love object. In a further parallel between the two pairs, just as Jim responds only occasionally and distractedly to Judy's words, so too, J.D. remains mostly quiet, with only his eyebrows and smirk registering a reaction to Veronica. Notably though, the discarded underwear points to actual intercourse having taken place in *Heathers*, whereas in *Rebel* this is merely implied. Further, J.D.'s casual demeanour contrasts with that of Jim in the earlier film, whose tentativeness conveyed the novelty of his romance with Judy. For J.D., however, such liaisons are routine. His remark that in 'seven schools in seven states, the only thing different is my locker combination' reveals that Veronica is merely the latest of his partners.

Reading J.D. as a citation of Jim Stark in a Butlerian sense invites a reflection on the latter character as a norm of juvenile delinquency. It is the retrospective view of the mansion scene in *Rebel* that constructs it as an idealised, romantic moment in the consolidation of the relationship between Jim and Judy, which *Heathers* knowingly subverts. However, the analysis earlier in the chapter has demonstrated that these scenes were beset with gender anxiety for Jim. In citing the youth delinquency film's generic past, its earlier films come to be reconstructed as innocent and uncomplicated. The juvenile delinquency portrayed in *Heathers* can be seen to correspond to Butler's contention that the citation of the norm does not necessarily uphold it, but rather has the capacity to change, or even to undermine it, in the present.

The following morning, Veronica and J.D. propose that a vomit-inducing hangover cure will be apt revenge for Heather Chandler. The two drinks that each character concocts correspond to the different models of rebellion discussed at the beginning of this case study. Veronica prepares a mixture of orange juice and milk, a temporary – albeit highly nauseating – punishment for Heather's cruelty and self-importance. Veronica's idea accords with the 'harmless mischief' model of teen rebellion (Shary 2002a: 83). This model of delinquency saw relatively affluent teenagers temporarily subvert normative rules of behaviour, while never really threatening the status quo. In contrast, J.D. proposes that a cup of drain-cleaning fluid would be an apt revenge for Heather Chandler. Tellingly, it is he who is placed in the foreground, granting more importance to his choice. His disregard for the drink's fatal properties aligns the character with increasingly pathological and violent presentations of the youth delinquent figure. The contrast in the generic norms to which the two characters belong is significant for identifying how J.D.'s performance style and actions place him between different contemporary iterations of the teen rebel.

J.D. is able both to deflect Veronica's better judgement as he pours the drain fluid into a cup for Heather, and to goad the latter into drinking it. Both of these actions are accomplished by invoking the spectre of cowardice. In Heather's case, J.D. offers her the drink by describing it as a hangover cure, dubbed 'an old family recipe', in reference not only to his rebel antecedents, but also to his father, Big Bud Dean (Kirk Scott), whose rambunctious predilection for explosives also codes him as violent. On its refusal, J.D. quietly turns to Veronica, stating 'I knew it would be too intense for her,' at which Heather takes the cup and defiantly drinks its contents regardless of the potential harm it might pose. In a similar manner to Buzz in *Rebel*, Heather knows that in order to maintain her status she must accept such challenges. Immediately upon swallowing the drain fluid, Heather clutches her throat and collapses into a glass coffee table. However, while the gang see Buzz's death with their own eyes, Heather Chandler is deified in her absence, as Veronica pens a convincing forgery that conveys the character's troubled profundity. With the removal of her signature, talismanic red scrunchie, her power is shown to be readily transferred elsewhere.

Kurt and Ram: From the Homosocial to the Homosexual

Roz Kaveney argues that in *Heathers*, 'social policing, through enforcement of heterosexual norms, is shown to be linked to homosociality' (Kaveney 2006: 57). This homosociality is both female, as exemplified by the hegemonic Heathers themselves, and male, as embodied by insecure jock twosome Kurt and Ram. Discussions of the homosocial earlier in the chapter observed Kosofsky-Sedgwick's assertion that there exists a continuum between homosocial and homosexual relations that is disrupted only by homophobia (Kosofsky-Sedgwick 1985: 25). Significantly, Kosofsky-Sedgwick argues that 'male homosocial bonds are suffused with entitlement' (Kosofsky-Sedgwick 1985: 1), which in *Heathers* is apparent in Ram and Kurt's repeated assertions that they're 'seniors, man', suggesting that this status alone should entitle them to a certain degree of respect. As both a figure of amorality and the film's moral centre, J.D. observes the latent homophobia among the high school students and the community at large, and seeks to dismantle the entitlement of the pair by orchestrating a situation that 'reveals' their homosexuality.

There is a contrast between the entitlement of the homosocial jocks and the moralistic – albeit radically antisocial – judgement of J.D. On the few occasions when J.D. does engage with his peers, his motive is manipulation, as with Veronica, or blackmail, which he attempts with Heather Duke, never expressly social. Kurt and Ram further attract J.D.'s disapproval when he sees them holding a younger student in a headlock for failing to respect his and Kurt's status as 'seniors, man'. The film cuts to a medium-long shot of J.D. riding past on a motorbike. The camera pans to follow the bike, as shown in Figure 3.5 below, and J.D.'s level stare at the scene unfolding in front of him. A further cut to a point-of-view shot to the scene from his perspective demonstrates the threat of that gaze, as its participants briefly pause, staring blankly back at J.D. as if frozen in fear.

J.D.'s pose is significant to his evocation of earlier juvenile delinquent figures and other models of masculinity. Clearly a cruiser designed to travel long distances, J.D.'s motorbike is far from the simple, affordable mode of transport a suburban teenager might use. Rather, the motorbike recalls that used by Johnny Strabler in *The Wild One*, wherein the arrival of his gang, the Black Rebel Motorcycle Club, precipitates a series of changes in the small town. What is more, J.D.'s level gaze evokes the moral insinuations of

Figure 3.5   J.D. (Christian Slater) watches the bullying unfold.

Clint Eastwood's 'man with no name'. The shot/reverse shot editing pattern, alongside the single harmonica note heard in the scene, references the opening scenes of *High Plains Drifter* (Clint Eastwood, 1973), where the unnamed man returns the townspeople's unabashed stares as he rides into Lago. In the cafeteria scene at the beginning of the film, J.D.'s gaze piqued Veronica's conscience, and likewise here, Ram and Kurt briefly pause their homophobic bullying while J.D. watches them intently. For Bingham, Eastwood's persona served to demonstrate the disjunction between 'the Western hero's gentlemanly manners and his brutality' (Bingham 1994: 172). Eastwood too is a considerably more adult and violent figure than is typically perceived of the juvenile delinquent. Similarly, J.D.'s bleakly utilitarian amorality pulls at the generic limits of permissible rebellion and violence.

Veronica and J.D. resolve to take revenge on Kurt and Ram after the pair spread a humiliating sexual rumour about her. The sequence in which they plan their revenge shows the extent to which Veronica and J.D. dissemble with each other along with Kurt and Ram, who must believe that a sexual encounter is going to take place. To achieve this, Veronica performs coquettish femininity, clutching the phone close to her face, speaking in a breathy voice, and giggling at Kurt's remarks. Veronica's performance is revealed as such when she must stifle her laughter at Kurt's request to 'write to Penthouse Forum' about the experience. For his part, J.D.'s murderous scheme once again requires Veronica's complicity. She must lure the pair to the woods behind the school with the promise of sex before Veronica and J.D. shoot the pair with what are tellingly called *Ich Lüge* (I lie) bullets, which will supposedly disorient and stun the pair, but not kill them. In order to secure Veronica's essential assistance in the plan, she too must believe that Kurt and Ram, though thoroughly humiliated, will not be seriously harmed. J.D.'s clothing provides a key persuasive vehicle in this scene, which is the only occasion in which he is without his long black duster coat. Instead, he is seen in pale blue jeans with a checked shirt over a grey vest that together recall not Clint Eastwood but Kevin Bacon's character, Ren McCormack, in *Footloose*. Although this clothing is typical of the fashion of the time, the film's intertextual play with other youth delinquency texts, along with Slater's physical resemblance to Bacon, invites Veronica, if not the film's audience, to interpret his plan as a comical, inconsequential teen caper.

Key to their plan, as both Veronica and J.D. perceive it, is the imposition of a 'hidden' homosexual relationship between Kurt and Ram. Although Veronica has penned a convincing suicide note describing their secret love affair, more persuasive still is J.D.'s assortment of artefacts that he believes will convince anyone finding the pair of their homosexuality. Pulling these items out of a large shopping bag he plans to leave at the scene, J.D. assembles an issue of *Stud Puppy* magazine, a box of chocolates, a Joan Crawford postcard, mascara, and 'the one perfecto thing', a bottle of mineral water. Importantly, J.D.'s invocation of the correct audience for his artefacts – he believes the Ohio police will immediately associate the effete mineral water with homosexuality – can be seen to correspond to Butler's theorisation of the importance of recognition to an individual's status as human (Butler 2004: 4). In this case, the audience for these items – a pair of Ohio police officers – is crucial to the functioning of these artefacts. Notably, these items assume their powers to convince as a result of the close relationship between the pair, and the easy slippage between the homosocial and homosexual relationship.

The suicide motif that pervades *Heathers* satirises both the labour that students must perform in order to count as popular in high school, and teenagers' supposed vulnerability. Heather Chandler, of course, was notorious even prior to her apparent suicide, while Ram and Kurt were, though not well-liked, known for their roles on the football team. Positioned as a trend, Martha sadly attempts to acquire some of the popularity that other students have attained in death, when she walks into traffic. While she fortunately survives, Martha's inability to perform suicide as effectively as Heather Chandler, Kurt and Ram appear to have done marks her out as a failure in *Heathers*. Even when J.D. and Veronica manipulate the norms of idealised gender such that they can only be instantiated by death, Martha is still unable to embody them and attain the popularity she so craves.

J.D. Loses his Cool

The conclusion of *Heathers* sees the death of J.D. and the inauguration of a new order presided over by Veronica, the 'new sheriff in town'. Throughout the film, J.D. has been characterised by a gift for linguistic invention and articulacy that contrasted him with the mumbling, improvisatory style of the Method performers discussed earlier in this chapter. It is thus fitting that his increased weakness should be signified by a declining mastery of language. When setting up his explosives in the boiler room immediately below the gym where a school pep rally is taking place, J.D.'s surprise is registered in his statement that 'the loose was too noose' in reference to Veronica's own staged suicide. J.D. quickly corrects himself, turning his head from her and brushing the back of his head with one hand as he does so, conveying his embarrassment and irritation at the slip. However, he soon regains his composure and disarms Veronica of her handgun while he resumes setting up his bomb. Here J.D.'s alignment with cool breaks down, instead becoming psychotic. As discussed previously, to be cool is to embody an attitude of benign defiance, rather than one characterised by decisive action (Pountain and Robins 2000: 19). J.D.'s plan to blow up the school in a nihilist vision to 'wipe the slate clean' thus goes against the attitudinal opposition signified by cool. Having thus transgressed the limits of the juvenile delinquent figure, he is no longer desirable to Veronica.

The pair's violent confrontation is frequently interrupted by the cross-cuts of the cheerleading rally taking place immediately above them in the gym. These cross-cuts serve to augment the scene's sense of suspense. More significantly, the school cohort becomes more enthusiastic and animated as the balance of power shifts from J.D. to Veronica. With its celebration of togetherness, the rally provides a sharp contrast to the cafeteria scenes with which the film opened. While those scenes showed students sniping at one another from inwardly-turned tables, the rally demonstrates their collective investment in the school as a united, communal identity. Veronica's alignment with the high school community is emphasised through costume, as the blue-tinted lighting of the basement is reflected in her dark blue blazer. This scene reveals that in order for a vision of utopia to prevail, certain subjectivities – in this case, J.D.'s psychotic nihilism – must be suppressed or disavowed.

Strapping a bomb to his body and looking towards the sky, J.D. commits suicide at the film's close. The ending of *Heathers* can be seen to recall Plato's murder at the conclusion of *Rebel*, if only for its narrative function in sealing the end of an old order and the inauguration of a new one, which necessarily brings with it the death of a rebel. Despite his death, and her ostensible championing of the flawed high school community, the film's final scenes demonstrate the extent to which Veronica has come to embody many of the traits previously associated with J.D. To his typically enigmatic question, 'What are you going to do now that you're dead?' Veronica silently takes a cigarette from her jacket and places it in her mouth, eyebrows raised as though daring him to detonate the explosives strapped to his body. Once he does so, her slow, jerking movements and cock of the head recall J.D.'s characteristically world-weary posture. When he finally does trigger the detonator, her face then emerges in close-up through a smoke-filled frame, indicating a new order in J.D.'s vision that ironically can only occur in his absence.

Heathers ends with Veronica's refusal of heteronormativity. Approaching Martha, Veronica asks if she would like to spend prom night with her. Significantly, the plans she proposes are away from the event itself, and concern simply watching videos. The film thus concludes with a bruised and bloodied Veronica walking despondently down the school corridor, accompanied by Martha in the wheelchair and neck brace she now needs as a result of her suicide attempt. The ending thus contrasts with the vibrant utopianism of *Grease* and *Rebel*'s mournful hopefulness. Instead, *Heathers* shows the violent consequences of sticking to one's principles, and, conversely, the possibility of refusing the prevailing matrix of gender norms.

Heathers is pitched as a deconstruction of the seemingly cosy politics of the 1980s high school film (Kaveney 2006). Yet even in this film, the high school continues to be constructed as an idealised space. When Veronica fights J.D. she does so not only on her own behalf, but in the name of the high school cohort as well. In winning this fight, and in depriving Heather Duke of the all-important red scrunchie, Veronica is seen to liberate the school from the Heathers' divisive reign. Nonetheless, the audience has seen her participate in the murder of other students, for which she receives no punishment. That Veronica is at once the evident champion of the high school cohort and a skilful murderer at large amongst them suggests a parody of the 'clean' endings of the other two films seen in this chapter, in which prior complexities are quickly – albeit unsuccessfully – erased.

Conclusion

This chapter has examined the performance style of three stars, each bearing a distinctive style across the youth delinquency subgenre. What has emerged is the way in which the rebels of the 1950s remain a significant reference point, either as a source of pastiche (as in *Grease*) or, paradoxically, as a time when 'cool' was a largely benign construct, as *Heathers* showed. Using Judith Butler's theorisation of gender, which understands gender identity as a performative construct, we might deem James Dean's incarnation of juvenile delinquency a masculine norm, which these later rebels seek to approximate. As Butler argues, though, this model of replication is not nearly as straightforward as it initially appears. Indeed, this analysis has demonstrated that the very model apparently instantiated by Dean in *Rebel* is itself beset with contradictions and slippages.

All three of these films provide examples of characters that are recognised as representations of idealised masculinity in a particular context. Throughout this chapter, we have observed a connection between heterosexual desirability, juvenile delinquency and cool. In *Rebel*, it is first Buzz, then Jim, who assumes the role of idealised masculinity, and that change in status is represented in concrete terms by Judy's quick switch of affections. In turn, Danny is introduced in *Grease* not only through his relationship with Sandy, but also at Rydell High, through his evident desirability to other girls. For his part, J.D. is positioned as an attractive outsider, a position that is shown not to be available to female outsider Martha, who is certainly not recognised as cool. The evident alliance between cool, rebellion and heterosexual desirability raises the question as to whether rebellion in and of itself has become a norm of teen masculinity. While Dean was emblematic of a masculinity in crisis, shorn of the certainties of previous generations, some aspect of rebellion now has come, paradoxically, to be regarded as a central component of masculine identity.

The dependence demonstrated by Buzz and Danny on the gangs they lead also brings these films together. While Buzz wants to befriend Jim, and is therefore reluctant to fight him, it is the gang that demand a face-off at the Chickie Run. In turn, it is the T-Birds that step in when Danny's affection for Sandy threatens the promiscuous, nonchalant image that is central to the gang's collective identity. While J.D. is something of an outlier in this instance, the characterisation of Heather Chandler shows that female cliques also impose demands on their members, where Veronica is expressly prevented from staying friends with those who might threaten the Heathers' elitist image. What is evident in all three of these cases is that these homosocial relationships are the key mode through which the embodiment of idealised gender is recognised.

There are two further implications of the apparent dependency of the leaders on their subordinates. Firstly, it is apparent that approximating to a greater degree the norms of idealised masculinity makes an individual more, not less, dependent on their subordinates to recognise their embodiment of those norms. There is some logic here, since one's embodiment of those norms can at least partly be viewed as an endorsement of them. Secondly, these films succeed in complicating, at the very least, one central tenet of Butler's theorisation of gender, namely that it is impossible to wholly instantiate idealised gender. Instead, these films have demonstrated the possibility that it is indeed possible to do so, if only in a clearly defined context. All three case studies show how attention to the performances of masculine rebellion reveals the contradictions, slippages and complexities in the construction of teen masculinity. The following chapter turns its attention to the transformation of femininity for the prom, an event that mandates adherence not only to a particular model of gender, but also of social class.

Notes

1. Notable among this body of work is Holmes and Redmond (2006), *Framing Celebrity*, and since 2010, the establishment of peer-reviewed journal *Celebrity Studies*.
2. Eddie Redmayne's Oscar-winning performance in the Stephen Hawking biopic *The Theory of Everything* (James Marsh, 2014) conforms to both of these criteria.
3. There are multiple examples of such instances. In 2016, the lack of ethnic diversity in both nominees and judging panel were a justified cause of controversy. See for instance Gray (2016).
4. See for instance Wexman (2004).
5. Nonetheless, some tentative summaries can be located. Of particular interest are Lloyd (2007), *Judith Butler: From Norms to Politics* and Brady and Schirato (2011) *Understanding Judith Butler*.
6. Butler (2004) revisits many of these issues in her lengthy discussion of John Reimer in *Undoing Gender*.
7. It should be noted that IMDB credits Ann Doran as 'Mrs Carol Stark'. See <http://www.imdb.com/title/tt0048545/fullcredits/> (last accessed 30 March 2017). Yet her name is never mentioned in the film, nor is it listed in the film's credits or in the script itself. See <http://www.dailyscript.com/scripts/Rebel_Without_A_Cause.html> (last accessed 30 March 2017).

8. Butler is particularly critical of *Tootsie* (Sidney Pollack, 1982) and *Victor/Victoria* (Blake Edwards, 1983) in this regard.
9. For a full description of the crash itself and the events leading up to it, see Spoto (1996), pp. 147–9.
10. It should be noted that Altman's description pertains particularly to studio-era Hollywood musicals. There are a number of more recent musicals that do not ascribe to this abiding structure, including *Dreamgirls* (Bill Condon, 2006), *Les Misérables* (Tom Hooper, 2012) and *Annie* (Will Gluck, 2014).
11. As if to emphasise the point, the star of the Beach Party films, Frankie Avalon, later makes an appearance as Frenchie's (Didi Conn) guardian angel.
12. Among which, Shary's (2005) assessment of the scene as celebrating a female character's transformation into the mould that suits her male partner.
13. For instance: 'Rama lama lama ka dinga da dinga dong; Shoo-bop sha wadda wadda yippity boom de boom; Chang chang changitty chang sha-bop; Dip da-dip da-dip doo-wop da doo-bee doo.'
14. Shary does point out a number of female-led juvenile delinquency narratives, yet these were released some years later, in the 1990s. It is also worth noting that the protagonists of these films are always normatively attractive.

4. MAKING OVER: GENDER AND CLASS AT THE HIGH SCHOOL PROM

The high school is one of the most recognisable features of the Hollywood teen movie, one whose setting itself usually guarantees a focus on its teenage inhabitants rather than on the adults that attend to them. However, prior to the mid-1980s, the genre largely focused on its protagonists' activities outside of the school, in youth-oriented spaces such as the drive-in cinema and, latterly, the mall. Even *Grease*, ostensibly set at Rydell High, has one of its narrative's key junctures – the final reunion between Danny and Sandy – occur at the carnival, an event staged to celebrate the conclusion of the characters' schooling.

That teenagers are now more often portrayed within high school can largely be attributed to the work of John Hughes, who wrote, directed and produced a significant number of teen movies in the 1980s. Chief among these was *The Breakfast Club*, which established a set of archetypal figures that have remained largely intact to this day: 'the princess, the athlete, the basket-case, the brain and the criminal'. Key to the appeal of Hughes's films was arguably their undramatic – even banal – content. To understand the impact of his work, it's worth recalling that most teen movies of the early 1980s portrayed their characters undergoing unusual experiences: from seeking greatness in the performing arts, as in *Fame* (Alan Parker, 1980), to evading murder in *Friday the 13th* (Sean S. Cunningham, 1980). In contrast, Hughes tapped into the ordinary lives of 'teendom's silent majority of average, middle-class, suburban kids' (Martin 1994: 67). The stories featured here were of a more everyday variety, exploring characters' struggle to fit in with the rules of the high school, and by extension the society in which it is located. Hughes's films took seriously the power of teenage cliques, and their powers to exclude members of the peer group.

One legacy of John Hughes's 1980s teen movies is the centrality of the high school within the contemporary teen movie. Shary, meanwhile, distinguishes the school film as a subgenre of the teen movie, defined simply as those 'whose main plot focuses on the setting of the high school or junior high campuses' (Shary 2014: 29). The ideological function of the high school within the school film can be elucidated through the work of genre theorist Thomas Schatz, who argues that Hollywood films may be divided into two principal groups: films of determinate space, and those of indeterminate space. While genres of determinate space, like the Western, provide the site for a conflict of value systems, genres of indeterminate space take place in an ideologically stable setting, whose conflict arises within an already established system of values (Schatz 1981: 14–29). The conclusions of genre films see the resolution of their central conflict, and as such, provide the strongest clues to the function of the film's setting. In the school film, the prom often provides the site of its denouement, demonstrating both the conclusion of the characters' high school experience, and with it, their progression into adulthood.[1] As I will show, the prom is heavily freighted with ideological baggage. The requirement to attend with a partner of the opposite sex, in a highly gendered outfit, reveals the event's heteronormativity, and with it that of the school film. I therefore position the school film alongside the melodrama, the romantic comedy and the musical – the heteronormative genres that Schatz identifies – as a genre of indeterminate space.

The significance of the prom as a narrative construct in the school film is further illustrated by Amy Best's ethnographic research examining the event's importance in the lives of real American teenagers. In its present-day incarnation, the prom is intended as a celebration of students' high school graduation. However, Best reveals that the prom's original purpose was rather different. In the wake of nineteenth-century reforms requiring compulsory high school education across the US, Best notes that the prom was initially intended to be a 'democratised version of the debutante balls' (Best 2000: 12). The prom, then, was always meant to assimilate upper-class norms of coming of age, wherein attendance would signal a young woman's readiness for marriage. However, while the debutante balls were attended by a tiny minority of America's young people, the prom was envisioned as a universal rite of passage. Best thus reveals the role of the prom, and by extension, the school as an arena for the heteronormative socialisation of American youth.

That the prom mandates students to adhere not only to gender, but also to classed norms of behaviour, is also apparent in the dress codes that continue to be observed in on-screen depictions of the event. Despite the adherence to contemporary fashions elsewhere in the teen movie, prom outfits remain forever preserved in the nineteenth century, transforming teenage casual styles into tuxedos and evening dresses. These outfits draw attention to heteronormative gender distinction, and by extension to the requirement to proliferate one's family line through marriage and heterosexual reproduction through exogamic, patrilineal kinship structures (Lévi-Strauss 1949: 137). The prom's legacy as a precursor to marriage is apparent in the event's gendered dress codes and continued requirement to attend the event as part of a heterosexual couple (Best 2000: 97–9)[2].

It is significant that the three films examined in this chapter, *Pretty in Pink*, *She's All That* and *Mean Girls*, portray their characters' negotiation with the gender and class norms mandated by the high school prom. These norms, then, are expressly portrayed as not natural or inevitable, but must be the object of concerted labour. This labour is typically manifested in some form of makeover, in which the protagonists are moulded into the ideal middle-class, feminine subject. Yet, as I will go on to explain, the very fact that of portraying such a transformation demonstrates the fragility and contingency of those gender and class norms that the characters must work to approximate. The prom serves as the goal of the protagonists' makeover, where the characters' acquisition of the norms of middle-class femininity are subject to the most acute scrutiny. As a consequence, it is possible to view the prom and the makeover practices that precede it as a locus not only of heteronormative gender interpellation, but also of interpellation into particular social structures. In all three of the films examined in this chapter, a lower-class or 'different' protagonist is transformed into a vision of middle-class femininity in preparation for their prom.

The work of delineating the norms of class as well as gender in this chapter's case studies is a complex one, not least because, despite ample evidence to the contrary, the USA continues to construct itself as a classless society (Scott and Leonhardt 2005: n.p.).[3] Even to raise the issue of class in the United States, Paul Fussell argues, is to undermine the country's myth of an egalitarian meritocracy (Fussell 1984: 12). Even when class is regarded as an applicable identity category, it evades clear description. David Halle's study of chemical workers in New Jersey found that they held multiple class identities simultaneously. In the workplace, although carefully avoiding the description 'working class', they would nevertheless describe themselves as 'working men', seemingly as a result of the physicality of their work (Halle 1984: 155). However, at home, these same workers identified their lifestyles as middle- or lower-middle-class in accordance with their standard of living (Halle 1984: 144). Individuals' experiences cannot, then, be captured by their economic categorisation alone, but consist in a complex negotiation of identifications and symbols.

In order to unpick these complexities, many scholars of social class have turned to the work of Pierre Bourdieu, whose conceptualisation of capitals as laid out in his 1986 work *Distinction* has emerged as a model for understanding the nuances of class as a lived social relation. Most significantly, he proposes that what he terms cultural and social capital work in addition to economic capital to affect an individual's experience of class and inequality. For Bourdieu, cultural knowledge, and most of all, knowledge of what he describes as 'highbrow' culture, which is officially endorsed by the education system, determines an individual's level of cultural capital, while social capital refers to the extent and importance of an individual's networks and connections. These types of capital all combine in the habitus, described by Rosemary Crompton as 'a system of dispositions shared by those who are products of the same conditioning' (Crompton 2008: 101). Inheritance is at the heart of Bourdieu's reading of class; over time, advantages accrued by high levels of social, economic and cultural capital accentuate and ingrain social inequalities.

Despite Bourdieu's apparent insistence on the entrenchment of class privilege, Crompton argues that his sociology of class is premised on the notion that 'inequalities are reproduced, sustained and modified through the daily actions of individuals' (Crompton 2008: 100). In other words, Bourdieu argues that social class may be altered through repeated individual behaviours. Class, then, is not conceived as a static picture of social life, but as a constant, active process of social differentiation, one that implicitly recalls Butler's description of gender as endlessly repeated approximations of a norm that come to coalesce into what looks to be a coherent gender identity (Butler 1990: 191). In a marked similarity between the two, Toril Moi likewise points out that Bourdieu is interested in the sociology of 'various ways of chewing one's food, different forms of dressing, musical tastes ... home decoration, the kinds of friends one has, and the kinds of films one likes to see', a description that recalls Butler's reading of gender as an aggregation of numerous, everyday actions (Moi 1991: 1020). Perhaps class, too, might therefore also be regarded as performative.

The latent similarities between the two theorists lead Terry Lovell to propose that, in order to analyse the ways in which gender and class inflect one another, Bourdieu's sociology of class must be combined with Butler's theorisation of gender (Lovell 2001: 31).[4] For Lovell, Beverley Skeggs's study of working-class women in north-west England exemplifies the type of analysis that becomes possible when the work of Bourdieu and Butler are successfully combined (Lovell 2001: 39). Significant to this chapter's case studies, Skeggs argues that class affects the lived experience of gender. What is more, she judges femininity itself to be a 'classed sign', that came to be defined in terms of 'delicacy, physical frailty and sexual propriety' (Skeggs 1997: 99). The physically demanding labour traditionally undertaken by working-class women – lighting candles, lifting chamber pots, preparing meals – led them to be regarded as 'healthy, hardy and robust', while also paradoxically a source of disease (Skeggs 1997: 99). To paraphrase Butler, working-class women are constructed as the Other against whom the feminine is made.

The construction of femininity as a middle-class competence leads Skeggs to observe that the working-class women she observed were reluctant to describe themselves as feminine. However, they recognised the conduct and appearance of femininity as bearers of cultural capital, as a result of which the women made substantial investments of both money and time in creating a feminine appearance. Commenting on a group's preparations for a night out, Skeggs argues that working-class women possess an ambivalent identification with femininity. The work to remodel themselves in a likeness of femininity is a costly, time-consuming, but nevertheless enjoyable and collective experience (Skeggs 1997: 105). The evident labour of their efforts can be seen to correspond to Butler's conceptualisation of gender as consisting of repeated approximations of an endlessly sought ideal, rather than an innate property. However, the 'raucous, outrageous' atmosphere of these gatherings belie the appearance of femininity these women work so hard to create (Skeggs 1997: 106). For these women, Skeggs argues, femininity is not an identity to which they fully belong, but a performance that can be applied and removed at will.

For Skeggs, working-class women's interest in fashion can be regarded as a form of disidentification, a means of distancing themselves from the fantasised Other they identify as working-class. Unlike their male counterparts, Skeggs finds that there is not a coherent and appealing working-class role with which women can identify, as a result of which they use clothing to 'present a picture of non-working-classness' (Skeggs 1997: 87). Such attempts to defy their working-class positioning are termed 'passing', an expression that is derived from queer studies, not least Butler's account of the negotiation of gender, racial and sexual identities seen in Jennie Livingston's 1990 documentary *Paris is Burning* (see Butler 1993: 129–33). Nonetheless, there is a substantial difference in the relationship of the trans individuals of Livingston's documentary, and those attempting to achieve an appearance of non-working-classness. Butler observes how Venus Xtravangaza, who features in *Paris is Burning*, confounds and destabilises the prevailing norms of gender, sexuality and race (Butler 1993: 125). In contrast, working-class women's endeavours to escape their class positioning are not attempts to trouble normativity, but to attain legitimacy in its terms (Skeggs 1997: 87). Consequently, when examining the respective transformations that take place in the films examined in this chapter, it will be important to observe the extent to which the prevailing matrix of gender and class norms are being destabilised or reinforced.

Clothing emerges as a key mechanism through which class and femininity are negotiated, echoing the respective contentions of Butler and Skeggs that markers of gender and class positioning are constituted on the surface of the body (see Butler 1990: 185; Skeggs 1997: 82). For Yvonne Tasker, Hollywood cross-dressing narratives are seen to transgress race and class boundaries as well as those of gender and sexuality. To illustrate, she cites the costumes in *Victor/Victoria* (Blake Edwards, 1982) where Victor's (Julie Andrews) tuxedo constitutes a masquerade of class and nationality as much as it does gender identity (Tasker 1998: 24). Tasker further identifies *Working Girl* (Mike Nichols, 1988) and *Pretty Woman* (Garry Marshall, 1990) as narratives of 'cross-class dressing' (Tasker 1998: 27) wherein the films' respective protagonists achieve a class ascension initially through their skilful assimilation of the costuming and behaviours of middle-class femininity as well as through a transformative heterosexual romance.

This chapter focuses on the school film, and the prom more specifically, as an arena in which these negotiations of gender and class norms take place in the Hollywood teen movie. As such, I will consider the event to be, in cinematic terms, an ideological locus of gender and class interpellation. *Pretty in Pink* and *She's All That* depict the transformation of a lower-class female protagonist, for whom the prom provides the final realisation of their makeovers and a test of their success. In contrast, *Mean Girls* depicts the gradual assimilation of middle-class cultural capital into postfeminist modes of teenage femininity. Although the prom occurs at the conclusion of these films, Best observes that the dance itself is a mere footnote of 'a series of practices, events and relations' that precede it (Best 2000: 12). Consequently, I will demonstrate that the prom not only provides the central focus of these films, but also permeates the narratives throughout. This chapter brings together the work of Butler and Skeggs in order to foreground the ideological mechanisms that compel attendance at the prom, and to observe how the films' characters negotiate the event's gender and class expectations. In doing so, I argue that despite Americans' traditional squeamishness about class, normative gender in the teen movie is always a classed discourse.

Pretty in Pink (Howard Deutch, 1986)

Written and produced by John Hughes, *Pretty in Pink* forms part of the small corpus of teen movies that he wrote, produced or directed, and which continue to define the genre's reference points today (see Shary 2002a and 2005; De Vaney 2002). While *Pretty in Pink* was filmed by Howard Deutch, a former director of music videos, the film retains Hughes's distinctive imprint, fusing a nostalgia for clean, virtuous adolescence with an incisive understanding of mid-1980s suburban youth. Among the features that mark out Hughes's teen movies is their portrayal of teen femininity. Jonathan Bernstein's study of the 1980s teen genre argues that female characters in Hughes's films are the exception to the majority of their contemporaries, who are merely tasked with displaying 'good-natured tolerance in the face of stalking, voyeurism, or fumbled attempts at seduction' (Bernstein 1997: 173–4). In contrast, Hughes depicts girls 'railing against cliques and caste systems' (Bernstein 1997: 5) and calling attention to the acute social divisions that were becoming increasingly apparent during the Reaganite 1980s.

Hughes's singular portrayal of girlhood owes much to his working relationship with Molly Ringwald, with whom he made three films between 1984 and 1986. *Pretty in Pink* constitutes the apex of this cycle, which began with *Sixteen Candles* (John Hughes) in 1984 and continued the following year with *The Breakfast Club*. Released soon afterwards, in 1986, *Pretty in Pink* was a star vehicle for Ringwald, capturing the actor's 'charismatic normality' as well as her widely imitated post-punk style (Kael 1992: 133). In turn, Anthony C. Bleach observes that Ringwald's characters engage in a 'struggle within or against the class constraints erected within their stable, suburban environs' (Bleach 2010: 25). In *The Breakfast Club*, well-to-do Claire Standish (Molly Ringwald) laments her material privileges and forges an unlikely alliance with the film's delinquent 'criminal', John Bender (Judd Nelson), while *Pretty in Pink* portrays Andie's (Ringwald) ostracism as a working-class 'mutant' apparently unworthy of Blane's (Andrew McCarthy) burgeoning affections. In Hughes's work, Ringwald provides a key figure through which gender and class requirements are worked out.

The intersection of gender and social class are central to this 'Marxist Romeo and Juliet' (Ansen quoted in Shary 2011: 580). *Pretty in Pink* depicts Andie Walsh, a working-class scholarship student attending a private high school. She has a distinct sense of style and is devotedly pursued by Duckie (Jon Cryer), a student with similarly idiosyncratic tastes and class background, while she in turn harbours affection for Blane (Andrew McCarthy), one of the school's upper-class 'richies'. The pairing of Blane and Andie receives widespread hostility, not least from Blane's friends, Steff (James Spader) and Benny (Kate Vernon), who disapprove of his association with a lower-class girl. Under increasing pressure, Blane reneges on his invitation to take Andie to the prom, as a result of which she decides to attend alone. Finally, as Blane stands up for Andie, the prom provides the scene for the pair's reunion and the film's ending. The film's portrayal of class disparity, combined with the heteronormativity of the prom, demonstrates how conflicting discourses of gender and class intersect in the Hollywood teen movie. Andie's relation to these gender and class norms is complex: certainly, Andie is shown to work hard at school, to aspire to the lavish suburban homes inhabited by her wealthier peers and to transcend her working-class background through her romance with Blane. However, her parodic performances of 'middle-classness' in her sartorial choices reveal a contempt for the gender and class norms invoked by that construct (Moseley 2002: 405). Andie's identity is thus portrayed as a complex negotiation of the heterosexual romance narrative, an ambition to transcend her class status through work, and her subcultural affiliation with Duckie and Iona (Annie Potts).

Inheritance and the Construction of Class Identity

While his portrayal of everyday adolescence has secured the longevity of Hughes's films, the director's persistent focus on white, high school suburbanites has also been regarded as evidence of his conservatism (see Kaveney 2006: 45). Ann De Vaney is more vehement still, arguing that Hughes's films are 'neoconservative' in their treatment of gender, race and class (De Vaney 2002: 204). A particular source of concern for her is the representation of teen girls, since she argues that the films stage a reassertion of the father's ownership and control over their daughters (De Vaney 2002: 210). Hughes, De Vaney argues, re-inscribes domesticity as the rightful domain of femininity, and can thus be seen to reflect a backlash against the significant advances that had been made towards gender equality by the mid-1980s.[5] What is more, De Vaney claims that Hughes's films contain the liminality of adolescence so that his female characters move neatly from girlhood to adulthood, thereby avoiding the tensions, repressions and prohibitions encountered in this liminal phase (De Vaney 2002: 210). In this way, she asserts, heteronormative gender identity is presented as undisputed and already fully finalised. In contrast, I argue that examination of the relationship between Andie and her father Jack (Harry Dean Stanton) allows us to consider the presentation of Andie's gender and class identity as one that exists in a tension between her inherited identity, and that which she fashions for herself.

Pretty in Pink opens with crane shots depicting a bare, unpopulated street, following an industrial vehicle as it passes slowly in front of a house and the railway that runs alongside the street. Positioned literally as 'the wrong side of the tracks', the presence of industrial equipment, combined with the lack of cars or people outside, signifies our positioning in a lower-class residential area. The film then cuts to lingering close-ups of Andie's hands, arms, legs and ears as she puts on her ostentatious clothing and jewellery, and applies make-up. Seeing Andie deploy the paraphernalia of femininity, rather than introducing her already fully clothed, the audience is already given to understood, echoing Skeggs's work, that the character is at a distance from the norms of this particular classed construction. What is more, the juxtaposition of class signifiers in these two scenes, between the unremarkable family home and the surface opulence of Andie's clothing, disputes De Vaney's claim that Hughes's work diminishes the liminality of adolescence. Rather, the opening scene portrays her indeterminacy, since Andie is shown to construct herself within the parameters of middle-class femininity while she remains geographically embedded in a working-class neighbourhood.

Once Andie is dressed, the film cuts to a medium-long shot of her standing in the doorway of her room, looking out of frame into the hallway to shout, 'Daddy! It's seven-thirty!' The shot scale allows us to take in the clothing, which (we assume) she put on in the previous sequence, and further underscores the contrast between her baroque, multi-layered apparel and the plain, unadorned hallway of her home. The non-diegetic soundtrack – the Psychedelic Furs' 'Pretty in Pink' – provides a further contrast with Andie's pearls and floral dresses, which typically denote older women. Rather than using music from successful mainstream artists of the mid-1980s such as A-Ha, the Bangles or Lionel Richie, Deutch selected a hitherto little-known British post-punk group to provide the title song for this mass-market teen movie.[6] The film's taste for the alternative continues into the rest of the soundtrack, which features tracks from the Smiths, New Order and INXS, most of which did not reach the top ten in the charts when released as singles.[7] Reports from the making of the film suggest that much of this music was suggested to Hughes by Ringwald herself, attesting to the authenticity of the film's evocation of contemporary teen tastes.[8] The scenes therefore suggest a complex layering of meanings, in which the glamour of Ringwald's precocious stardom underlays the portrayal of Andie's aspirations to transcend her working-class positioning.

In her interactions with her father, Andie is shown to be both a daughter and a carer for the indolent yet protective Jack. As she enters her father's bedroom, a medium-long shot follows her in, allowing us to observe its cluttered interior. Jack's rumpled sheets, combined with his vague allusions to 'getting in late', work to signify possible alcoholism, although this is never explicitly stated. The film thus establishes Jack as a failed patriarchal figure who is unable to provide adequately for his child. His low status in the scene is reinforced by Jack's complaint that Andie is 'nagging him all the time', placing her in the role of a persistent spouse rather than a daughter. As their conversation develops, Jack enquires how 'things are going at school'. Probing no further into Andie's shrugging response that 'it's okay', he turns his attention instead to the prom and the thorny matter of whether she has yet managed to find a partner with whom to attend. Jack's interest in his daughter's heteronormative socialisation over her academic education reflects the relative priorities of the high school as portrayed in the teen movie, whose narrative is governed not by academic or sporting achievement, but by social success.

Clues to the shame that Andie seems to experience, as she reveals that she has not been asked to the prom, can be elucidated by Best's observation that in high school, popularity – or social capital, to use Bourdieu's term – is 'bound up with normative constructions of masculinity and femininity' (Best 2000: 72). Further, she observes that girls' popularity in particular was accrued from their apparent attractiveness to the opposite sex (Best 2000: 72). Consequently, social capital is shown to intersect with heteronormative femininity. Andie's shame therefore consists in her recognition that she has fallen short of the gender and class norms upheld by the prom. Jack's questioning can be seen to represent not only Andie's working-class inheritance, but also the continued weight of familial heteronormative expectation.

Subculture and Performances of Respectability

Rachel Moseley argues that *Pretty in Pink* allows for and celebrates difference through 'attention paid to spaces [Andie] inhabits and details of her dress' (Moseley 2002: 405). Given that Andie is positioned throughout the film alongside two other individuals, Iona and Duckie, who share her post-punk style, it is possible to position the group collectively as a subculture. For Dick Hebdige, a prominent theorist of such factions, subculture is defined simply as an 'opposition to the mainstream' (Hebdige 1979: 82). Significantly, Hebdige identifies subculture as the preserve of the working classes who aim to subvert the (middle-class) mainstream. In *Pretty in Pink*, the opposition of Andie, Duckie and Iona to the elite comprised of Blane, Steff and Benny is demonstrated in their hostile attitude and their occupation of specific spaces, such as Iona's record shop, Trax, and Cats, a bar they frequent.

In *Pretty in Pink*, subcultural opposition is expressed through more than simple contrarianism and hostility. In what Ken Gelder describes as 'anachronistic self-fashioning' (Gelder 2007: 92) and Kaja Silverman more simply as 'retro' (Silverman 1986: 150), the clothing worn by Andie, Duckie and

Figure 4.1 A subculture: Andie (Molly Ringwald), Duckie (Jon Cryer) and Iona (Annie Potts).

Iona is shown to re-appropriate the styles of the past, thereby refuting the imperative for conspicuous consumption associated with perpetually changing mainstream fashion. Andie's clothing is comprised of thrift-shop finds intermingled with her own creations and offset by copious jewellery. Although her pearls, smart jackets and dresses evoke the conventionally respectable mores of middle-class femininity, the clashing colours, patterns and layers of Andie's outfit create what Duckie aptly terms her 'volcanic ensemble', marking her clothing as excessive.

Duckie's unusual combinations of smart blazers and trousers, overlaying flamboyant braces and other accessories, demonstrate a similar fondness for plunder and bricolage. His clothing both references smart masculine attire of the past and mocks the look epitomised by Michael Douglas's performance as Gordon Gekko in *Wall Street* (Oliver Stone, 1987), associated with financial services workers during the 1980s. Like Andie's clothing, Duckie's outfits are comprised of the mainstays of middle-class attire and accessorised with numerous rings, belts and watches. The evident contempt Andie and Duckie inspire at their high school – and their awareness of the low esteem in which they are held – invites their invocations of 'middle-classness' to be perceived as efforts to distance themselves from their designation as working class, a tendency that Skeggs observed in her research participants, who felt similarly disparaged (Skeggs 1997: 86). However, in contrast to the attempts at class passing that Skeggs found, where working-class women sought to assimilate middle-class tastes and sensibilities, Andie, Duckie and Iona's invocation of respectability through fashion is clearly intended as ironic mimicry. Their clothing succeeds in denaturalising these norms of middle-class dress, and invites the viewer to question the gendered conventions on which notions of respectable clothing are founded.

Andie's clothing denaturalises discourses of middle-class femininity. However, her opposition to, and dislike of, Steff and Benny is problematised by her evident aspiration to transcend her class position. Following a shift at Trax, Andie drives to the suburb inhabited by many of her more affluent classmates, and imagines a life for herself there. The scene foretells her later return to the area as Blane's guest at Steff's party, and prefigures her symbolic class ascension at the film's conclusion. Considering Anzia Yazierska's 1923 novel, *Salome of the Tenements*, which charts the class ascension of its Russian-Jewish protagonist, Catherine Rottenberg argues that the American Dream discourse, which holds out the promise of ascending the class hierarchy to any American citizen, is predicated on the individual's ability to assimilate the norms of 'determination, hard work and moral uprightness' (Rottenberg 2004: 69). Andie certainly embodies these ideals: her determination is demonstrated by her insistence on attending the prom despite the absence of a date; her work ethic is shown in her job at Trax and in her critical attitude to her father's unemployment. Finally, her moral uprightness is established by her honesty and candour throughout the film (which, crucially, contrasts with Blane's cowardice). Consequently, there is an ambivalence in Andie's urge to mock gender and class norms and her fit with established narratives of social mobility.

The complexity of Andie's mockery of gender and class norms is reflected in the relationship between thrift shops and mainstream fashion. Although seeming to refute the mania for endless consumption and the thrill of the new, thrift shops flourish only within a thriving economy where clothing's utility outlives its desirability. Since this very phenomenon is dependent on mainstream fashion, the group's second-hand clothing shows their wider ambivalence towards consumer culture. In Trax, Andie's mildly hostile 'American Express Platinum card maybe?' to Blane's prospective record purchase, illustrates this paradox. While the record shop depends on wealthy teens' disposable income, Iona and Andie remain dismissive, even antagonistic, towards their customers. Similarly, *Pretty in Pink* is unquestionably an artefact of mainstream culture, yet its construction of subculture within the narrative enables the film to carve out a place for critique of gender and class norms from within.

The meaning of the subculture constructed in *Pretty in Pink* is further elucidated by the work of sociologist Sarah Thornton, who takes up Bourdieu's conceptualisation of capital in relation to social class to propose 'subcultural capital' as a means of articulating how youths carve out distinctions among themselves (Thornton 1995: 12). As with Bourdieu's cultural capital, Thornton argues that subcultural capital may be embodied by dressing in a certain way and objectified through the conspicuous possession of certain items. However, in contrast to cultural capital, which is determined by mastery of 'legitimate culture', as defined by the most powerful classes (Anderson and Hansen 2011: n.p.), Thornton notes that subcultural capital is instead reliant on a peer network in which 'hipness' is constantly redefined and redistributed (Thornton 1995: 195). Consequently, while Iona's record shop demonstrates that subcultural capital is readily convertible to economic capital, Thornton contends that it is substantially less class-bound than cultural capital (Thornton 1995: 203). Rather, subcultural distinction obfuscates class status such that when Iona meets pet shop owner Terrence (Jamie Anders) she is surprised to discover that she likes this 'yuppie', even though, as small business owners, they appear to occupy similar class positions.

Thornton argues that 'subcultural capital confers status on its owner in the eyes of the *relevant* beholder' (Thornton 1995: 185; my emphasis). As such, when Andie attends Steff's house party with Blane, the film portrays the preppy guests' failure to recognise the significance of her subcultural style. As she and Blane walk through the house, the camera tracks behind them, enabling the film's spectators to observe how the pair are scrutinised by the other party guests. One girl they pass, riding piggyback on another student, accosts Andie and remarks: 'Hey, aren't you the girl in my art class?' When Andie does not respond, the girl taunts, 'nice pearls – this isn't a dinner party, honey', sneeringly highlighting Andie's reference to middle-class respectability, even as she misses its subversive excess. Indicating the importance of space for the perception of subcultural capital, patterns from Andie's paisley twinset are echoed in the soft furnishings of Steff's house. Presumably selected by Steff's parents, the paisley upholstery signifies the middle-class comforts of an older generation, such that the ironic dissociation that Andie intends is not recognised here. The majority of those attending Steff's party are clad in plain, off-white clothing, indicating their belonging to an entirely different taste culture.

Attempting to escape the bacchanalian excesses of the party, Andie and Blane head upstairs, only to encounter Steff and Benny. Clearly aghast at Blane's choice of partner, Benny performs a double-take before exclaiming loudly 'am I having a nightmare?' Swiftly accompanied out of the room by Steff, whose leering smirk makes clear his agreement with Benny's invectives in spite of his outward solicitousness, Benny declares Blane an 'asshole', while to Andie she simply states 'I don't even know what you are.' Benny's inability to locate vocabulary to describe Andie, and the guests' ignorance of her name despite sharing a class with her, indicate their inability to place her according to conventional descriptors of class and gender. Later, Steff refers to Andie as a 'mutant' in a bid to dissuade Blane from further association with her. That Andie does not seem to conform to a recognisable identity recalls Butler's theorisation of recognition as an essential constituent of subjectivity. However, while Butler considers that unintelligibility of one's gender, racial or national identity might cause a subject not to be recognised as such, she does not consider the consequences of flouting the norms of classed gender (Butler 2004). Nonetheless, it is in the merging of these otherwise recognisable axes of identity in particular that Andie is not deemed a viable subject for Benny and Steff.

Class, Labour and the Prom

The sequence in which Andie creates her prom dress conveys the labour of the construction of gender and class identity. As the event inches ever closer, Andie receives two prom dresses as gifts. One comes from her father, who, spotting it in a second-hand shop, deduces that Andie would be able to alter it to her liking. The other dress comes from Iona, whose nostalgia for 'the only time I ever looked normal' is matched by her affection for her friend and employee. Each dress represents two distinct – though equally significant – alliances for Andie. The gift from her father represents Andie's status as

Figure 4.2 Andie (Molly Ringwald) makes her dress.

a daughter, her inherited gender and class status and the tacit requirement to maintain his lineage through heterosexual coupling. In turn, the dress from Iona stands for Andie's subcultural affiliation, musical tastes and subversive style. As I demonstrate, she succeeds in combining these dresses in order to create a space for her own identity within the heteronormative framework of the prom.

Despite the dresses' distinct meanings, there are substantial similarities between the two garments; both are pink, albeit in different shades, and both are cut in the traditional hourglass silhouette, which is wide at the shoulders and tight around the waist, below which a full skirt emphasises a feminine figure, and with it, female reproductive potential. Indeed, the conventional prom dress calls on the event's legacy as a democratised version of the debutante cotillions (Best 2000: 7), in which attendance was bound up with marriageability. That the dresses are presented as second-hand, yet do not appear discernibly anachronistic, attests to the timelessness of the prom dress's style, and by extension, the consistent expectations for the event's female attendees over time. Indeed, either of the two dresses would be suitable for the event without alteration. Andie's decision to made radical changes to them is therefore significant to her construction of gender and class identity, which embodies yet slyly subverts heteronormative, classed femininity.

In her bedroom, Andie lays the two dresses on the bed in order to examine their differing fabrics and textures. The scene continues with close-ups and medium close-ups of Andie's labours in creating the dress, sketching ideas on her notepad, ripping apart seams and sewing new ones in their place, before assessing the results in a full-length mirror. As will shortly become apparent, the dress that Andie creates embodies the complex position she occupies – between normativity and rebellion. Significantly, Andie's is no instantaneous transformation, but one that is the result of her expertise and labour.

Cross-cuts in this scene to other characters' preparations for the prom demonstrate that Andie's work ethic is an exceptional one. Other characters are shown in a state of inactivity, not least Duckie, whose scowling face in medium close-up portrays his unproductive anger in contrast to Andie's concerted efforts. Likewise, cross-cuts to Blane and Steff show their minimal preparations for the prom. Throughout *Pretty in Pink*, work and consumption have been portrayed as mutually exclusive: those who work do not consume, while those who consume are not seen to work. The counter in Trax which initially divided Andie from Blane provides the physical manifestation of this dichotomy. Here too, while the increasing speed of Andie's sewing, combined with increasingly faster editing indicates a sense of urgency, the still shot of Steff and Blane shows the pair lounging around in their (presumably purchased) tuxedos. That said, as Steff scrutinises his image in the mirror, *Pretty in Pink* does highlight an alternative form of labour for Andie's wealthier peers: the fraught anxiety of failing to live up to a fictionalised, masculine ideal. The scene shows that there is always labour behind the quest for gendered and classed acceptability, which transcends social rank. The division between work and consumption enacted in the earlier sections of the film is thus spurious.

Figure 4.3 Andie (Molly Ringwald) tentatively enters the prom venue.

The sequence concludes with Andie showing off her dress for her father's approval. Narrow at the neck and slim-fitting to the knee, Andie's dress is the converse of the 'hourglass' silhouette typical of most prom dresses. Although she is clad head to toe in pink, a traditional signifier of heteronormative femininity, Andie has literally reversed the traditional cut of the prom dress, demonstrating her ambiguous positioning with regard to the hereditary principles upheld by the event. Accordingly, she surprises her father by revealing that she plans to attend the prom alone, without a male partner.

The prom, then, constitutes a privileged space of gender and class interpellation, respected even by those whose subcultural positioning would usually lead them to shun such an event. The longevity and tradition of the prom is key to its normalising function. Our first view of the event is a static medium close-up of the back wall of the dance hall on which a monochrome photograph of big band musicians in identical black and white suits is seen. As the camera zooms out and cranes over the hall, we see another, much smaller collection of musicians at work at this prom, here administering to synthesisers and a backing track. Examining the crowd of teenagers dancing in heterosexual pairs, the male teenagers are universally wearing the black and white ensemble seen in the old photograph. The prom is thus established as an eternal, unchanging fixture in the socialisation process of all young adults. Although music tastes and technologies may change over time, this process of heteronormative socialisation will remain.

Andie's reunion with Blane at the prom provides the film's narrative closure. Moseley argues that the film's ending is 'too easy, almost trite' (Moseley 2002: 406), while for Kaveney the film's ending is problematic given that Blane never fully repents for his earlier humiliation of Andie (Kaveney 2006: 32).⁹ Indeed, foreclosing the possibility of any alternative or unfulfilled desire, Duckie – with a wry smile to the camera – is quickly paired off with an attractive female prom attendee. Cementing the characters in heterosexual pairs, the film's conclusion demonstrates the force of the prom's gender and class interpellation. The high emotion is further reinforced by the ecstatic, sweeping chords of Orchestral Manoeuvres in the Dark's 'If You Leave'. Consequently, the scene permits no question of the couple's suitability, nor an interrogation of the class disparities that were previously explored in the film.

Having rejected Steff's threats, Blane and Andie are reunited in the car park, where the film ends as their kiss affirms their successful reunion. Appropriating what Marc Augé describes as a 'non-place' for action that would normally be associated with the prom, the scene invites the possibility that Andie and Blane have coined their own value system (Augé 1995: 78). Looking back at their date earlier in the film, their relationship is seen to flourish only in other non-places, such as on the street and alone in the stables at the hunting club. However, as the non-diegetic soundtrack associated with the prom continues to accompany the scene, the car park is presented as an extension of, rather than an alternative to, the prom. The event's status as a privileged site of interpellation is reinstated as omnipresent, even for those who sit on the margins of intelligibility. *Pretty in Pink* demonstrates how the parodic, excessive citation of middle-class heteronormativity might open a space for critique within its boundaries.

SHE'S ALL THAT (ROBERT ISCOVE, 1999)

Thirteen years after *Pretty in Pink*, Robert Iscove's 1999 adaptation of *Pygmalion*, titled *She's All That*, was released to a film-going public now well versed in the conventions of the high school teen movie. In fact, 1999 was dubbed 'the year of the teen movie' (Brook 1999: n.p.)[10] owing to the volume in which such films were released and the commercial success, and often critical acclaim, with which they were received. Considering the teen movies of the 1990s from the vantage point of the early 2000s, Robin Wood argues that a canonical literary source was a central component of the genre, one that he attributes to an 'ambition to construct a resonance' beyond the genre's otherwise blandly commercial aspirations (Wood 2003: 319). Wood is certainly correct that the 1990s saw numerous teen-oriented literary adaptations. Following the success of *Clueless* in 1995, 1999 alone saw the release of two teen-oriented Shakespeare adaptations, *Ten Things I Hate About You* (Gil Junger, 1999), a reworking of *The Taming of the Shrew*, and *Never Been Kissed* (Raja Gosnell, 1999), an adaptation of *As You Like It*, as well as *Cruel Intentions*, Roger Kumble's take on *Les Liaisons Dangereuses* (1999).[11]

Wood's comments speak to the extent to which the teen movie continues to be regarded as a base form that must acquire prestige by association with more highly regarded literary works. In contrast, Howard Davis observes that the adapted texts are those that are studied in American high schools. As a result, rather than seeking a spurious cachet as Wood argues, film-makers working in this mould continue the time-honoured tradition of the 'pre-sold' film, which has the considerable commercial advantage of a ready and waiting audience (Davis 2006: 53; King 2002: 54). More significantly, Davis argues that the self-contained environments presented within these literary works are analogous to the hermetic ecosystem of the contemporary high school (Davis 2006: 53). Consequently, the literary inspiration behind many a 1990s teen movie is no empty quest for status, but should in fact be regarded as one that demonstrates continuity between the trope of the 'final festival', common in many of these literary works, and the ideological function of the prom.

She's All That introduces us to Zack Siler (Freddie Prinze Jr), class president and captain of the football team. It is understood early on that he and his girlfriend, Taylor Vaughan (Jodi Lyn O'Keefe), are destined for the titles of prom king and prom queen respectively. However, when she leaves him for laughable reality star Brock Hudson (Matthew Lillard), Zack makes a bet with his friend Dean (Paul Walker) that he can transform any girl into a prom queen. Accepting the wager, Zack's friends select Laney Boggs (Rachel Leigh Cook), whose art, politics and standoffish attitude mark her as 'scary and inaccessible'. Zack gradually coaxes Laney into attending social events and gives her a makeover, as a result of which she becomes an unlikely prom queen candidate. In contrast to *Pretty in Pink*, in which Andie's makeover is an active choice, *She's All That* sees Laney's unwitting co-option into Zack's crass scheme. As a result, it will be important to consider whether, and if so, how, Laney is able to retain a sense of agency in this process.

Constructing Status at the High School

As an adaptation of *Pygmalion*, the film must immediately establish the differences in status of the film's two key players, and the reasons for which one of them must be transformed. Laney is introduced from the very first frames of the film through quick close-ups of her hands first soaking newsprint and then painting a large canvas, which we later learn concerns a riot in Mogadishu. These shots can be seen to recall the attention paid to Andie's clothing and make-up at the beginning of *Pretty in Pink*. However, in contrast to her 1980s predecessor, Laney's actions are not only politically motivated and therefore directed towards the world beyond that of the high school, but also shown to be problematic. Her intense scrutiny of the canvas before her in this scene, for instance, leaves her untroubled by the paint splattered onto her clothing and face. That Laney's political interests are to be regarded as pathological is even reinforced at school, where, after seeing the completed canvas, her art teacher (Debbi Morgan) remarks somewhat sarcastically, 'That's wonderful, Laney. Now tell me something: which part represents you?' Thus, *She's All That* establishes the parameters for transformation: Laney must learn to orient her work and creativity away from far-off political conflict, and towards a concentrated labour on the self.

Having hinted at why Laney must be transformed, the scene in which she and Zack independently arrive at the high school that day speaks a great deal to the contrasting positions the two characters occupy there. A crane shot of a street scene centred on a school bus is overlaid by the school radio DJ's voiceover, which situates the film as taking place immediately following spring break, with eight weeks remaining before high school graduation. The camera pans to follow the bus as it stops in front of the school. However, confounding expectations that Laney will emerge from the vehicle, the camera moves closer to spot a small van behind it, which then comes to a stop. The camera remains centred on the bus, with the implication that the social life contained within is where Laney truly belongs. However, having chosen to arrive at school in her father's van suggests that Laney has rejected the school community, and that she possesses limited social capital.

In contrast, Zack is positioned at the very centre of the high school community, which is indicated not only by his status as class president, but in the star casting of Freddie Prinze Jr.[12] Accordingly, his arrival at school is heralded by a medium-long shot of a large yellow sports utility vehicle bearing a personalised number plate that reads: 'Mr Prez'. As if to emphasise the point, this car pulls into a parking space marked 'student body president – reserved'. Zack's high levels of social capital are shown to correspond, and be bolstered by, his equally elevated economic capital. The camera follows Zack, keeping him at the centre of the frame as he walks into the school, firstly showing his legs leaving the car, and only gradually moving up to reveal more of his body. In this, Zack's arrival at the school corresponds with Orpen's conception of the 'delayed and fragmented' star entrance, whose conventions were flouted to dramatic effect at the beginning of *Rebel* (Orpen 2003: 91). In contrast, here we are only granted a view of Zack's face when he notices a smiling portrait of himself on a wall, at which point he pauses to assume the pose in the photograph. Both intra- and extra-textually, then, Zack is clearly indicated as the film's star.

Yet Zack's star positioning in the film does not make him any less anxious about his ability to fulfil his role. Recalling Cary Grant's famous lament that 'even I want to be Cary Grant', Zack poses in front of his own photograph, which adorns the school corridor, and adopts the smiling pose of success it depicts. For Zack, the portrait seems to represent an ideal self that even he, the individual represented in the portrait, cannot quite approximate. Zack's elevated positioning is further punctured when he notices a girl he recognises walking in the opposite direction. When he greets her with an assured, 'What's up, Connie,' the girl (Ashlee Levitch) shyly returns his greeting, while her friend (Vanessa Lee Chester) corrects her, stating: 'Your name is Melissa.' Zack remains oblivious to the error, the scene indicating his self-absorption and hinting at his transformation by the end of the film.

Zack's girlfriend, Taylor, is introduced as 'the one all the girls want to be and all the guys want to nail'. As Zack's gendered opposite, she is the school's embodiment of idealised femininity, whose coronation as Prom Queen is all but inevitable. As discussed in relation to *Pretty in Pink*, Best's research reveals that heteronormative attractiveness is central to the popularity of high school girls (2000: 58). However, Best does not discuss the role that socioeconomic classification per se might play in the construction of idealised femininity. In this, too, Taylor is Zack's mirror image, with

GENDER AND CLASS AT THE HIGH SCHOOL PROM

Figure 4.4 Zack (Freddie Prinze Jr) notices his picture.

her own car and reports of an extravagant spring break vacation in Miami. However, in contrast to Zack, whose Ivy League ambitions suggest that he possesses high cultural capital, Taylor's claim that her sister, cousin, mother and grandmother have all been Prom Queen at their respective high schools calls attention to the role of inheritance in social capital. Bourdieu's work on hereditary advantage focuses principally on access to high cultural capital, which has currency within the education system (Bourdieu 1986b: 90). However, Taylor's assertion of hereditary advantage calls not only for the prom to be considered as an ancillary part of the education system, but also for an alternative reading of cultural capital that accounts for the labour on the self and expertise in the feminine that is accumulated by individuals like Taylor.

When Zack makes a bet with Dean (Paul Walker) and Preston (Dulé Hill) that he can make any girl into a potential prom queen, Taylor is the model against whom they assess all others. When Dean and Preston select Laney as the most unlikely girl to become prom queen, the audience understands that she is deficient in qualities that Taylor possesses. Significantly, Laney's difference from Taylor is conveyed primarily through movement. In contrast to Taylor's confidence and poise, Laney is seen here hurriedly ascending a flight of stairs in an awkward, jerking walk while carrying bulky art equipment. Laney is dressed androgynously, in paint-splattered overalls worn over a lurid tie-dyed T-shirt. Her hair is tied up but not otherwise styled, while her small face is dominated by a pair of large, unfashionably-shaped glasses.[13] In contrast to the other girls Zack's friends suggest, Laney is distinct for her combination of ungainliness, political interests, androgyny and lack of care in her appearance, all of which signify her as lacking in sufficient middle-class feminine competences to be a viable prom queen candidate.

For Sarah Gilligan, Laney's presentation as awkward and undesirable is characteristic of the 'make-under', which establishes the parameters of 'wrong' femininity to be reformed during the course of the makeover narrative (Gilligan 2011: 168). Typically, Gilligan argues, this 'wrong' femininity is signified by 'heavy brows, no make-up and glasses', precisely the appearance that Laney has here (Gilligan 2011: 168). Once this appearance has been remedied, the character's 'real womanhood' can find expression (Gilligan 2011: 169). However, reflecting Butler's contention that the normative construction of gender works to conceal its fragile foundations, this 'true self' can only be recuperated through specialist knowledge and labour that creates a spectacle of effortlessness. Significantly, too, Laney's dungarees and T-shirt can be seen to reference the fashions of 1970s feminism, indicating in advance the unlikelihood that Laney will refuse Zack's attempts to mould her into a prom queen (Gilligan 2011: 170). The flaws in Zack's instantiation of idealised teen masculinity, contrasted with Laney's integrity, emerge as the pair are brought together over the course of the film.

Transforming Laney and Zack

While *She's All That* is explicit in its intent to transform Laney, Zack is shown also to require change to make himself worthy of her. We'll examine here how both characters' transformations are portrayed in the film. Having accepted the terms of the bet, Zack incorrectly believes that, just as with his encounter with Melissa in the previous scene, Laney will be easily flattered by a sudden flurry of attention from the class president. However, simply accosting Laney proves unsuccessful, and Zack finds himself at the Jester Theatre in order to show an interest in her experimental theatre group. In this subcultural space, Zack's plain white T-shirt and black trousers are conspicuously dull amid the other attendees' striking, multi-coloured clothing and elaborate hairstyles. The theatre therefore presents an alternative social system within which Zack does not represent idealised masculinity. Rather, the flamboyant, exhibitionist Mitch (Alexis Arquette) is the focus of the audience's attention. Perhaps as a consequence, frequent reaction shots of Zack depict his unease as he shifts in his seat and glances around at the other members of the audience. Revealing his lack of experience of this type of performance, on perceiving a break in the action, Zack moves to applaud before quickly noticing the studious silence of the audience around him. While the theatre is clearly marked as Laney's space, the audience's sympathies remain with Zack, a normative figure who must negotiate this otherworldly environment.

Aiming to test Zack's apparent interest in experimental theatre, Laney invites him to perform an improvised set on stage. Initially awkward and self-conscious on stage, Zack produces a small 'hacky sack' beanbag from his pocket and begins to demonstrate the skills that have earned him the captaincy of the school football team. As he continues, however, the performance begins to take on a different tone. Talking to himself, shouting 'everyone's watching you, Zack' and 'don't let the ball drop', his performance demonstrates the pressures that come from his elevated position in the high school. Just as the gang leaders of *Grease* and *Rebel* found in the previous chapter, Zack discovers that his status as class president in fact leads to greater scrutiny from the student body. His performance itself sees Zack repeatedly kicking and balancing the hacky sack on each foot, before finally letting it drop to the ground. He is therefore seen to perform the repeated compulsion to approximate the position of idealised masculinity as well as its inevitable, ultimate failure. Zack's performance earns the applause of the theatre attendees, including Mitch, indicating that his high levels of cultural, social and economic capital translate even to this subcultural environment. The exhilaration he so evidently feels at having expressed his status anxiety through performance arguably provides the first step in Zack's gradual extrication from the demands of Harrison High.

In contrast to the incremental changes in outlook that Zack undergoes throughout the film, Laney is subjected to a significantly briefer and more superficial transformation. In fact, she undergoes a staged makeover that draws heavily on the conventions of makeover television, which came to prominence in British and American lifestyle programming during the late 1990s.[14] For McRobbie, programmes such as *What Not to Wear* (BBC 2001–7; TLC 2003–13) typically portray a lower-class protagonist moving 'from one state which is unacceptable to another which is a greatly improved state of good-looks and well-being' (McRobbie 2009: 124). As the participant's tastes are mocked by the presenters, who are constructed as arbiters of 'middle-class good taste', McRobbie argues that these programmes constitute a form of symbolic violence that works to denigrate the (already substantially diminished) cultural capital of working-class women (McRobbie 2009: 125). While Laney submits to the process engineered by Zack and his sister Mackenzie (Anna Paquin), I argue that she is able subtly to resist the cultural logic of the makeover.

For McRobbie, the makeover demands a move from a 'frumpy, asexual positioning to a state of glamorous individuality' (McRobbie 2009: 125). That state of glamorous individuality constitutes a complex nexus of heterosexual desirability, femininity and class. However, this is not a state that, once granted, is permanently present; the participant must continually renew her appearance in accordance with the changing demands of fashion. Even when the participants have succeeded in following the advice provided by the show's experts, they are never able to assume equal status with them. This continued disparity between the show's presenters and participants calls to be read in terms of Bourdieu's reading of habitus. That is, while we see the process in which the participants acquire knowledge and expertise, those of the presenters appear effortless, demonstrating what Bourdieu would doubtless describe as their 'instinctive feel for the game' (Bourdieu 1986: 33). In this context, McRobbie finds few possibilities for participants to subvert the cultural logic of the makeover programme.

However, understanding power relations in such scenes not as centralised and unilateral, but as diffuse and contingent, leads to an alternative proposition. As Butler argues, each citation of a norm creates the occasion for the subversion of that norm (Butler 1993: 108). Consequently, the imposition of a particular stylisation of femininity that occurs in the makeover may equally set up the possibility of subverting the primacy of this normative construction. Whereas McRobbie's reading of the habitus restricts interpretation of the makeover to an instance of symbolic violence, Butler's work allows Laney's transformation to be read as an example of ambivalence of interpellation under the heterosexual matrix. As McRobbie argues, the makeover's success is determined by the participant's ability to accept and follow the experts' guidance without continued monitoring. However, the very surveillance that is performed one year after the transformation itself demonstrates

Figure 4.5 Zack (Freddie Prinze Jr) is surprised by Laney's (Rachel Leigh Cooke) appearance after her makeover.

the possibility that the participant might refuse to comply with the advice she receives, or indeed that 'mistakes' with her sartorial choices might mean that her appearance signifies differently from the intention desired by the programme-makers.

Turning to Laney's transformation itself, a fade out of the makeover scene cuts to a long (re)establishing shot of the Boggs family home in front of a setting sun, creating an ellipsis to indicate the time (and by extension, the labour) taken on Laney's makeover. Our first view of Laney's transformed appearance is heralded by the introductory chords of 'Kiss Me', a single released concurrently with the film's cinema exhibition and which therefore indicates the importance of this scene.[15] Mackenzie announces Laney's arrival to the waiting audience of Zack, her younger brother Simon (Kieran Culkin) and her father (Kevin Pollack), drawing on the conventions of the television makeover as she declares, 'Gentlemen, may I present the new, not improved – but different – Laney Boggs.' That Laney is 'not improved' indicates in advance the slippage between the desired appearance and the reality of Laney's transformed identity, a possibility that is further implied by her missing Mackenzie's carefully calibrated cue. Nonetheless, the soundtrack duly increases in volume before the film cuts to medium shots of Simon and Zack, who stand in expectation to see her.

A close-up of a red, high-heeled shoe on the staircase as the song's vocal track kicks in signals Laney's entrance into the scene. As she walks slowly and deliberately down the stairs, the camera tilts slowly up Laney's body, ensuring that the audience has taken in her red dress, lack of glasses, made-over face and restyled hair. Lingering shots of Laney's body underscore her new positioning as 'an object of erotic spectacle' (Gilligan 2011: 173). Indeed, a cross-cut to Zack's open-mouthed expression indicates his surprise that he now desires her. Thus positioned as an object of spectacle, Laney now seems to have moved from her androgynous appearance to one that demonstrates her femininity.

Disrupting the spectacle, Laney soon missteps in her vertiginous heels and stumbles awkwardly into Zack's arms. An abrupt change of shot scale and sudden halt to the non-diegetic soundtrack indicates that Laney's fall brings an end to the silent reverie that preceded it. In this, we see evidence of Laney's continued clumsiness, a quality that, according to Dean and Zack, made her an impossible candidate for prom queen. However, in contrast to earlier scenes, in which Laney falls abruptly face first, here she falls so delicately and slowly that Zack has sufficient time to move across the room to catch her. Since Laney's fall is precipitated by her shoes, an evident signifier of femininity, her fall reveals an unease with her new heteronormative positioning. Although Laney's makeover newly casts her as sexually available and desirable, her continued maladroitness with the conventional apparatus of femininity can be seen to indicate the contingency of this status.

The role of bodily movement and grace in Laney's transformation can be further illustrated with reference to *Pretty Woman*, which depicts the gradual transformation of Vivian (Julia Roberts), a prostitute, into a partner for wealthy businessman Edward (Richard Gere). The parallel is particularly relevant, as the conclusion of *She's All That* sees Laney describe herself as feeling like 'Julia Roberts in *Pretty Woman*'. Tasker is attentive to the ways in which Vivian's low social class is signalled through bodily gestures, highlighting her raucous laughter and belching as evidence of her working-classness (1998: 28). As in *Working Girl*, working-class femininity is indicated through bodily excess that is gradually tempered as the character learns to assume the conduct of 'respectable' middle-class femininity. In this context, it is notable that although Laney assumes much of the conduct and appearance of middle-class femininity, she retains her clumsiness throughout the film. While reading Laney's makeover in the light of Butler's work foregrounds the labour and the construction of that gender identity, establishing that gender as a classed discourse provides a further layer of complexity in the scene and demonstrates how classed gender may be established, reproduced and indeed refused through forms of action and bodily movement.

Alternative Values and the Prom

Following her makeover, Laney attends Preston's party with Zack. As Taylor arrives at the party wearing a short red dress similar to that which Zack selected for Laney, it is clear both that Taylor remains his model of an ideal female partner and that, as the current front-runner for prom queen, she embodies the type of femininity valorised by the high school cohort. Confronting Laney, Taylor asks, 'Isn't your father my pool man?' drawing attention to her rival's lower social status outside, as well as within, the high school. The interaction culminates with Taylor intentionally spilling her drink over Laney's dress, a gesture that legitimates her as a credible threat to Taylor, and so indicates the success of Laney's makeover. Here, I will examine the nature of Laney's candidacy for prom queen to argue that she constitutes a site of ambivalent resistance to the event's gender and class strictures.

Returning to school after the party, Taylor's and Laney's campaigns for prom queen are distinct for the values that the two characters are respectively seen to embody. Significantly, Laney's campaign appears to have been instigated without her knowledge, as she is handed a leaflet inviting her to vote for herself. Rather, she is positioned as a stand-in for other political interests that transcend the school. Thus, she is the 'pro-choice choice', and endorsed by the 'Gay Students Union', 'The Oppressed Prisoners Club' and the 'Hygiene Squad'. In contrast, Taylor's campaign is focused on her own totemic presence, with her campaign posters simply emblazoned with 'Taylor Vaughn', her name in itself providing reason enough to vote for her. While Laney's candidacy provides a platform for the articulation of political dissent for causes that transcend the high school, that of Taylor represents the values of individualism and entitlement. Dressed in a cheerleader outfit, which demonstrates her economic and social capital within the school, Taylor's non-slogan, 'Taylor Vaughn' needs no further embellishment.

There is some irony in Laney's makeover authorising her as a site of political mobilisation. Certainly, as was observed at the beginning of the film, her political interests have previously been regarded as problematic, and a substantial obstacle to her potential desirability. For McRobbie, postfeminist culture requires a repudiation of political consciousness in order to 'count as a modern sophisticated girl' (McRobbie 2004: 258). This 'girl' should not concern herself with evidence of continued sexism, which requires a concerted feminist response. In an environment in which the aims of feminism have supposedly been fully realised, to suggest the contrary is to position oneself as belonging to the past (McRobbie 2004). Rather, she must 'just lighten up', as Zack suggests to Laney when she brings up the issue of sewage waste in the Pacific Ocean. However, in *She's All That*, Laney's newly glamorous appearance does not diminish her political voice, but provides her with a platform from which to articulate her views. Further, she becomes the site for the articulation of previously oppressed viewpoints within the student body.

While the positions of Prom King and Queen have governed much of the film's narrative, events at the prom itself undermine the importance of the status attached to these roles. Here, unsurprisingly, Zack is elected Prom King, while Taylor narrowly beats Laney to become Prom Queen. For Wood, Taylor's victory 'defies the logic of the film thus far', which, he argues, should further validate Laney's transformation by cementing her as Prom Queen at the film's conclusion (Wood 2003: 325). However, Zack's acceptance speech reveals the meaninglessness of the accolade, as he remarks, 'For a lot of us, this is as good as it gets . . . but the truth is, we're just getting started.' In doing so, he constructs the titles of Prom King and Queen, and with them the idealised status they imply, as the meaningless trivia of high school, an institution with which he has definitively concluded his association. Taylor's win is therefore something of a pyrrhic victory, demonstrating her continued entrapment within these juvenile strictures, of which Zack and Laney have since grown tired.

The prom's centrality in the lives of its teenage attendees is further undermined when the final reunion between Zack and Laney occurs not at the event, but at Laney's home. Indicating her desire for a relationship with Zack that is removed from his high school status, she refuses his initial offer of a 'last dance', and instead proposes a 'first dance', the first, that is, of their relationship that flourishes best away from the high school. In contrast to the conclusion of *Pretty in Pink*, which celebrated Andie's apparent class ascension through her relationship with Blane, *She's All That* sees a levelling of its two principal players. Contrary to Zack's earlier plans to attend an Ivy League university, he now intends, like Laney, to enrol in art school, in his case to pursue his new-found interest in performance art. While art school lacks the cultural capital of the more prestigious institutions he previously pursued, this choice amounts to Zack's self-actualisation, since it marks the first time in which he has made a decision untroubled by the consequences for his social standing. Laney's is certainly the more spectacular of the two transformations. Arguably, though, that which Zack undergoes is shown to have more significant consequences for the film's construction of identity. Indeed, in contrast to Laney, who remains much as she has been throughout the film, Zack's outlook changes substantially. As Laney and Zack's coupling is endorsed at their high school graduation, their relationship can be seen to demonstrate that despite the seemingly oppressive gender and class norms upheld by the school, there are in fact a number of ways of constructing identity and value within that normative space.

Mean Girls (Mark Waters, 2004)

In its central focus on the perils, travails and labour of attaining and maintaining female popularity, *Mean Girls* owes much to *Heathers* and even to *Clueless*.[16] While *Heathers* portrayed the viciousness of the eponymous group, *Clueless* charted the coming of age of Cher (Alicia Silverstone), a sympathetic figure characterised not only by her seemingly vapid consumerism, but also by her flair for invention and creativity. *Mean Girls* marks a return to a portrayal of teenage girlhood as uniquely malicious. The film is especially distinctive for its demarcation of the norms of femininity, and its lament on the extent to which these norms have changed over time. Indeed, the film's very title assumes a contrast between the saccharine norms of girlhood and the slyly aggressive practices of *this* generation of girls in particular, one that was central to the moral panic that both inspired the film's inception and surrounded its release.

Mean Girls cannot be considered a literary adaptation in the same way that was discussed in relation to *She's All That*. Nonetheless, Tina Fey's knowing screenplay does possess a written antecedent in the form of *Queen Bees and Wannabes*, a self-help book by Rosalind Wiseman. Written in 2002, Wiseman's book identifies particular forms of psychological abuse practised by teenage girls at the beginning of the twenty-first century. Tellingly, the book's subtitle, 'Helping your daughter survive cliques, gossip, boyfriends and the new realities of Girl World', specifically identifies other teenage girls as the principal perils of female adolescence. In an interview with the *New York Times* shortly before the release of her book, Wiseman confounded expectations that girls are 'sweet and nurturing', calling on her readers to observe the divisive power plays between teenagers (Wiseman in Talbot 2002: n.p.). What is at stake, then, is the ways in which contemporary girls' behaviour has strayed from traditional forms of femininity. In this, Wiseman observes the work of Finnish psychologist Kaj Bjorkvist to argue that girls' supposedly 'natural' empathy makes them particularly dangerous, since they 'know better how to harm' others (Bjorkvist in Talbot 2002: n.p.). We are thus positioned in a postfeminist universe, where girls are no longer regarded as victims of their male peers, as they had been in feminist accounts of girls in education (Ringrose 2012: 32). Nor, for that matter, can a bond based on sisterhood be counted on. Rather, Wiseman presents teenage girls as newly individualised antagonists, whose supposedly natural ability to build relationships is now used in the service of creating and breaking alliances to further their own ends.

Wiseman's book is expressly intended for a concerned adult audience. Yet Fey's screenplay and Waters's direction position *Mean Girls* as part of the teen genre, cultivating Cady (Lindsay Lohan) as the locus of the audience's sympathy. Formerly home-schooled in Africa (a more specific locale is never supplied), Cady's ignorance of the social and educational norms of an American high school makes her an ideal proxy for the audience's (re)introduction to the unwritten rules that structure contemporary adolescence. In particular, it is the conventions of the high school teen movie that are conveyed, not least because Cady's unusual circumstances mean that she is ignorant of much of the popular culture that is familiar to the other characters. In *Mean Girls*, Cady is soon adopted by The Plastics, an elite all-female trio headed by Regina George (Rachel McAdams), whose regal nomenclature recalls the poisonous Queen Bee of Wiseman's tome. Accordingly, Regina is shown to manipulate Cady, who must navigate her own growing popularity, acquired through association with the Plastics, and her own, less well-regarded abilities in maths.

In Wiseman's account, contemporary girls' behaviour has strayed from an idealised feminine norm such that it requires careful management during the *sturm und drang* of contemporary adolescence.[17] Teenage girls are thus presented as pathological in a way that their more traditional forbears were not. Yet it should be noted that Regina and her acolytes are shown to contain their emotions and refuse physical aggression, tendencies that recall the repressive behaviours associated with middle-class femininity (Skeggs 1997: 99). The film's mean girls therefore embody a complex combination of conventional and heteronormative femininity, alongside a dangerously insidious aggression. Analysing how Cady gradually comes to assimilate these norms, I demonstrate how the film stages a complex negotiation between traditional understandings of girlhood, and the contemporary mores that seem to mandate increasingly aggressive behaviour in high school.

Cultural Capital in 'Girl World'

Mean Girls principally portrays Cady's acquisition of social and cultural capital at high school.[18] As a result, it is important that the beginning of the film conveys the absence of these qualities. In *Mean Girls*, Cady's lack of social and cultural capital is represented through her appealingly childlike innocence, an Edenic state that is on the point of being utterly transformed. With a close-up, low-angle shot of two parents (Ana Gasteyer and Neil Flynn) earnestly asking if she has all that is necessary for her first day at school, the audience is cued to expect the object of their ministrations to be a young child. We are therefore surprised when a cut to a wider shot scale sees a high school-age girl quickly stand up and leave the house. As Cady's voiceover explains, having spent her childhood in Africa, her research zoologist parents have home-educated her, such that her first day at school in fact occurs at the age of sixteen. Despite Cady's childlike positioning in this initial scene, she is definitively placed within the teen genre: initial scenes present the principal topoi of the high school,[19] while her family's decision to relocate to Chicago positions her in the midwestern centre of John Hughes's well-known teen output. Demonstrating that Cady is at a remove from American popular culture, while making clear that the audience's sympathies lie with her, the opening scenes of *Mean Girls* make the mores of the high school appear all the more strange, arbitrary and contingent.

Caught between the norms of childhood and adolescence, Cady's liminality is reflected in the stardom of the actor who plays her, Lindsay Lohan. Leaving her parents, Cady walks uncertainly into North Shore high school, where long point-of-view shots see feral students setting fire to objects while others blankly bump into her and obstruct her path. The movement from parental control to the apparently uncontrolled world of the high school can be seen to mirror Lohan's own progression from her work for Walt Disney Studios – in which she starred in children's films, among them *The Parent Trap* (Nancy Meyers, 1998) and *Freaky Friday* (Mark Waters, 2003) – to this, her first film made outside of the studio in the quintessential generic milieu of the teen movie. Lohan's stardom also provides an important reference point for the way in which girlhood itself is perceived as being under threat in *Mean Girls*. As Sarah Projansky observes, this was the last film Lohan made without the 'cloud of the "crash-and-burn girl" surrounding her', which would become unavoidable by the following year (Projanksy 2014: 101). Like Lohan, Cady is the innocent who comes to be corrupted by the insidious girl culture at the high school.

Cady's lack of social and cultural capital at the beginning of the film is also indicated through costume. Her indifference to fashion, and, it follows, her lack of femininity, is conveyed through her functional blue plaid shirt and jeans, while her hair is tied up in a ponytail. This costuming has more in common with that of maths teacher Ms Norbury (Tina Fey) than with her classmates, indicating both Cady's strong abilities in the subject and her fellow students' disregard for it. As if to signal that aptitude for maths is antithetical to the construction of idealised femininity, Ms Norbury is constructed as a social and economic failure, being divorced and working as a bartender in order to boost her income. Further, the Mathletes team is so male-dominated that they are particularly eager to secure a rare female recruit. Through costume, then, Cady is both masculinised and aligned with an embodiment of inadequate femininity.

Cady's ignorance of American popular culture and her disdained knowledge of African wildlife and maths leads many students at North Shore High to regard her as an 'alien'. For the other students, there is no value in these areas of knowledge, demonstrating the necessity for a community that recognises its importance in order for it to count as cultural capital. In contrast, the description of North Shore High itself as 'girl world' is key to the articulation of cultural capital in *Mean Girls*. For Kathleen Rowe Karlyn, 'girl world' is a 'liminal time and space between childhood and adulthood, where girls rule' (Karlyn 2011: 78). In contrast to Wiseman's descriptions of 'girl world' as a perilous one from which girls must be protected, Karlyn constructs the high school as a temporary respite outside of which girls and women do not possess such power. Nonetheless, it is clear that in 'girl world' it is principally the construction of idealised, middle-class femininity that counts as cultural capital. As such, Cady's areas of expertise are not regarded positively.

A crucial overview of the school's social hierarchy is contained in the high school cafeteria. As was briefly observed in relation to *Pretty in Pink*, communal spaces within the school grounds are particularly fraught locales for the delineation of youth identities. In this case, Janis (Lizzie Caplan) describes the esoteric tribes of North Shore High, helpfully providing Cady with a map of the cafeteria tables in which these groups congregate. We are thus introduced to 'girls who eat their feelings, girls who don't eat at all, [and] sexually-active band geeks' as well as to the Plastics, comprised of Regina, Gretchen (Lacey Chabert) and Karen (Amanda Seyfried), and 'the greatest people you will ever meet', a group that consists of Janis herself and her friend Damien (Daniel Franzese). To paraphrase Bourdieu, this type of rigorous social discrimination always classifies the classifier, such that Janis's assessment of her own social position should be understood as relational.[20] Indeed, it should be noted that neither Regina, Gretchen nor Karen ever refer to themselves as the Plastics, and that they themselves dub Janis and Damien 'art freaks'. These descriptions are therefore a function of the characters' own self-perception within the high school.

Referring to 'unfriendly black hotties', 'cool Asians', and 'wannabes', among others, Janis's descriptions suggest that attractiveness is the key

Figure 4.6 Cady (Lindsay Lohan) meets the Plastics (Rachel McAdams, Lacey Chabert, Amanda Seyfried) for the first time.

uniting factor in the social capital of these tribes. This certainly corresponds with Best's research, which further observes that for girls in particular, social capital is accrued through adherence to a normative standard of attractiveness, as judged by their male peers (Best 2000: 72). The high school thus provides one more arena in which, as John Berger memorably observed, 'men look at women; women watch themselves being looked at' (Berger 1972: 45). In the case of *Mean Girls*, though, Berger might also have added, '... and ascribe social capital accordingly'. In 'girl world' it is not teenage boys but girls who deem Cady to be a 'regulation hottie', and 'really pretty', as Janis and Regina respectively describe her. *Mean Girls* positions girls, not boys, as the arbiters of social capital in the high school.

It is precisely because Cady is 'really pretty' that she is permitted to sit with Regina, Karen and Gretchen in the cafeteria and granted privileged access to the many arbitrary rules to which they subject themselves. Gretchen informs her of the following series of norms and prohibitions: while wearing pink on Wednesdays is obligatory, 'you can't wear a tank top two days in a row ... you can only wear your hair in a ponytail once a week ... [and] you can only wear jeans or track pants on Friday'. The triviality of these rules, combined with Gretchen's earnest delivery, is clearly intended for comedic effect. However, the consequences of failing to comply are rather more serious. When, later in the film, Cady is denied the possibility of eating with the other girls, she finds herself eating alone in a stall in the girls' toilets. As such, she is positioned as an abject non-person, recalling Butler's conception of de-realisation, wherein failure to approximate the norms of idealised gender causes the subject to lose recognition as a viable subject (Butler 2004: 34). If the approximation of idealised gender can be partly conferred, it can also be swiftly removed.

Mean Girls and Relational Aggression

Cady's first brush with meanness in *Mean Girls* occurs when the seemingly 'sweet' Regina scuppers Cady's nascent relationship with Aaron (Jonathan Bennett). Having done so, Regina tauntingly invites Cady to admire her beau's hair, prompting Lohan's character to speculate how the dispute would be resolved in 'the animal world'. A version of events is duly supplied by her mind's eye, in which Cady sees herself pouncing on Regina and pinning her to the ground. However, the film cuts to the original scene, where Cady straightforwardly complies with Regina's request, as the voiceover reminds us that in 'girl world' such anger must be expressed in alternative 'sneaky' ways. Here, then, an appropriate feminine response to anger is shown to be a repression of the untutored, instinctive impulse to attack.

For Jessica Ringrose, the 'sneaky' forms of aggression to which Cady alludes can be described by Nicki Crick's term, 'relational aggression' (Crick 1996 in Ringrose 2013: 32). As stated in the introduction to this case study, the very title of *Mean Girls* implies that girls' behaviour has been irrevocably transformed from the nurturing norm. Similarly, relational aggression can be read as a modifier of a normalised, masculine model of aggression, which is centred on the expression of physical violence (Ringrose 2013: 32). In this scene, references to the 'animal world' construct physical violence as the natural way of resolving differences, in contrast to the artificial, rarefied mores of 'girl world'. As a result, relational aggression is portrayed as doubly perverse; not only does aggression itself disrupt the norms of femininity, but the girls' underhandedness differs from the physical, direct and masculinised norms of aggression.

Relational aggression is constructed as pathological in *Mean Girls* and educational literature alike. Nonetheless, these behaviours remain consistent with the norms of middle-class femininity that require women to suppress their emotionality and corporeality. As discussed in relation to *She's All That*, middle-class femininity is signalled by the extent to which bodily excess is successfully contained. In turn, the white, middle-class mean girl who is *au fait* with sneaky, relational aggression stands in contrast to working-class femininity, whose violent aggression codes such girls as abject, 'low-down, masculine and deviant' (Ringrose 2012: 30). To examine relational aggression as a classed phenomenon, it is instructive to compare the *modus operandi* of Waters's *Mean Girls* with that of the 'angry girl' cycle of the late 1990s (Roberts 2002: 217–34). In one such film, *Freeway* (Matthew Bright, 1996), working-class Vanessa (Reese Witherspoon) must fight off a serial killer while on the run.[21]

Class distinctions in the ways that female characters express aggression are also apparent in the films discussed in this chapter. When working-class Andie confronts Blane in *Pretty in Pink*, she does so directly and forcefully, shouting that he is a 'fucking liar' before physically cornering him.[22] In *She's All That*, Laney only becomes adept at expressing her anger following her makeover, when she comes to be signified as an embodiment of middle-class femininity. An impossible double bind is seen here; while the norms of femininity require repression of bodily instinct, the assertion of aggression by other, non-physical means is portrayed as pathological. Girls are thereby granted no means of legitimately expressing their anger.

Mean Girls portrays Cady's gradual slide into behaviours associated with relational aggression. Consequently, she works with Janis to sabotage Regina's position as an embodiment of idealised femininity. To identify how best to dent Regina's popularity, Janis draws up on a blackboard the three key aspects on which her Queen Bee position is contingent:

> her high-status man-candy [points to first line on blackboard, which reads 'Aaron Samuels'], technically good physique [points to second line: 'Hot' body], and evil band of loyal followers [points to third line: Army of Skanks].

To put it another way, Regina's status is predicated on her attractiveness to the opposite sex, thinness and high levels of social capital. Despite the efforts of Janis and Cady, so strong is her status within the high school that when Cady switches Regina's facial moisturiser for peppermint foot cream, or Janis cuts large holes out of Regina's vest, other girls, sensing a trend, soon follow suit. Other girls' ready acceptance of these practices indicates not only the arbitrariness of the norms of attractiveness, but also the unthinking compliance of the high school girls. However, when Cady tricks Regina into putting on weight, the other students' acceptance and imitation of the trends she establishes come to an end. As a result, while Janis determines that Regina's 'hot body' is one of three crucial aspects that together contribute to her Queen Bee position, it in fact turns out to be thinness that is the single most important factor in her dominance.

The acute self-surveillance of female bodies portrayed in *Mean Girls* is, as Diane Negra observes, symptomatic of postfeminist culture (Negra 2009: 119). The Plastics are shown comparing their bodies in Regina's floor-length mirror, identifying real and imagined flaws. When they glance over at Cady, who has so far remained silent, she finds that she too must identify some aspect of her body to disparage, eventually offering up 'really bad breath in the morning'. There is a ritual quality to this exercise, as one girl's flaw must be rebuffed by another, who must likewise come up with some inadequacy.

What is clear, though, is that the female body is a locus of constant labour and scrutiny, one that should be seen to be 'underfed, over-exercised' (Negra 2009: 119). The fat body is thereby constructed as the abject abnegation of this labour and surveillance.

As has been apparent in other female bodily norms discussed in this chapter, fatness possesses class connotations that in turn have consequences for Regina's social capital. As discussed previously, Skeggs argues that femininity is a classed construct that effectively delimits its belonging from working-class women. Yet unlike their male counterparts, working-class women have not found that class status to be a worthwhile identity to rally under. Instead, Skeggs finds, working-class women recognise and reject their positioning as abject, and, observing the cultural capital that accrues from (middle-class) femininity, dissociate themselves from their class identity (Skeggs 1997: 74–9). Such complex processes of recognition, identification and dissociation occur at a bodily level, as Skeggs observed that her research participants were keen to distance themselves from those of their acquaintance who were perceived to have 'let themselves go' (Skeggs 1997: 83). Their fat bodies, it is implied, are beyond regulation and discipline, and thus cannot 'aspire' to become middle class (Skeggs 1997: 84).[23] It is the lack of attention to controlling the body, as was apparent in the discussion of unregulated displays of emotion and aggression, that is at stake in the maintenance of the controlled, middle-class body.

In *Mean Girls* the class connotations of fatness are particularly apparent when Regina can no longer fit into the designer dress she planned to purchase for the forthcoming Spring Fling dance. Much to Regina's chagrin, the assistant at the chichi boutique (Jo Chim) snootily informs her that the larger sizes are only stocked at Sears, a mass-market department store. Despite Regina's continued ability to afford the dress, her fatness causes her no longer to be recognised as a viable consumer in the exclusive shop. Rather, she is dismissed as undeserving of the assistant's attention. What is at stake in this scene is the question of recognition, the key component on which Regina's hegemony at the high school depends. This scene demonstrates that recognisability of classed gender, and the constraints and privileges that come with it, are constantly formed and reconfigured on the very surface of the body.

Soon after Regina's economic capital fails to be recognised, she finds that her fatness causes her to lose social capital. In the cafeteria Gretchen shrilly tells Regina that in accordance with the rules stipulated earlier in the film to Cady, Regina cannot sit at the Plastics' table, since she is wearing tracksuit bottoms on a day that is not Friday, the day on which these garments are tolerated. Regina's humiliation is further compounded when, attempting to rush out of the cafeteria, she bumps into a student who warns her to 'watch where you're going, fatass', prompting the entire student body to erupt with laughter. Regina's fatness has moved her from a positioning in which she was both admired and feared to one in which she is the object of casual derision. As Katherine Sender and Margaret Sullivan observe in their analysis of weight-loss programming such as *Biggest Loser* (NBC, 2008–) or *Extreme Weight Loss* (ABC, 2004–), the fat body, and most especially the fat female body, is derided as one that lacks the requisite self-control and self-esteem (Sender and Sullivan 2008: 573). Sender and Sullivan conclude that viewers respond to these fat bodies as 'figures of fun or failure' whose subjectivity is never considered apart from the size of their bodies (Sender and Sullivan 2008: 574). The scene ultimately demonstrates the fragility of classed gender norms, given how quickly Regina has moved from being regarded as an embodiment of idealised femininity to an abstractly-conceived figure of derision.

Becoming Plastic

The previous section showed that relational aggression is the logical consequence of norms of femininity that mandate the repression of emotional and bodily excess. What is more, girls' bodies are subject to constant monitoring and scrutiny, and must achieve a particularly stringent criterion of thinness. Within this environment of heightened surveillance, it is hardly surprising that Cady would succumb to the perils that afflict all double agents, and aspire to become like the Plastics themselves. *Mean Girls* consequently does not feature a single makeover sequence in the same way that *Pretty in Pink* and *She's All That* did. Rather, the film portrays Cady's gradual assimilation of the mores of 'girl world', as well as the high school cohort's increasing acceptance of her as the new 'Queen Bee'.

Changes in Cady's costuming and hair reflect the extent of the changes in attitude that are taking place in her character. As discussed, Cady begins her school year wearing a plaid shirt and jeans, with minimal make-up. However, as her inculcation into the Plastics takes hold, her clothing becomes increasingly pink – a heavy-handed analogy of her acquisition of the norms of hegemonic femininity. The silhouette of her clothing also changes to reflect those of Regina, Gretchen and Karen, who are typically seen in V-neck jumpers or T-shirts accompanied by A-line skirts, the obvious femininity of which recalls the fertility implied by the traditional prom dress. It is therefore clear that Cady has definitively moved from her childlike positioning to one of adult, middle-class femininity.

Striking though these changes in costume may be, close-ups of Cady draw attention to her face and hair as the principal locus of her girlhood gone astray. As a model and later a contracted actor for Walt Disney Studios, Lohan was known for her vibrant red hair. Certainly, the star remarks that her hair colour allowed her to stand out from the blonde, blue-eyed child models who constituted the majority of her competition (Croft 2012: 16). What is more, her red hair draws Lohan into a lineage of actors, such as Molly Ringwald and Ron Howard, whose youthful virtuousness was underpinned by their red hair, pale skin and freckles. Gaylyn Studlar's analysis of girlhood in classical Hollywood cinema takes up John Hartley's account of 'juvenation', which consists in 'communication via the medium of youthfulness' (Hartley in Studlar 2013: 2). For Studlar, juvenated stars not only allow the audience to, however briefly, be addressed as youthful, but also serve as arbiters that patrol the boundary between child and adult identities (Studlar 2013: 2–3). Although Studlar refers to child stardom in classical Hollywood cinema, Lohan's status as a studio-employed actor – thus conforming to the employment practices used during the classical era – makes Studlar's observations relevant here. In *Mean Girls*, the blonde streaks in Cady's hair draw attention to her rejection of girlhood and movement into adult, sexualised femininity.

Changes in Cady's outlook are also signalled by her use of language and talent for dissimulation. As discussed, maths is shown in the film to be an unusual area of skill for girls. So rare a find is the female Mathlete that Kevin (Rajiv Surendra) assures Cady that they will double their funding if they have a girl on their team. Recognising that her abilities do not fit with the prevailing norms of femininity, Cady stages a performance of feminine deference for Aaron, playing with her hair as she denies knowledge of concepts in which she is fully proficient. Underscoring the disparity between her actual level of understanding and the performance of ignorance, a voiceover allows the audience to hear Cady mentally correcting Aaron's explanations and answers, even as her words and submissive body language suggest that she holds his abilities in high regard. An analogy with Joan Rivière's well-known essay on womanliness as masquerade suggests itself here. Rivière observes how, for intellectual women in particular, a performance of feminine modesty and compliance serves as a defensive mechanism towards men, who might otherwise feel themselves under threat (1929). Yet in *Mean Girls* it is Cady's performance of femininity that has adverse consequences, not least her failing the advanced maths class in which she is enrolled.

What *Mean Girls* therefore suggests is the sense in which the norms of femininity are not within the control of the agents who seem to be in the driving seat. As Butler argues, such approximations of idealised femininity cannot be taken as the design of 'the performer's will or choice' (Butler 1993: 95). Instead there are a whole suite of gender norms that govern not only how the approximation of gender norms occurs, but how it is likely to be received by its audience. In this way, then, *Mean Girls* is seen to stage a critique of the contemporary norms of femininity that mandate girls' submission to their male peers. Further, when Cady does agree to participate in the Mathlete championship, her knowledge of the norms of femininity, cemented through weeks of immersion with the Plastics, disrupts her performance. Although she must solve the maths problem within a strict time limit, Cady finds herself mentally enumerating her female opponent's flaws, cattily taking in the '99 cent lip-gloss on her snaggle tooth'. However, scrutiny of this girl's inferior gender and class positioning comes at the expense of calculating the answer to the question, which Cady can only arrive at by focusing on the task at hand. This scene shows that knowledge of the mores of middle-class femininity can impede other areas of expertise.

Attending the Spring Fling in her (masculinised) Mathlete garb, Cady can be seen to erode the event's implied heteronormativity. Certainly, her earlier performance at the competition itself has given the lie to the assertion that any attempt to combine maths with femininity is nothing less than 'social suicide'. It should be acknowledged that, in contrast to the proms in the two previous case studies, the *Mean Girls* Spring Fling merely heralds the end of the academic year rather than high school graduation. It does not, therefore, possess the ritual significance attached to the prom. Nonetheless, with the exception of Janis and Damien, who attend in matching tuxedos, the Spring Fling sees most characters uniformly donning the highly gendered costuming we have seen elsewhere in the chapter, particularly the respective candidates for Spring Fling King and Queen. Yet when Cady receives her accolade of Spring Fling Queen still wearing her Mathlete uniform, as seen in Figure 4.7 below, her victory appears to celebrate the diversity of the high school cohort.

For Projansky, celebrations of uniqueness and diversity such as the one instantiated by *Mean Girls* are somewhat disingenuous. Projansky notes a recent surge in films that praise exceptional examples of girlhood, highlighting Katniss Everdeen (Jennifer Lawrence) in *The Hunger Games*, whose rare combination of skill and ethics makes her an ideal figurehead of a nascent rebellion movement. Such inimitable examples of girlhood are easily praised. Yet, for

Figure 4.7   Cady (Lindsay Lohan) is crowned Spring Fling Queen.

Projansky, the very uniqueness of girls like Cady or Katniss only serves to foreground the sameness and conformity of the majority of their peers (Projansky 2014: 124). The film initially appears to be in favour of Cady's hybrid identity, which blends her masculinised maths skills with her role as Spring Fling Queen. However, *Mean Girls* clearly positions Cady as an exception to the majority, who continue to comply with the previously stipulated norms of 'girl world'. As if to demonstrate that heteronormativity remains intact, for instance, a long shot depicts the students coupled off into opposite-sexed pairs as the Spring Fling concludes.

The end of *Mean Girls* sees the dissolution of the Plastics, with Regina now channelling her aggression into lacrosse. The danger represented by her anger is now therefore contained, not to mention masculinised, through its expression in sports. However, the impression that Cady's actions have forever transformed the behaviour of high school girls is soon dispelled as she and Janis spot a new, younger trio of girls, who have the characteristic clothing and disdainful demeanour once possessed by Regina, Gretchen and Karen. *Mean Girls* draws attention to the cyclicality of the high school, where, it is implied, the learning process that Cady and her peers have endured must be undertaken again and again by the generations to come. The film's conclusion is therefore bittersweet; while gender norms may be temporarily undermined and critiqued, the fundamental structures will remain largely unchanged.

Conclusion

Pretty in Pink, *She's All That* and *Mean Girls* speak to the constructions of gender that are valued within the high school teen movie; that is to say, which identities count as culturally intelligible, and which are sidelined. These films portray the prom as the site at which these judgements are formally made, often, as in *She's All That* and *Mean Girls*, presenting the conferment of idealised gender as one that is made by an official process and bestowed by a figure of authority. Even characters who are not put forward for such garlanded positions do not escape the event's scrutiny. Certainly, as was claimed on multiple occasions in this chapter, the prom requires adherence to particularly rigid gender and class norms, as a result of which many characters are shown to undertake, or to undergo, transformations that will see them better assimilate those ideals.

The prom is undeniably a normative space. However, in this conclusion, I want to consider how, when all three case studies are viewed alongside one another, the prom can conversely provide an arena in which individual subjectivity can find expression. In *Pretty in Pink*, Andie is forced through financial necessity to make her own dress, which will allow her to attend the prom. The event is therefore figured as something of a barrier that stipulates a particular threshold level of economic and social capital in order for a student to attend. Nonetheless, as the analysis demonstrated, Andie's pink, narrowly-fitting dress ambiguously suggests not only her desire to be accepted at the prom, but also to subvert the traditional prom-dress silhouette denoting heteronormativity and fertility. Andie is thus able to showcase something of a hybrid identity that embraces her desire for normativity, her positioning as a daughter and her love of subcultural bricolage.

In *She's All That* Laney is deceived into undergoing a makeover, which could be regarded as limiting her agency. Nonetheless, it is striking that only in the wake of Laney's Prom Queen candidacy, itself enabled by her makeover, can her political interests be validated. It is in this way that the disparate causes supporting her candidacy can find voice within the ordinarily conservative realm of the high school. While the end of the film seeks to undermine the positions of the Prom King and Queen as a juvenile irrelevance, it is notable that the prom brings the relationship between Zack and Laney into being, and is therefore partly responsible not only for his change in academic direction but also for her acceptance into art school. In turn, the concluding scenes of *Mean Girls* see Cady, incongruously clad in her Mathlete uniform, celebrated as the ultimate endorsement of teen femininity, the Spring Fling Queen. In those scenes, too, Cady is shown to distribute parts of the crown around the cohort in a bid to diffuse the hostilities that had characterised the high school up to that point.

To reiterate, it is not the ambition of these concluding remarks to deny that the high school, and the prom as its final flourish, are extremely normative spaces. Indeed, the secondary aim of the education system is to socialise teenagers into the ways of the world. Nonetheless, as these examples show, it is possible to identify sites of resistance and complexity within those spaces. The work of Butler and Skeggs read together reminds us that while teenagers might be interpellated into these rigid ideals of gender and class, this does not necessarily mean they are straightforwardly obeyed. The following chapter examines the construction of the past in the teen movie, with particular attention to the gender roles of those past eras. Here it will be important to observe how the characters regard their own future prospects, as much as they are themselves embodiments of the past. In the light of the contradictory gaze of the postfeminist perspective, the chapter will investigate whether, and if so how, a return to the past is presented as desirable.

Notes

1. It should be acknowledged that by no means all high school films conclude at the prom; however, it is an event which occurs in many such films, and is at least referenced in numerous examples of the subgenre. The prom is central to understanding the role of the school within the teen movie.

2. Best does acknowledge that some students have successfully campaigned to attend prom as same-sex couples, or indeed as part of a group of friends. Yet the overwhelming majority are still expected to attend as part of a heterosexual couple.
3. A poll conducted in the *New York Times* found that 40 per cent of Americans believed that the chance of moving from one class to another had risen over the last few years. In fact, the opposite is true (see Scott and Leonhardt 2005).
4. It should be noted that the two theorists have expressed disagreement with one another over the potential for subversion in their two seemingly allied theories. See Butler (1997), p. 147, and Bourdieu (1998), p. 110.
5. See Faludi (1992).
6. It should be noted that the Psychedelic Furs recorded the song five years prior to the release of *Pretty in Pink*. On the understanding that the song was to provide the film's title, the group recorded a new version, which is heard in this scene.
7. See <http://www.billboard.com/#/album/original-soundtrack/pretty-in-pink/65041> (last accessed 30 March 2017).
8. Hadley Freeman reports that Hughes liked to discuss his young actors' tastes in music. One product of these discussions was the inclusion of the Psychedelic Furs' music in *Pretty in Pink*. See Freeman (2014).
9. Originally, Andie was to be united with Duckie at the film's conclusion. While reports suggest that test audiences preferred to give Andie a 'fairytale ending' with Blane (Brammer 2009), Shary's investigations point to a number of factors prompting this change in romantic partners, among which was Ringwald's illness in the final days of shooting and her lack of chemistry with Jon Cryer. In a 2008 interview, Cryer states that the reaction shots from the assembled richies were seen to 'lack oomph', and that this was why audiences disliked the film's ending (Shary 2014, p. 366).
10. Brook (1999), 'Teen power storms US box office', <http://news.bbc.co.uk/1/hi/special_report/1999/03/99/tom_brook/290955.stm> (last accessed 30 March 2017).
11. In addition to those mentioned above, we might also consider *Whatever It Takes* (David Raynr, 2000), adapting *Cyrano de Bergerac*; *Get Over It* (Tommy O'Haver, 2001), adapting *A Midsummer Night's Dream*; *Deal of a Lifetime* (Paul Levine, 1999), based on *Faust*; *Crime and Punishment in Suburbia* (Rob Schmidt, 2000), from the Dostoyevsky text; *Sleepy Hollow High* (Chris Arth, Kevin Summerfield, 2000), from the Washington Irving short story; and *O* (Tim Blake Nelson, 2001), adapted from *Othello*. *Easy A*, one of the next chapter's case studies, is adapted from Nathaniel Hawthorne's *The Scarlet Letter*.
12. Although the teen movie is not typically regarded as a star text, Prinze Jr earned a following from teen slasher hits *I Know What You Did Last Summer* (Jim Gillespie, 1997) and its follow-up *I Still Know What You Did Last Summer* (Danny Cannon, 1999), and provides the biggest star presence of this film.
13. While this style of glasses has since come to be fashionable, I am referring here to the film's textual frame and the time of its release.
14. In reference to British television in particular, Rachel Moseley describes this new wave of makeover programming as a 'takeover' (Moseley 2000).
15. Notably, 'Kiss Me' by Sixpence None the Richer was also used in teen drama series *Dawson's Creek* (WB 1998–2003) and subsequently parodied in Joel Gallen's *Not Another Teen Movie* (2001), indicating the song's iconic positioning in the genre.
16. Roz Kaveney observes that *Heathers* was written by the brother of *Mean Girls* director Mark Waters, speaking to the similarities in tone and content.
17. Conveniently, Wiseman has such a solution in the form of her 'Empower Program', which she toured around American high schools. She now runs a similar program,

'Sharing Culture of Dignity'. See <http://culturesofdignity.com/> (last accessed 30 March 2017).
18. Economic capital does not appear to be a factor in *Mean Girls*, with all teenage characters seemingly occupying the same suburban, upper-middle-class demographic.
19. For Adrian Martin, the principal accessories of the high school constitute the teen movie's semantic level; that is, the visual ingredients an audience expects to see upon encountering any teen movie. These include lockers, the cafeteria, cliques and sports teams (Martin 1989, p. 9).
20. 'Taste classifies, and it classifies the classifier' (Bourdieu 1986, p. 6).
21. Outside of Hollywood, too, *Bande de filles* (Céline Sciamma, 2014) portrays a gang of violent working-class girls on the outskirts of Paris.
22. Significantly, this is the only occasion in which such expletives are uttered in any of the films that John Hughes wrote, produced or directed in the 1980s.
23. We might think in this regard of Deirdre Kelly, better known as 'White Dee' in the Channel 4 documentary *Benefits Street* (2014–). Here, it is Kelly's positioning as fat and working-class that allows her to be presented as the abject Other of the 'future-oriented, individualistic and entrepreneurial neoliberal citizen' (Allen et al., 2014, n.p.).

5. LOOKING BACK: NOSTALGIA, POSTFEMINISM AND THE TEEN MOVIE

Throughout this book, it has been clear that the Hollywood teen movie has close links with the youth culture of its time. Yet as this chapter will demonstrate, this equation between contemporary youth culture and the Hollywood films that claim to represent it is not nearly as clear-cut as one might expect. For Timothy Shary, the genre is trapped in a peculiar double bind that determines its relationship with the past: while film-makers aggressively target a youth audience, young people themselves lack the experience or means to produce a mass-market feature film, as a result of which, these representations of youth are 'filtered through an adult lens' (Shary 2002a: 2). An oblique refraction of the youth culture of the past – often that of the director themselves – can therefore be regarded as a central feature of the genre as a whole.

Lesley Speed observes the contradiction in the teen movie's claim to represent contemporary adolescent experience while the films are produced by those whose teenage years are some years past (Speed 1998: 28). However, in contrast to Shary, who regards this peculiar relationship between past and present as a given throughout the teen movie, Speed argues that this conflict is apparent only in a specific sub-category of the genre, the 'nostalgic' or 'rite-of-passage' teen movie, which is set in the past and portrays the process of the protagonists' maturation (Speed 1998: 25). Unlike the majority of films in the genre, the nostalgic teen movie uses narrative devices such as the retrospective voiceover heard throughout *Stand by Me* (Rob Reiner, 1986), which privileges an adult reflection on youthful experiences of the past. Adolescence is thereby contained within an adult narrative perspective.

Retaining the focus on the construction of identity and sexual coming of age that has been present throughout, this chapter will examine what is at stake in these refractions of the past in the teen movie. Examining *American Graffiti* and *Dirty Dancing*, both of which are set in the early 1960s, the analysis will examine the genre's presentation of the past. Despite their similar period settings, the films' perspectives on that epoch are quite different. Released in 1973, *American Graffiti* is widely regarded as the paradigmatic nostalgia film (Jameson 1991; Speed 1998; Dwyer 2015) and portrays a group of teenagers whose Kennedy-era optimism is soon to be dramatically punctured by the ideological uncertainties of the Vietnam War. In contrast, *Dirty Dancing* calls attention to the already existing structural inequalities of the early 1960s, and is instead optimistic for the future. The chapter's final case study, *Easy A*, is not set in the past. However, featuring clips from well-known 1980s teen movies, the film demonstrates how the contemporary trend for retro (Reynolds 2011) inflects the construction of identity in the contemporary teen movie. Here it is expressly the films of the 1980s, rather than the period per se, that are cast as privileged objects of nostalgia.

My description of these films has referred both to their representation or evocation of the past as nostalgic. This terminology is certainly a reflection of the literature as it currently stands. However, it seems clear that 'nostalgia' does not adequately account for the complex relationships created by these films with the past eras they represent or reference. As Linda Hutcheon observes, nostalgia is one of many ways to look back to the past: 'you can look back and reject. Or you can look and linger longingly' (Hutcheon 1998: 4). Nostalgia is indisputably associated with the latter approach. Derived from the Greek *nostos* (return) and *algos* (home), nostalgia was originally conceived as an acute form of homesickness. Only in the eighteenth century did the term acquire its contemporary meaning, so that rather than the (usually) possible wish to return to a particular place, nostalgia came to describe the impossible desire to return to a lost time, most frequently a time of youth (Hutcheon 1998: 4).

Nostalgia undoubtedly retains traces of its former status as a pathology. Writing in 1979, Fred Davis argues that the proliferating media representing the 1950s in the 1970s constituted a retrenchment from the social and political upheavals of the 1960s (Davis 1979: x).[1] Davis thus characterises this 'nostalgia boom' as a conservative phenomenon wherein audiences rejected the reality of the present in favour of an idealised, uncomplicated past. Yet the relationship constructed between past and present in the nostalgia text is rarely as straightforward as Davis claims. Beyond the teen movie, we might consider *Pride* (Matthew Warchus, 2014), which depicts the victimisation of LGBT activists and Welsh miners alike in the mid-1980s. No right-thinking person could look back longingly on such incidents. However, in its portrayal of the collaboration between these groups, *Pride* may be regarded as nostalgic for the galvanising potential of the movements that followed, which have since resulted in substantial legislative changes for gay rights.² In the wake of historic legal changes permitting same-sex marriage across much of the western world, there is now a sense that the potential of the movements depicted in *Pride* has been fully realised in the eyes of many activists (Nelson 2016). The complex interplay between the celebration of, and disillusion with, the achievements currently enjoyed in the present is echoed in the postfeminist mindset, which informs this chapter and which will be discussed further.

Paul Grainge's work usefully unpicks the complex function of nostalgia in popular culture. In particular, he distinguishes the nostalgia mood, an emotional state he terms a 'yearning for the past', from the nostalgia mode, its manifestations in popular culture, prominently associated with the work of Fredric Jameson (Grainge 2000: 28). For Grainge, the nostalgia mood constitutes a form of 'idealised remembrance' such that the nostalgic's longing both results from, and further contributes to, their idealisation of the past (Grainge 2000: 28). Nostalgia, then, is a self-perpetuating phenomenon. Complicating matters still further, Susan Stewart argues that since the nostalgic must know that the object they seek is irretrievably lost, they must be 'enamoured of distance, not of the referent itself' (Stewart 1993: 143). The affective dimension of nostalgia consists in mourning the inevitable loss of the past, rather than the reality of the past itself. That loss can, in and of itself, create the conditions for the nostalgia mood will be significant for the analysis of gender relations throughout this chapter.

The nostalgia mode, by contrast, is not characterised by the complex affect of the nostalgia mood. Rather, Jameson conceives it as the prevailing cultural form of the postmodern era, which signals its positioning in what he calls 'late capitalism' (Jameson 1984: 66). This conception of the postmodern as the latest in a sequence of epochs is significant, since Jameson appears himself to be nostalgic for the modern era, which, he claims, possessed individual styles that could be effectively subverted through parody (Jameson 1991: 22). In its place, he argues that the advent of postmodernism has brought with it the demise of the bourgeois ego as a unique self, and with it, the death of the artist. Consequently, parody has been replaced by pastiche. Unlike Dyer, who argues that the discrepancies and distortions evoked by pastiche engender affectivity (Dyer 2007), for Jameson pastiche is merely 'blank parody' that demonstrates the collapse not only of history but of historicity (Jameson 1991: 17). What remains, then, is the 'nostalgia film', which holds the promise of representing the past, yet instead conveys only a sense of '"pastness" by the glossy qualities of image' (Jameson 1991: 19).

As this chapter's case studies will show, Jameson's conception of the nostalgia film is unduly pessimistic. Following Hutcheon, who is particularly vociferous in her criticisms of Jameson's work, I will demonstrate that Jameson is not attentive to the ways in which these undeniably postmodern constructions of the past expose how historical meaning has always been textual and consequently 'unstable, contextual, relational and provisional' (Hutcheon 2010: 64). Indeed, Hutcheon argues that postmodern culture reveals how the past only becomes known through 'textual traces available in the present' (Hutcheon 2010: 78), such that no objective, transparent access to the past is, or was ever, possible.

It is significant that although there has been much scholarship discussing the meanings of nostalgia, and of the nostalgic teen movie in particular, the representation of gender in these films has rarely been considered. In reference to its 1970s manifestation, including *American Graffiti*, Shary contends that the film's principal appeal is to young men, who can marvel at the power they once commanded over their female contemporaries – a power that has now been undermined in the wake of second-wave feminism (Shary 2005: 45). Similarly, Barbara Creed argues that it is the presentation of 'true heroes and distressed heroines' – that is, the illusion that there were once stable, clearly defined gender roles, which are no longer nearly so stark – that is the key draw of the nostalgia text (Creed 1988: 54). This chapter will dispute the claim that the construction of gender in the past is presented as simple and clear-cut in such films. Rather, the case studies discussed here are complex and contradictory, celebrating women's freedoms in the present, yet also looking back – sometimes with affection – to the past in which those freedoms were not possible.

Postfeminism is proposed as a lens through which to view the construction of gender in the nostalgic teen movie. Here, as in Chapter 4, I take up McRobbie's account of postfeminism, which is attentive to the historical context from which the term is derived, since she claims that postfeminism 'takes feminism into account', with the result that, women's equality having been achieved, it is no longer required (McRobbie 2004: 252). In this, she draws from Sarah Projansky's account of postfeminist culture, in which feminism is presented as 'victorious and ultimately failed' (Projansky 2001: 66). Consequently, feminism is expressly cast as a movement whose radical impetus for change is one that belongs to the past, specifically to the 1970s and 1980s (McRobbie 2004: 255). Further delineating what she terms the 'postfeminist sensibility', Rosalind Gill argues that the contemporary media landscape presents a contradictory 'emphasis on self-surveillance, monitoring and discipline' alongside a 'focus on individualism, choice and empowerment' (Gill 2005: 149). Within this framework, women and men are seen to enjoy the (economic) benefits of increased gender equality, while postfeminist texts portray the allure of gender roles of the past (see Negra 2009). As this analysis demonstrates, the construction of gender in the three films examined here is a complex one that shows the continuous processing of feminist and postfeminist ideas.

The work of Lynn Spigel and Hilary Radner demonstrates the type of analysis that becomes possible when representations of the past are analysed in the context of postfeminism. Discussing the early-1960s setting of *Mad Men* (AMC 2007–15), Spigel argues that the show stimulates a nostalgia for the 'pre-feminist' era, one in which undercurrents of proto-feminist discontent were apparent, yet more overt movements demanding widespread change had not yet occurred (Spigel 2013: 272). The series observes the sexism faced by the female characters, yet, in placing them in a 1960s period setting, couches it safely in the past where, following McRobbie, feminism strictly belongs. Consequently, Spigel argues that the series presents a nostalgic version of the 1960s that anticipates the ideal postfeminist subject: a woman who is 'independent, career-focused, yet hyperbolically feminine in their embrace of fashion, shopping and dating' (Spigel 2013: 273). There is, then, a complex interplay between the time of the series' setting and that of its release, which is used in the service of valorising the highly contradictory state of gender relations in the present.

In turn, Hilary Radner argues that one of this chapter's case studies, *Dirty Dancing*, which is set in the 1960s and was released in 1987, anticipates the need for feminism, particularly in its portrayal of abortion. However, in a similar vein to Spigel's discussion of *Mad Men*, Radner argues that the film's heroine, Baby (Jennifer Grey) is positioned as an embodiment of postfeminist femininity, whose interests move away from social justice and towards her own sexual fulfilment. The most radical transformations of gender relations – which occurred in the period following the film's conclusion, yet before the audience's viewing in the late 1980s – are relegated, Radner argues, to 'feminism's future past' (Radner 2013: 137). Taken together, the work of Spigel and Radner draws attention to the interplay between the epoch represented and that which is inhabited by the audience, and its significance in analysing the construction of gender in the past. What is more, Spigel and Radner show how the contradictions of postfeminism, with its curiously retreatist impulses, elucidate the nostalgic pull of past eras when women's roles were considerably more limited than today.

It should be noted that the films analysed in this chapter are not only set in past eras, but allude to representations of the past in the present. Further, as I have argued elsewhere in the case of two recent romantic comedies, *Crazy Stupid Love* (Glenn Ficarra and John Requa, 2011) and *L'Arnacoeur* (Pascal Chaumeil, 2010), *Dirty Dancing* now constitutes an object of nostalgia in its own right (Smith 2014). In these films, the male characters' knowledge of the *Dirty Dancing* choreography, in particular the 'lift' that Baby and Johnny (Patrick Swayze) perform at the film's conclusion, allows them to win over their female love interests, who are fans of the film.[3] The chapter's final case study, *Easy A*, is not set in the past, yet in Olive's (Emma Stone) lament that her life is 'not directed by John Hughes', the film portrays the character's desire to return to a simulacrum of 1980s teen movies. This highly allusive film invites the audience to question whether, as Olive believes, gender relations in the 1980s teen movie were preferable to those she experiences in the present day.

These moments call to be read in the context of the current positioning of the 1980s as a privileged site of nostalgia (Smith 2016). For Christina Lee, this is the result of Generation X nostalgia for the popular culture of their own past (Lee 2010).[4] In contrast, Hadley Freeman's recent work on 1980s films argues persuasively that the appeal of that decade's films goes beyond those who directly experienced them at the time of their initial release, and is instead the result of a loss of quirky, mid-budget Hollywood cinema that studios, in search of a global audience, are now increasingly reluctant to entertain (Freeman 2015: 19). In addition to examining the effect of the films' representation of the past, this chapter will therefore also be attentive to the ways in which the films may themselves be regarded as sites of nostalgia.

AMERICAN GRAFFITI (GEORGE LUCAS, 1973)

Released in 1973, *American Graffiti* swiftly won many admirers. Earning $55m at the box office at its first run, from a budget of only $750,000, the film was an extraordinary commercial success (DeWitt 2010: 47). The film also garnered widespread critical acclaim, attracting five Oscar nominations including Best Picture, Best Director and Best Screenplay. Although set in 1962, only eleven years prior to its release, *American Graffiti* portrays the early 1960s as a historical period whose practices and ideals have largely been confined to the past. Certainly, a number of significant changes had taken place between the time of the film's setting and its release. The setting of 1962 prefigures the assassination of President Kennedy the following year, and by extension the collapse of innocence provoked by this incident.[5] It also anticipates the 'British invasion' inaugurated by the success of the Beatles, which transformed American pop culture forever. By 1973, however, the Beatles had split up and the Vietnam War, for so long a locus of countercultural discontent, had incurred heavy American losses. With the tagline asking 'Where were you in '62?' the film hails the now aged teenager of the 1960s and informs them that the time in which they grew up is now confined to the distant past.

Jameson's view that *American Graffiti* constitutes a regressive amalgam of pastiche images of the past has been so widely influential that the film's description as 'nostalgic' has become almost inevitable.[6] Yet, as Michael D. Dwyer notes, Jameson's interpretation of Lucas's film is itself historically contingent (Dwyer 2015: 56). Writing in 1984, Jameson positions *American Graffiti* as the impetus for a number of works in the 1970s and 1980s that

NOSTALGIA, POSTFEMINISM AND THE TEEN MOVIE

attempted to recapture the innocence of the Eisenhower era (Jameson 1984: 67). However, Dwyer observes that upon its release *American Graffiti* was considered a part of the American New Wave, quoting the *New York Times*, whose review hailed the film as 'the most important American movie since *Five Easy Pieces*, maybe since *Bonnie and Clyde*' (Dempsey 1973, quoted in Dwyer 2015: 57). Thanks to the overwhelming success of his later *Star Wars* films (1977; 1980; 1983; 1999; 2002; 2005; 2015; 2016), the director of *American Graffiti*, George Lucas, is now predominantly associated with the high-concept blockbuster. However, it is clear that his prior positioning as one of the 1970s film-school generation, alongside Martin Scorsese and Francis Ford Coppola, was central to the reception of *American Graffiti*. Many of those directors' films, including those cited by the *New York Times*, were principally concerned with debunking and destabilising the values on which American society supposedly rested.

It is in the context of debunking the myths of an idealised past that I examine the construction of gender roles in *American Graffiti*. My aim is not to reposition Lucas's film as a feminist text; Pauline Kael's assertion that the film marginalises the experiences of young women and ethnic minorities remains undeniable (Kael 1975: 53). However, as I hope to demonstrate, the film's overt focus on only the male characters, particularly at its conclusion, can in itself be regarded as something of a commentary on the gender relations of the early 1960s. Examining the intersections between the film's construction of gender and its representation of the past, I argue that *American Graffiti* provides a more complex engagement with the period than has previously been acknowledged.

Constructing the Past at Mel's Drive-In

American Graffiti begins at Mel's Drive-In, a location that immediately establishes the film's setting and provides a point of convergence for its disparate group of teens in the small town of Modesto, California. Aurally, though, the film opens to indistinct snatches of voice and music – the sounds of a radio being tuned in – before finding and settling on XERB, a 'border blaster' station, so-called because while catering to the American youth market, its operations were based in Mexico in order to bypass American broadcasting regulations (Dwyer 2015: 65). With the evocation of the sound and experience of tuning in a radio, XERB is marked as a distinct choice from a wider selection of options on the radio's spectrum. The narrative that follows, it is implied, depicts just one version of events, while a number of other possible stories remain unseen. Consequently, while (as Kael points out) *American Graffiti* does not dwell on the experiences of those who are not young white men, the film does at least implicitly acknowledge other experiences of the past, even if it ultimately chooses not to portray them. The film's opening chimes with Hutcheon's contention that the postmodern exposes the 'unstable, contextual, relational and provisional' character of history, despite its pretence at a single, universal meaning (Hutcheon 2010: 64). From the very beginning, then, the spectator is invited to consider what alternative histories are sidelined when we choose this particular station.

The song currently playing, 'Rock Around the Clock' by Bill Haley and the Comets, is likewise a revealing choice. As David Shumway notes, since the song was released in 1955, seven years prior to the film's diegetic period, it was unlikely to be heard on a popular radio station in 1962 (Shumway 1999: 41). However, this is not to say, as Shumway goes on to claim, that the song is intended merely to evoke the past in a general sense. Since 'Rock Around the Clock' is widely hailed as the 'first rock and roll song', as Shumway himself acknowledges (1999: 42), it immediately evokes the inauguration of a particular generation and its counterculture. In this opening scene, though, there is a disjunction between the long, still shot of Mel's Drive-In, backlit only by the setting sun, and the exuberance of the song's tempo and lyrics. While Haley urges movement, literally to 'rock around the clock', the image his song purportedly illustrates is morosely still and defies the song's energy.

'Rock Around the Clock' also recalls the beginning of *Blackboard Jungle* (Richard Brooks, 1955), whose opening sequence featured the song. The violence depicted in Brooks's film, combined with Haley's call to a collective youth culture, reportedly provoked isolated cases of riots following initial screenings (Simmons 2008: 383). In contrast, the setting sun at Mel's Drive-In indicates that the type of youth rebellion portrayed in *Blackboard Jungle* and embodied by 'Rock Around the Clock' may no longer be possible. However, as

Figure 5.1   Mel's Drive-In.

I later argue in relation to the characterisation of John Milner (Paul Le Mat), this is no straightforward evocation of nostalgia. Rather, *American Graffiti* is seen to look forward to a move away from individual, atomised instances of rebellion, to a mass counterculture with the capacity to bring about widespread political and social change.

The music gradually becomes less prominent as the camera pans to the main car park to provide a roll call of the film's leading players, each of whom is heralded by their respective vehicles. Jack DeWitt draws attention to the significance of these cars for the characterisation of their owners. Terry (Charles Martin-Smith) is first to appear, arriving clumsily on a white Vespa. Later charitably described by Debbie (Candy Clark) as 'almost a motorcycle', Terry's scooter signals his emasculation, to be temporarily alleviated when class president Steve (Ron Howard) lends him his customised 1958 Impala. For DeWitt, the Impala foretells Steve's conventionality, since its tuck-and-roll upholstery and sky-blue paint demonstrate good taste and expense though little sense of originality or personality (DeWitt 2010: 48). In turn, DeWitt observes Laurie's (Cindy Williams) arrival in a 1958 Edsel, a family car widely held as a commercial and technological failure in the American automotive industry (DeWitt 2010: 58). Curt's (Richard Dreyfuss) Citroën 2CV positions him exotically outside American teenage car culture and anticipates his later departure from Modesto. Lastly, John's customised yellow 1932 Ford Deuce is far older than the others, and, DeWitt argues, constitutes the quintessential hot-rod car (DeWitt 2010: 49). The evocation of these period details is consequently not incidental; the vehicles are freighted with meaning about the film's key personalities.

The over-signification of the characters' cars calls to be read in terms of Dyer's, rather than Jameson's, conception of pastiche. In contrast to Jameson's derisive description of blank parody devoid of the capacity for critique, Dyer suggests that pastiche is 'an imitation that you are meant to know is an imitation' (Dyer 2007: 1). The clarity of the allusions to 1950s car culture and the multitude of high-shine surfaces in this opening scene hold similarities to the highly stylised evocation of the 1950s seen in Todd Haynes's *Far From Heaven* (2002), which Dyer regards as pastiche (Dyer 2007: 174). For Dyer, the complex affectivity of Haynes's film can be attributed at once to its painstaking recreation of the 1950s melodramas of Douglas Sirk and Max Ophüls, and to the discrepancies and distortions in that representation (Dyer 2007: 176). The potent combination of similitude and difference, Dyer argues, speaks to the perennial ambiguity of the past, that we can never be certain of the truth of a particular time (Dyer 2007: 177). The opening scenes of *American Graffiti* likewise demonstrate the shaky ground on which our perceptions of the past rest, which, as later sections show, has consequences for the film's construction of gender relations in the past.

Rebels of the Past and Future

John Milner embodies two figures of American masculinity that by 1962 had become largely outmoded, and in 1973 were very much figures of the past: the Western hero and the juvenile delinquent. To examine the Western hero first, there are clear echoes in John's aspiration to possess the 'bitchinest car in the valley', and many a Western hero's 'fastest guns in the West', as James Curtis observes (Curtis 1980: 596). Just as the protagonists of *Shane* (George Stevens, 1953) and *The Gunfighter* (Henry King, 1950) find that their power has waned in the passing of the West, so too John discovers that the demise of the town's drag-racing subculture diminishes his own significance. That his long-standing tenure is likely to be overthrown by the film's conclusion is prefigured by the growling sounds of Bob Falfa's (Harrison Ford) black 1955 Chevy, heard in the distance from Mel's Drive-In.

While John's status within Modesto recalls the Western hero, the iconography that surrounds him, not least the tight white T-shirt, blue jeans and his ostentatious yellow car, evoke the 1950s juvenile delinquent, most obviously James Dean in *Rebel Without a Cause*. The film's high-saturation colour, showcased by the vibrant yellow seen in Figure 5.2 below, recalls the lavish Warner Color of Ray's films. However, whereas Dean was a celebrated figure in 1950s youth culture, John is not an aspirational figure here. Discussing their plans to leave for college, Steve warns Curt that staying in Modesto might cause him to 'end up like John', an outcome that is clearly to be avoided. John exposes the extent to which a character can be cast outside of their time.

The sense that John embodies roles that are no longer viable is compounded by the presence of Carol (Mackenzie Philips), a precocious fourteen-year-old who John is duped into taking with him in his car. Carol's youth provides a useful counterpoint to John's age, and reveals the film's ethos concerning

Figure 5.2   John (Paul Le Mat) and his yellow Ford Deuce.

changes in youth culture between the 1950s and 1970s. When Carol changes the radio station to select one playing the Beach Boys, John objects, stating, 'I hate all that surfer shit. Rock and roll's been going downhill ever since Buddy Holly died.' John's preference for Buddy Holly, who died in 1959, marks his musical tastes as outdated. His predilection for early rock and roll also demonstrates his alignment with the 1950s youth culture most emphatically expressed by such music, which was regarded as unknowable, unpredictable and part of a perceived moral decline (Doherty 2002: 40). In contrast, the younger Carol is aligned with the Beach Boys.

The film initially appears to lament the passing of this subversive form of rock and roll music, whose power has subsequently become diluted. The waning powers of the juvenile delinquent are brought into focus when a police officer pulls John over during their drive. The conversation that ensues reveals that John is a familiar figure to the police. Indeed, when he passes Carol the citation handed to him by the officer, she discovers a glut of other screwed-up citations in the passenger door compartment, leading her to exclaim 'you're a real J.D.!' Carol's declaration demonstrates the extent to which understanding of the juvenile delinquent had developed by 1962. Far from the unknowable danger that such figures presented in 1955, the routine manner with which the police officer deals with John, and the facility with which Carol can identify him as conforming to a particular type, reveal that by the 1960s the teen rebel figure had become known, documented and categorised and therefore not nearly so unknowable, dangerous or subversive.

In contrast to John's declining fortunes, Carol's youth and quick wit seem to look forward favourably into the future. A key distinction lies in the two models of rebellion instantiated by Buddy Holly and the Beach Boys. As discussed in Chapter 3, a central tenet of the 1950s juvenile delinquent's appeal was shown to be their embodiment of 'cool', a 'permanent state of private rebellion' (Pountain and Robins 2000: 70). Doherty's historical account of teenage rebels in the 1950s echoes this, observing that the 1950s rebel generally engaged in localised confrontations with authority figures in their immediate surrounding areas in small, localised groups (Doherty 2002: 42–4). Conversely, Carol's taste for the Beach Boys prefigures Brian Wilson's later musical experimentation, and with it the well-documented youth-led mass movements of the later 1960s and 1970s. The contrast between John and Carol can consequently be conceived as a move from 'contraculture to counterculture' (Doherty 2002: 38) – a movement away from the unfocused rebellion of a few isolated individuals towards mass movements that would bring about a generational shift in society's mores.[7] Tellingly, it is Carol, a young woman, who is marked as a figure of hope for American youth. While she is a relatively marginal figure in the film, *American Graffiti* certainly indicates that the future will be shaped by those like her, rather than John.

Going Steady in *American Graffiti*

In the film's two couples, Steve and Laurie and Terry and Debbie, *American Graffiti* provides a reflection on the gender relations within heterosexuality, which were the subject of so much attention in the 1960s and 1970s. Shary's contention that the film, in tandem with many others that represent the past in the 1970s and 1980s, harks back to a time when 'men still felt a sense of superiority over women' (Shary 2005: 45) casts the film's couples in a reactionary, conservative light. However, examining these relationships over the course of the film's mythic fifteen hours, I argue that *American Graffiti* shows the characters coming to terms with increased sexual freedoms, which, following the FDA approval of the contraceptive pill in 1960, were starting to become apparent by 1962 (Marks 2010: 79). Analysing the pairing of Steve and Laurie, I will show how their patriarchal coupledom comes retrospectively to be idealised despite the evidence that both parties are dissatisfied with their relationship.

From their initial interaction with each other at Mel's Drive-In, it is clear that Steve and Laurie have very different expectations for their relationship. When Steve is hesitant, Laurie correctly guesses that he is 'leading up to something kind of big' but mistakenly infers that he is plucking up the courage to propose marriage, not to state his plans to 'date other people at college'. The position of the camera immediately adjacent to Laurie as the pair sit in Steve's car grants priority to her disappointment. As such, although Laurie is shown to be without agency in this scene, merely waiting for a hoped-for request from her boyfriend, *American Graffiti* does show sympathy for her misguided aspirations. In this regard, the film can be usefully compared with *Mad Men*. While Spigel shows that the series glosses over the achievements of feminist activism in favour of a postfeminist subject, in highlighting Laurie's disappointment and limited horizons *American Graffiti* foregrounds the need for an increased interrogation of the heterosexual couple whose power relations remain sharply imbalanced. Significantly, this line of enquiry reached its apex shortly after the release of *American Graffiti*,[8] demonstrating an awareness of the film's temporal positioning in the midst of the second-wave feminist movement.

Later scenes at the hop show how the dominant view of gender relations of the past as simple and uncontested comes to be constructed. At the dance, Laurie and Steve independently confide in their friends about the likely future of their relationship. While Steve's brief exchange merely confirms his intention to 'screw around' while away at college, Laurie's conversation with Peg (Kathleen Quinlan) reveals the pair's contrasting attitudes to dating. Peg advises that Laurie's status as senior prom queen will ensure that a number of possible boyfriends will be available to her, while Laurie sighs wistfully, 'I just wish I could go with him or something.' To this, Peg rolls her eyes dismissively, stating, 'Jeez, Laurie, come on,' as she walks out of frame and back to the dance. Laurie's desire for marriage and monogamy before she has even completed high school seems to be regarded as embarrassingly retrograde even in 1962.

The parallelism created between Steve's and Laurie's conversations is also significant to the articulation of clearly defined gender roles. While Steve and his friend are in agreement that promiscuity at college is preferable to retaining a monogamous, long-term relationship, constructing their preference for promiscuity as the dominant, masculine one, Peg's rejection of Laurie's rose-tined romanticism complicates Laurie's ability to stand for the female position. Nonetheless, Laurie's status as head cheerleader as well as senior prom queen, with the elite standings those positions imply in the teen movie, ensures that it is her stance that is privileged over Peg's.[9] Presenting multiple examples of femininity while making clear that only one of these models is to be idealised, *American Graffiti* can be seen to reveal the mechanisms through which historians 'suppress, repeat, subordinate, highlight and order' the reality of the past in order to provide a single, coherent account of a given period (Hutcheon 2010: 64). However, it is in the very foregrounding of this process that the film succeeds in critiquing and destabilising the possibility of such an account. *American Graffiti* exposes the mechanisms through which one single ideal comes to be privileged as the 'true' model of femininity of the period.

The couple's later slow waltz reveals the disillusion felt by both Laurie and Steve. Announced as the 'former class president and current head cheerleader', they are constructed as the ideal representatives of their cohort and asked to take centre stage as the opening refrain of The Platters' 'Smoke Gets in Your Eyes' is heard. While the song's evocative vocal quality and gentle rhythm seemingly create the ideal conditions for a romantic slow dance, the lyrics persistently claim that 'all who love are blind', constructing romance as a state of self-deception and inevitable disillusionment. The scene thus acknowledges the powerful lure and promise of romance (and, indeed, of nostalgia), yet affirms that romance is ultimately and tragically impermanent.

The stability of this representation of the past is also undermined by the fragility of personal memory, which is made apparent in this scene. During the dance, Steve claims that he initiated their relationship and that their first kiss occurred at the canyon. However, Laurie reminds him that it was she who asked Steve out on 'backwards day' – itself a revealing indicator of the gendered expectations of the period – and that their first kiss occurred at the lake. The instability of memory, and the consequences for the retrospective construction of history, are demonstrated in the scene's editing. The film cuts between a medium shot of the couple dancing, a privileged position that allows us to see that Laurie is crying as she clutches Steve, and a long shot of the pair from the presumed perspective of the other students at the hop, from which we see only a couple sharing a loving embrace. Given the numbers in the crowd, it is likely that this is the version of events that would be recounted by the majority of students at the 1962 high school hop, and by extension, in popular memory. In turn, the *mise-en-scène* of the dance strongly suggests the possibility of distortion, as a spotlight frequently shines directly into the camera, dazzling the viewer and obscuring their view of the dance. As such, *American Graffiti* exemplifies how multiple perspectives may be formed on the same event. Rather than blocking our access to the past, as Jameson claims, the film exposes how, to paraphrase the Platters, smoke gets in our eyes, such that one prevailing version of events comes to mask the dismal reality of Laurie and Steve's slow waltz.

While Laurie and Steve are presented, at least superficially, as ideals of their high school cohort, the evident inadequacies of the film's other couple, Terry and Debbie, constitute a pastiche of the teen dating rituals of the period. As previously discussed, Terry is alone among the main characters in not owning a car, a feature that, alongside his boyish, bespectacled appearance, marks him as insufficiently masculine in the context of Modesto's macho cruising culture. In contrast, Debbie constitutes a hyperbolic spectacle of femininity. As Terry watches her from within Steve's Impala, the audience is invited to share his perspective and to take in her appearance. Her blue and white patterned dress, overlaid with a cropped white cardigan, follows the model of the cinched-in waist and wide, billowing skirt that characterised Christian Dior's New Look. Introduced in Paris in 1947, this style was widely considered passé by the 1950s and was more outdated still in 1962 (Bruzzi 2011: 163). In contrast to the pared-down clothing of Carol and Laurie, Debbie totters on kitten heels in a full face of make-up and bearing an arresting bouffant of platinum-blonde hair. As Terry states excitedly, Debbie is a 'real babe' and, like the driver of the white Thunderbird whom Curt fruitlessly pursues, is marked as an embodiment of spectacular femininity.

Debbie's stipulations for what constitutes an ideal partner can be seen to lampoon the presumed gender roles of the era. Accepting a ride from Terry, believing him to be the owner of Steve's Impala, she is extremely specific in what she requires from him: he must possess a good-looking car, ideally with tuck-and-roll upholstery, drive aggressively and pay for all food and alcohol. The unlikelihood that Terry will be able to live up to these expectations soon emerges when he is unable to pass as an adult to purchase alcohol, and another customer absconds with his money. He must therefore submit to the worst humiliation of them all; asking Debbie for money. Aghast at this tampering with the natural order of things, Debbie pronounces, 'Girls don't pay, *guys* pay!' Nonetheless, she hands over the money, destabilising the fixity of the gendered expectations of which, only seconds before, she had seemed so certain. Later, when Terry confesses that he lied about his car collection and 'hunting ponies', Debbie once again rewrites her expectations of a male partner to accommodate him, remarking that 'a scooter is almost a motorcycle, and I just love motorcycles'. Characters in *American Graffiti* thus undermine the supposed stability of gender roles in the past, disputing the claim that they were ever simple and undisputed.

Debbie is shown to possess the ability to reconstruct the recent past. Contradicting her angry, dismayed reaction to the evening, which saw the pair lose the Impala to a gang who then beat up Terry, Debbie states that she had a 'great time' with Terry. It is an experience, she claims, that she would be happy to repeat. Although many characters discuss the past in *American Graffiti*, only the events of Debbie's recollection are actually shown on screen. On this occasion alone, then, the audience are able to assess for themselves the veracity of the vision of the past being presented. Listing their misadventures, Debbie notes that she and Terry 'saw a hold-up, got your car stolen, and then [. . .] got into this really bitchin' fight. I really had a good time.' Following such a calamitous evening, Debbie's romanticised recollection should be understood both to bring into question the reminiscences of other characters, and to pastiche the process through which the past – however catastrophic – might come retrospectively to be idealised.

Leaving Modesto

Ultimately, *American Graffiti* stages Curt's eventual decision to leave Modesto. As discussed, his unusual Citroën 2CV places him at a remove from the signifying economy of the town's car culture, and foretells his departure at the film's conclusion. Yet Curt's decision is one over which he agonises, and he seeks the advice of a number of characters throughout the film, notably sympathetic teacher Mr Wolfe (Terence McGovern) and quasi-mythical DJ the Wolfman (Wolfman Jack). The lupine tie between these two otherwise disparate men reveals their shared status in Curt's eyes as sympathetic adults in whom, perhaps, the teen sees his future self.

At the hop, Curt discusses his potential departure with Mr Wolfe, who recounts that he spent a mere semester away before returning to Modesto. He was not, he says, 'the competitive type'. Although the teacher ostensibly promotes the virtues of going away for college, Curt echoes Mr Wolfe's sentiments, stating that he too may not be 'the competitive type'. Their discussion is interrupted by a female student, whose over-familiarity with Mr Wolfe makes it clear that the teacher is involved in some sort of relationship with the girl. *American Graffiti* thus portrays Curt's disillusion with his teacher, who is revealed to be a lecherous, middle-aged man preying on the misguided adulation of teenage girls. Contrary to those who argue that *American Graffiti* celebrates the patriarchal dominance displayed here, the scene conveys Curt's clear disappointment with the situation, thereby looking forward to an era in which such dominance might no longer be possible.

The collapse of a further masculine ideal occurs when Curt visits the Wolfman to ask him to deliver a dedication to the mysterious Thunderbird driver, for whom he has spent the evening searching. The DJ's distinctive, rasping voice pervades individual cars and the non-diegetic soundtrack to create what Shumway terms a 'nostalgic sonic space' (Shumway 1999: 28). The Wolfman's faceless yet ubiquitous presence makes him the object of feverish speculation among Modesto's teens. Carol claims that he 'broadcasts from a plane that flies around and around in circles' while rebel gang the Pharaohs debate whether his programme is transmitted from the Mexican border, or indeed if, as one (correctly) argues, his studio is located just outside the town. The hearsay concerning the Wolfman constructs the DJ as a glamorous, mythic figure who embodies the hedonistic promise of early 1960s youth culture.

Figure 5.3   The Wolfman as myth.

Figure 5.4   The Wolfman in reality.

Curt tracks down the Wolfman in a small, isolated radio station at the edge of town in order to request a dedication to the driver of the white Thunderbird. The darkness at Modesto's town limits, punctured only by the dim lights of the station and the headlamps of the 2CV, indicate the related mysteries of what lies beyond Modesto's dark fringes, and in Curt's future. As he enters, a glass wall divides him from the DJ, obscuring the latter's face to create the emblematic silhouette seen in Figure 5.3. When granted access to the studio itself, Curt discovers that this man is not the Wolfman but an employee at the studio charged with playing his recorded voice, such that, as the DJ puts it, 'the Wolfman is everywhere'. Nonetheless, the man is keen to play up the Wolfman's mystique, referring admiringly to 'the places he's been, the things he's seen'. Like Mr Wolfe, the Wolfman urges Curt to experience the world, yet the adult characters' minor duplicities undermine the adventurous message they impart. As Curt leaves the studio, he discovers that the studio employee really was the Wolfman. His explanation of the DJ's absence demonstrates his need to create a mythical persona for himself, one that the sight of him eating rapidly defrosting popsicles alone in an isolated studio would soon dispel.

The collapse of the Wolfman's enigmatic persona follows a number of events that puncture the idealism of the era; when Terry reveals that he is not the owner of an Impala, but a Vespa, John loses the drag race to Falfa, and Curt realises that he will never discover the identity of the elusive Thunderbird driver. For Dwyer, the film's intention is not to show 1962 as an idealised period that would foreground the nostalgia mood. Rather, *American Graffiti* is shown to acknowledge the affective tug of the past, while also portraying the moment in which a particular 'fantasy of innocence' was permanently ruptured (Dwyer 2015: 59). Significantly, the disillusionment brought about by these events demonstrates the need to move forward into the upheavals of the later 1960s and 1970s. It therefore comes as no surprise when Curt resolves to leave Modesto the following morning.

Once Curt reaches this decision, the film moves quickly to his departure, cutting immediately from his resolution to his arrival at the airfield where his friends and family have assembled to bid him farewell. The contrast between the darkness in which the majority of the film has taken place and the bright, blue skies of the airfield creates the impression of the inauguration of a new era. While the previous evening saw Steve persuading Curt of the benefits of leaving and attempting to divest himself of his relationship with Laurie, this new order sees Steve clutching his girlfriend, providing evasive reassurances that he will join Curt the following year. The unlikelihood of his doing so is indicated through costume, as Steve's yellow shirt echoes the hue of Laurie's dress and Terry's shirt, signalling his affiliation with the characters who will remain in Modesto.

The camera follows Curt onto the plane, positioning the film's perspective away from Modesto and into the future, before dissolving to a long shot of the plane as it moves across a cloudless blue sky. With only the gentle whir of the engines heard in the background – the nostalgic sonic space of Modesto now far behind – the futures of the four male lead characters are slowly listed in sequence: 'John Milner was killed by a drunk driver in December 1964; Terry Fields was reported missing in action near An Loc in December 1965; Steve Bolander is an insurance agent in Modesto, California; Curt Henderson is a writer living in Canada.' For Speed, this epilogue demonstrates the film's fundamental conservatism by portraying the lasting significance of what seemed to be relatively inconsequential behaviour (Speed 1998: 27). Thus, John is killed by someone who was driving dangerously, much as he is shown to do in the film, while Terry's comical clumsiness assumes an ominous quality in the light of his near-certain death in Vietnam. Steve's decision to postpone college that particular year means that he is destined never to leave Modesto. Equally, having departed, Curt never returns to the town.[10]

For Vera Dika, the epilogue portrays the 'literal or symbolic' deaths of the film's male characters as a result of the Vietnam War (Dika 2005: 94). However, we are not told what the future holds for the three female leads. Wood argues that this omission might have been understandable in the case of Carol or Debbie, who we only meet during the course of the evening. However, as he observes, Laurie is unquestionably a principal character, introduced at the same time as the male leads at the beginning of the film (Wood 2003: 219). That Laurie, Carol and Debbie are not considered here is therefore the result of their gender, rather than their narrative significance. These characters, the film implicitly claims, would not have destinies of their own that could be similarly squandered. While the loss of male potential is mourned here, the film implies that the female characters never had any potential that could have been lost. Nonetheless, Dwyer notes that following the silence of the epilogue, the credit sequence is once again accompanied by a pop track, one of which Carol would surely approve: The Beach Boys' 'All Summer Long'. Released in 1964, two years after the film's diegetic setting, Dwyer argues that the film's ending literally 'pushes the viewer out of 1962 further into the 1960s' (Dwyer 2015: 76). That Carol appears to have had the last word of the film hints at the inauguration of a new, considerably more feminist era to emerge in later years.

DIRTY DANCING (EMILE ARDOLINO, 1987)

Like *American Graffiti*, *Dirty Dancing* is also set in the early 1960s. However, released in 1987, the film's allusions to feminist activism and its subsequent (re)processing in postfeminism are far more overt. For Radner, *Dirty Dancing* anticipates the need for feminist victories of the 1960s and 1970s, particularly in its portrayal of abortion. However, in a similar vein to Spigel's critique of *Mad Men*, Radner then claims that the film's heroine Baby (Jennifer Grey) is positioned as an embodiment of postfeminist femininity, whose individual desire for sexual fulfilment ultimately trumps her quest for social justice. The most radical transformations in gender relations, which occurred following the film's conclusion but before the audience's late-1980s perspective, are relegated, Radner argues, to 'feminism's future past' (Radner 2013: 137). As such, she claims that *Dirty Dancing* dodges the rather more radical and challenging possibilities of second-wave feminism in favour of 'neofeminism', a conflation of individualist and consumerist tendencies that are loosely allied to feminist thought, but which have far more in common with the tenets of neoliberalism (Radner 2013: 139). In Radner's view, then, *Dirty Dancing* possesses a complex relationship with its construction of the past and its representations of gender relations.

As well as its 1960s setting, *Dirty Dancing* must also be understood as part of the 1980s teen dance musical cycle alongside *Fame* and *Flashdance*. Yet, in contrast to these films, *Dirty Dancing* had an unusually difficult journey to the box office. As Freeman reports in a recent interview with the film's screenwriter, Eleanor Bergstein, no studio would take it on. Bergstein and the film's producer Linda Gottlieb eventually accepted an offer from a small independent studio who proposed making the film for $4m, around a quarter of the budget for most films of the period (Freeman 2015: 20). Central to studios' reluctance to make the film was its abortion subplot, which, fearing that the 1973 Supreme Court Decision allowing the procedure might soon be reversed, Bergstein refused to edit out (Radner 2013: 134). *Dirty Dancing* is a complex offering, presenting the utopian pleasure offered by the musical alongside a glimpse of the period prior to the installation of legislation permitting women to access abortion.

The positioning of *Dirty Dancing* as an object of 1980s nostalgia should also be acknowledged. Recent screenings of the film at events such as The Secret Cinema and nostalgia-led sing-alongs at London's Prince Charles Cinema call attention not only to the film's 1960s setting, but also to its status as a quintessentially 1980s release.[11] As Claire Molloy (2013) notes, much of the film's audience discovered *Dirty Dancing* via word of mouth, resulting in audiences cultivating a personal relationship with the film.[12] Despite the odds against it, the film was shown on no fewer than 900 screens for seventeen consecutive weeks, attesting to a remarkably sustained popularity.[13] It is arguably this nostalgia – for the audience's 1980s youth as much as for the film's evocation of the early 1960s – which has led to a film sequel,[14] a successful stage show in the West End and on Broadway, and even a mooted remake.[15] This case study will therefore be attentive not only to the film's construction of the 1960s but also to the way in which, in its anachronistic and generic positioning, the film has itself been taken up as a locus of nostalgia for the 1980s. Told from the retrospective point of view of its female protagonist, Frances 'Baby' Houseman, *Dirty Dancing* portrays her romance with dance instructor Johnny Castle (Patrick Swayze), whom she befriends when she offers to stand in for Penny (Cynthia Rhodes), whose illegal abortion appointment clashes with one of her contractual performances. The film depicts a complex negotiation between the desire to look back to an idealised past, and an examination of the era's gender and class inequalities.

'That was the summer of 1963'

The opening scenes of *Dirty Dancing* convey both the film's representation of the past, and its belonging to modes that, with hindsight, are now predominantly associated with the 1980s. The credit sequence opens with a vertical wipe to portray dancers moving slowly to the Ronettes' 1963 hit 'Be My Baby'. The use of this song, along with its contemporaneous release date in August of that year, immediately position the film in the early 1960s. Medium close-ups of the dancers' indistinct faces dissolve to show parts of their bodies as they move in slow motion to the music. The grainy image and black and white film stock suggest the position of a contemporary viewer looking back to the past through an archive. This, the film implies, is an era whose practices and music have long been confined to the past.

The sense of looking back to a distant moment in the past is disrupted by the quintessentially 1980s pink, slanted scrawl in which the film's title is displayed across the screen. This style of text echoes the similar scripts used in the promotional materials of other contemporary teen dance musicals, not least *Footloose* and *Flashdance*. The title sequence therefore works to position *Dirty Dancing* generically, and has consequences for its construction of the past. Bergstein describes the film's teen musical packaging as something of a lure, which works to draw unwitting audiences into its feminist message. In this, the film is a retort to those who would regard nostalgia as denoting an unthinkingly positive portrayal of a past era and a retreat from the complexities of the present (see Davis 1979). Instead, the film's opening titles use the promise of a look back to the past, and the principles of pleasure associated with the film musical, to interrogate the liberal hypocrisies of the early 1960s middle classes.

The contrast between the representation of the early 1960s and its instantiation within cinematic modes predominantly associated with the 1980s also has consequences for the film's feminist politics. Anecdotally, audiences report that it was initially the songs and the romance between Baby and Johnny that led them to become fans of the film. However, in the decades since its release, *Dirty Dancing* has become more widely credited with portraying the necessity of the feminist movement, which gained traction in the years after 1963.

As Susan Faludi memorably observed, the late 1980s saw a backlash against the gains that women had earlier secured (1992). It was for this reason that Bergstein was adamant that the portrayal of Baby's sexual awakening was also accompanied by an exposure of the grisly consequences of backstreet abortion. The rose-tinted idealism of the musical is thereby used to undermine nostalgia's claim to represent a better reality.

Following the credit sequence, *Dirty Dancing* opens with a long shot of a family saloon car driving on a wide, near-deserted highway, where the film's periodisation is made specific. This tale, Baby's voiceover tells us, takes place in 'the summer of 1963'. Baby demonstrates the importance of this period to American popular culture, remarking that the holiday occurs 'before Kennedy was shot' and 'before the Beatles came'. Thus, the film is positioned at a cultural threshold, a sentiment echoed by Christine Sprengler's belief that the President's ill-fated trip to Dallas on 22 November of that year called an end to the Fifties as a self-mythologised time of prosperity and innocence (2009: 64). Further, Tamar Jeffers McDonald identifies the summer of 1963 as a liminal period in the history of the women's movement. As the film's events affirm, *Dirty Dancing* takes place prior to the widespread availability of birth control, and yet some months after the publication of Betty Friedan's *The Feminine Mystique* in February that year (Jeffers McDonald 2013: 45). Baby is thereby situated in a period in which stirrings of feminist discontent are beginning to make themselves felt. Indeed, espousing many a liberal cause himself, Baby's father Jake (Jerry Orbach) is proud to tell resort owner Max Kellerman (Jack Weston) that 'Baby's gonna change the world someday.' Nonetheless, as the film's events demonstrate, the mores of Jake Houseman and the society he represents remain very much of the past.

That Baby finds herself caught between the liberalism of the future and the conservatism of the past is underscored by an abrupt change in the film's soundtrack. The Ronettes, who provided the soundscape for the writhing bodies dancing in the credit sequence, suggest the heady claustrophobia of the 1960s basement dance floor, to which Billy (Neal Jones) later alludes. By contrast, the Housemans' journey is accompanied by the Four Seasons' 'Big Girls Don't Cry', in which the falsetto refrains of the lead singer, Frankie Valli, suggest an adult masculinity unnaturally constricted to the vocal patterns of childhood. Similarly, called Baby, Frances is shown to be saddled with a childlike identity that no longer fits. The contrast between the musical worlds evoked here is further emphasised by the eras with which the Four Seasons and the Ronettes are associated. While the former enjoyed success in the latter part of the 1950s, and indeed the early 1960s – 'Big Girls Don't Cry' enjoyed a five-week reign at the top of the Billboard Top 100 in 1962[16] – the 'Wall of Sound' effect of Phil Spector's production of 'Be My Baby' prefigures experimental pop music released in the latter part of the decade. There is, then, a clear distinction made here. While Baby and her family remain mired in the Fifties, the dancers of the credit sequence look forward into the 1960s. The film's work will therefore be to move Baby into this latter, progressive period.

'Three weeks here, it'll feel like a year:' Troubling Utopia in *Dirty Dancing*

Richard Dyer argues that the film musical presents its audience with the idea of utopia, understood simply as 'the idea of something better into which to escape' (Dyer 2002: 20). Utopia is not a political manifesto that directly proposes how societal ills might be combatted. Rather, like the nostalgia mood, it is a sensibility that presents an idea of how such a society might feel in the most general sense. In *Dirty Dancing*, Kellerman's resort does its utmost to present itself as a utopian location, one that, in a similar manner to the nostalgia mood, promises a temporary respite from everyday life. It is in this context that Max assures the overworked Dr Houseman (with no small irony) that 'three weeks here, it'll feel like a year'. Sheltered in the Catskill mountains with a seeming abundance of entertainments on offer, Kellerman's resort certainly looks like the relaxing getaway it purports to be. However, a number of events work to disrupt the resort's conscious positioning as an idyllic place of escape, and by extension, to disrupt the film's positioning of the 1960s as an idealised period in the past.

Almost immediately after the Housemans' arrival at Kellerman's, *Dirty Dancing* portrays the patriarchal gender roles and equally entrenched class disparities that the resort advocates. As will become apparent, dance later provides the principal means through which these norms will be undermined in the film. However, the first dance class that Baby attends encapsulates in miniature the conservative gender politics promoted at Kellerman's, and by extension, of the era represented by the resort. Leading the class, 'former Rockette' Penny advises her female acolytes to submit to their male dance partner, advising that 'on the dance floor, he's the boss', drawing attention to the performance of patriarchal dominance in which she invites the dancers to participate.[17] Penny further instructs that class that 'when I say stop, you'll find the man of your dreams!' Yet the *mise-en-scène* undermines Penny's claim. The small wooden summer house in which the class takes place is so crammed with customers that the dancers can only blankly shuffle in regimented lines. Further, the noise of their heavy rhythmic stomping on wooden floorboards obscures the deft Latin music that ought to inspire their movements. Penny's promise certainly does not materialise for Baby, who finds herself jammed between two older women, neither of whom could realistically qualify as the man of her dreams.[18] *Dirty Dancing* thereby demonstrates the mode through which Baby's sexual awakening will occur, but also shows that it will not arrive through the means officially sanctioned by the resort, nor indeed by her family.

Baby's transformational decision to enter the staff leisure space sees her not only flout multiple signs warning errant customers to return to their sanctioned areas, but also her family's expectations of the social sphere she will inhabit during the holiday. She is initially paired off with Max's odious son Neil (Lonny Price), who revels in telling Baby about the 'two hotels' he stands to inherit following a spell at Cornell to study hotel management. It is clear that the family regard Neil as a worthy suitor, as Jake accepts his request that Baby assist him with the magic show, while a quick cut to Baby's aghast expression tells of her annoyance at her father's having spoken on her behalf. The family's expectations of their two daughters are revealed through the limited characterisation of their mother, Marjorie (Kelly Bishop), and the rather banal concerns raised by Baby's sister Lisa (Jane Brucker). While Jake is unquestionably the dominant force in the family, for whose affections Lisa and Baby compete, Marjorie is presented as little more than a sideshow, her input limited to reassuring Lisa that ten pairs of shoes is probably a sufficient number for a three-week holiday. Marjorie can be seen to embody the position of middle-class women prior to the feminist movement (what I will term 'pre-feminist woman'), as an individual whose concerns and sphere of influence have been constricted to the domestic through her role as a housewife.[19]

Lisa seems content to replicate the role of her mother, consulting her on such matters as lipstick shades and honeymoon destinations, thereby signalling her positioning as a wife-in-waiting. In contrast, Baby demonstrates no such interests; while Lisa is seen in the matching dresses and heels that echo their mother's style, Baby is most often found in jeans, showing her practicality, egalitarianism and rejection of femininity. As a result, Baby enjoys a close relationship with her father, who acknowledges and nurtures her wider horizons. Nevertheless, Jake continues to foster a relationship between Baby and Neil, indicating that he continues to harbour rather conventional aspirations for Baby, namely that soon after college she will marry someone not dissimilar to Neil and establish a family of her own. As Baby leaves Neil, then, she signals her dissatisfaction with the trajectory on offer to her, which was nevertheless typical of young middle-class women of the period. The film can therefore be seen to reject pre-feminist ideals, and, within this nostalgic construct, paradoxically to look forward to a period in which greater self-determination will be possible for women.

Entering the instructors' leisure space on the pretence of carrying a watermelon, Baby is confronted by a considerably more sexual spectacle than the dances found in the resort's main areas. A shot/reverse shot pattern between Baby's intrigued yet intimidated expressions and the dancers' bodies conveys her surprise at the spectacle she has encountered. For Shumway, Baby's positioning in the scene, innocently asking Billy where 'they learned to dance like that' represents the novelty of rock and roll music, when it was 'new and felt to be subversive' (Shumway 1999: 46). Certainly, in contrast to the Kellerman's family foxtrot, the dancing here does possess the shock of the new. However, there are notable similarities between the 'official' dances advocated by the resort's management, and the staff dancing, which is depicted in the film as clandestine and, as the very title of the film announces, 'dirty'. Indeed, Penny's earlier instructions that 'on the dance floor, he's the boss' are echoed in the exaggerated sexual submission she performs with Johnny, as she lifts one leg over his shoulder while he spins her around. This continuation between the two dances calls attention to the limits of the utopian escape offered by dance. In portraying the ineffective promise of utopia, the film demonstrates the need for more substantive changes that will demonstrably improve the characters' lives.

The construction of Kellerman's, and with it the early 1960s, as an idyllic utopian space is most radically disrupted not by Neil's cloying affections, but by the portrayal of Penny's unwanted pregnancy and her resulting abortion. Presenting the procedure as both costly and dangerous – Penny's crooked physician is equipped with only a 'dirty knife and a fold-out table' – *Dirty Dancing* makes it clear that abortion was illegal in 1963.[20] Crouched alone on the floor of the hotel's kitchen, Penny's distraught appearance conveys the demise of utopia. Still clad in the dance attire that connotes the glamour of show business, her posture is hunched and despondent, while her make-up is smeared by tears. Penny's abortion is to be read alongside Bruce Babington and Peter Evans's contention that the post-studio era musical, of which *Dirty Dancing* is an example, stages the meeting of two competing drives: an urge for utopia, and the representation of reality (Babington and Evans 1985: 273). Such an encounter can be found in Penny and Johnny's frequent rebuffs to Baby, who is dismissively dubbed 'Miss Fix-it', and advised to 'go back to your playpen' when she proposes what the dancers believe to be naïve solutions.

Penny's abortion, of course, is an unusual dose of reality for the Hollywood film musical, and, as discussed, one that Bergstein was urged on multiple occasions to remove from her script. Although it is never explicitly stated, the audience is invited to appreciate the considerable developments that have occurred in the intervening years between the time of the film's setting and its 1987 release, not least the Supreme Court decision dubbed 'Roe v. Wade', which legalised abortion across the United States. That the film regards these changes as givens would advocate Radner's view that the representation of women prior to feminism, embodied notably by Lisa and Marjorie, gives way to that of postfeminism, in which, to use McRobbie's phrasing, women's equality has been taken into account (Radner 2013). However, with a focus on the construction and negotiation of nostalgia, I differ from Radner's assessment that the postfeminist is privileged in *Dirty Dancing*. Rather, I argue that in portraying the absence of freedoms enjoyed in 1987, the film in fact foregrounds the need for the feminist movements that occurred in the intervening years. Indeed, it was Bergstein's desire to portray the consequences of losing these rights that made her disinclined to remove the abortion subplot. *Dirty Dancing* can therefore be seen to deploy its utopian mode, the musical, and its idyllic, prelapsarian setting – Kellerman's resort in the summer of 1963 – precisely to demonstrate that neither this period nor this place could conceivably be regarded as utopian.

'Some people count, and some people don't'

Uttered by Robbie (Max Cantor), this line shows his disregard for his former girlfriend, Penny, for whose abortion fees he refuses to pay. Robbie's worldview is supported by his well-thumbed copy of Ayn Rand's *The Fountainhead*, so beloved that he has scrawled a number of 'notes in the margin'. As we will see, Robbie's callous view of the working-class staff, without whom Kellerman's would cease to function, is by no means isolated. To Baby's dismay, she discovers that the brusque manner with which the entertainment staff are regarded by other members of the staff and management has transferred to the dancers' own perception of their self-worth. It is through his relationship with Baby that Johnny gradually learns not to see himself as the 'nothing' he initially believes himself to be.

Robbie's snootiness is encouraged by the resort's management. One of Baby's first encounters with the class disparities engendered by the resort occurs as she watches Max divide the employees by the role they perform, and by extension, their social class. Believed to be of a similar standing to the resort's clientele, the Ivy-League-educated waiters are deemed worthy to make conversation, and even to flirt, with the customers. By contrast, the working-class entertainment staff are expressly forbidden from doing so. Their interactions with the customers are to be limited to providing classes for which they are expressly paid, such that there is no question of their socialising on an equal level. As Baby observes unseen through a narrowly open door, the scene is constructed as a 'backstage' moment which would be undesirable for customers to witness. In addition to portraying the class disparities that characterised the era, the scene also shows the disdain in which the entertainment staff in particular are held. To reveal why this might be, consider that the waiters' expertise lies in remembering the details of various dishes, and in coming up with flirtatious patter to flatter the customers. While the act of bringing food and drink to the table is a physical one, it is the intellectual dimension of the waiters' job that is emphasised in *Dirty Dancing*. In contrast, the skill of the entertainment staff consists primarily in the physical capabilities of their bodies.

It is in this contrast between intellect and physicality that Johnny finds himself falling short. Comparing himself unfavourably to Jake, he states that 'people treat me like I'm nothing 'cos I'm nothing'. Baby is surprised to discover the precarious existence of such a skilled dancer as Johnny, who, she learns, spends most of his year as a jobbing house-painter and became a dance instructor only through a chance encounter. As a result of his economic precarity he allows himself to be condescended to by Neil, and to prostitute himself to some of the older, female customers, exemplified by the predatory Vivian (Miranda Garrison). However, *Dirty Dancing* can be seen to valorise precisely Johnny's expertise, and, in the time-honoured manner of the musical, to foreground the capacity of music and dance to liberate individuals from their everyday concerns. While cowed by Max and Neil, his dance skills allow him to be quietly mischievous with Baby on their first meeting at the staff quarters, beckoning her over and instructing her in a few basic moves. In order to capitalise on his dance capabilities, though, he requires Baby's high ideals, which see her stand up for Johnny when he is unjustly accused of theft. Her defence of Johnny not only makes her vulnerable for knowing a resort employee at all, and thereby stepping out of her class boundaries, but also through the clear sexual defiance of her father. Their relationship is thus one that combines social justice and sensuality.

Baby and Johnny's final dance at the resort's end-of-season show celebrates the meeting between idealism and dance skills instantiated by the couple. As we will see, the dance that concludes the film looks forward into the future. In contrast, the beginning of the show is marked by the nostalgia mood, since it marks the end of summer at the resort. As Max discusses the ups and downs of Kellerman's over the years with band leader Tito Suarez (Honi Coles), he appears to sense an incoming cultural change that will soon sound the death knell for the resort. The show, then, not only marks the end of summer, but also the conclusion of the era most obviously represented by the resort, namely the 1950s. The show begins with a mournful tone as a group led by Neil sing 'Kellerman's theme', with a piano accompaniment. The song's slow pace and melancholic key belie the lyrics' claims that 'joy, laughter, voices, hearts' characterise the Kellerman's experience. The choral ensemble accompanying him, with their curiously regimented, linear choreography, corresponds to an idea of collective enjoyment for the resort's management. However, cutting to a medium shot portraying the yawning disinterest of the diegetic audience, the film can be seen to demonstrate the failure of their idea of community. A further cutaway to the dance staff standing at the periphery shows their pointed exclusion from the proceedings, demonstrating the wider gender and class inequalities embodied and enacted by the resort. Despite Neil and Max's doleful words, then, *Dirty Dancing* shows that the demise of the resort is not to be mourned.

Johnny's unexpected return to Kellerman's to perform the final dance sets in play the creation of a new type of community without the acute divisions that

NOSTALGIA, POSTFEMINISM AND THE TEEN MOVIE

have hitherto typified life at the resort. Making a speech that Baby 'taught me about the kind of person that I want to be', before inviting her on the stage to dance with him, the moment amounts to Johnny's self-actualisation. With the sure knowledge that he understands dance and music better than Neil ever could, Johnny reclaims his position in defiance of the resort's management. His speech also marks an instance of what Altman calls 'personality dissolve', according to which the Hollywood film musical sees a fusion of the personalities of its central couple (Altman 1987a: 84).[21] While Baby was previously associated with ideals and intellectualism, her ability to join Johnny on stage in dance reveals the sensuality that has been brought out by her relationship with him. In turn, Johnny's speech reveals that he has acquired Baby's idealism. As a result, both physicality and intellectualism are valued equally in the film's finale, pointing to a more egalitarian future.

In what appears to be Baby's final dance with Johnny, she is able effortlessly to follow his lead. The routine is similar to that which the pair performed at the Sheldrake hotel, when Baby covered for Penny earlier in the film. Yet unlike that dance, which was punctuated by Johnny's terse instructions and culminated in Baby's failure to perform the final lift, this performance appears natural, graceful and unforced. The camera's close position shows their ease and enjoyment in each other's company. On this occasion, no instructions are needed and the pair are able to respond naturally to one another's movements. Finally performing the lift for the assembled crowd, Baby provides the symbolic bridge between the resort's guests and its workforce, creating, as

Figure 5.5 Baby (Jennifer Grey) is held over the audience at the conclusion of *Dirty Dancing*.

she does so, a new, more egalitarian community, and looking forward into the 1960s.

The record that accompanies Johnny and Baby's dance, '(I've Had) the Time of My Life', is significant to the scene's construction of nostalgia. Of course, the song's very title points to an idyllic event that has now come to a close. However, as Shumway has noted, '(I've Had) the Time of My Life', is a 1980s creation, which combines the 1960s sounds of Righteous Brother Bill Medley with a distinctly 1980s production quality (1999).[22] For Shumway, this and the film's other anachronistic songs push the audience out of the 1960s frame that the film's visual aspect otherwise maintains. As a consequence, the audience's attention is drawn to their view of the events in hindsight, leading to speculation as to what occurred following the dance. For Chris Jordan, Dr Houseman's apology to Johnny indicates that he accepts the dance instructor as Baby's future husband (Jordan 2003: 112). However, if we recall Baby's voiceover at the beginning of the film, the holiday at Kellerman's is positioned as taking place prior to her joining the Peace Corps, where it seems unlikely that Johnny would accompany her. I argue, therefore, that the film's romance is positioned as formative and yet finite, and that our knowledge that the pair must surely soon part ways is what contributes to the bittersweet quality of the film's conclusion. In this, the film is unusual for a teen romance, most of which suggest the possibility of a lasting relationship. *Dirty Dancing* at once contrasts an individual's idealised memory with a depiction of the past that is far from idyllic. The nostalgia demonstrated by the scene is thereby individualised.

EASY A (WILL GLUCK, 2010)

Easy A is undeniably distinct from the first two films discussed in this chapter. While *American Graffiti* and *Dirty Dancing* both purport to represent the early 1960s, albeit in a highly stylised fashion, *Easy A* is not expressly set in the past, but in the present. Nonetheless, in its knowing evocation of both the 1980s and the 1990s Hollywood teen movie, and oblique adaptation of Nathaniel Hawthorne's *Scarlet Letter*, *Easy A* shares with the other two films examined in this chapter a preoccupation with changes in women's social roles and courtship rituals over the past thirty years.[23] It is the protagonist's disillusion with the sexual double standards of the present that prompts her to desire a return to the Eighties teen movie, a descriptor I will shortly discuss more fully.

Easy A centres on Olive (Emma Stone), who inadvertently starts a rumour – shown in the film to be untrue – that she has lost her virginity to 'a guy at community college'. When Brandon (Dan Byrd), a gay student keen to hide his sexuality, discovers that Olive has not only lied, but been readily believed, he spies an opportunity to masquerade as heterosexual, by spreading a rumour that the pair have had sex. Olive soon makes a lucrative business of other male students paying to claim that she has had sex with them. The film portrays the fluctuations in Olive's social capital, where she is first the object of fascination and thinly-veiled jealousy, before she is quickly branded a 'slut' and a 'whore'. Such a conflicted view of female sexuality is reminiscent of the contradictions of postfeminism, in which performance and knowledge of sexuality is celebrated, while actual promiscuity remains undesirable. In this, *Easy A* depicts and critiques a continued sexual double standard wherein male students are lauded for their sexual potency, while the same behaviour is not permitted for their female peers.

Embroiled in the complex sexual politics of the contemporary postfeminist landscape, Olive is nostalgic for the apparent 'chivalry' of the Eighties Hollywood teen movie. In using 'Eighties' rather than 1980s, I draw from Sprengler's distinction between the Fifties and the 1950s, wherein the former is a nostalgic construct of popular mythology, and the latter, the decade between 1950–9 in all its complexity (Sprengler 2009: 64). In *Easy A*, Olive does not show an interest in the events of the 1980s. Rather, she is nostalgic for the gender politics of the decade's teen movies, particularly those made by John Hughes. Consequently, I argue that it is the Eighties for which Olive is nostalgic. Significantly, *Easy A* is not the only recent teen movie to express nostalgia for its Eighties forbears. In *Pitch Perfect*, Jesse (Skylar Austin) tells Beca (Anna Kendrick) that the closing scene of *The Breakfast Club*, where Judd Nelson raises his fist in defiance as he swaggers through the school sports fields, is 'the most perfect film ending in cinema history'. Though sceptical here, Beca later co-opts Simple Minds' 'Don't You Forget About Me', which provides the soundtrack to *The Breakfast Club*, into her a cappella group's winning routine. In both cases, there is an expectation that contemporary teen audiences will not only understand, but appreciate, these references to films that are over thirty years old, speaking not only to the increased exhibition opportunities that television, DVD and streaming services have afforded (Garrett 2007: 24) but also to the Eighties' current status as a privileged object of nostalgia.

For Christina Lee, the current trend for Eighties nostalgia is one that plagues Generation X spectators and film-makers, who, having come of age in the 1980s, are now the taste-makers of the present (Lee 2010). However, as Freeman observes, the contemporary evocation of the Eighties encompasses more than those who had direct experience of the decade (2015: 18). For her, the films of the Eighties recall a film-making past in which greater freedom of expression was possible in Hollywood cinema. Noting the contemporary trend for the global superhero blockbuster, she laments the demise of mid-budget Hollywood cinema, whose dialogue-driven narrative makes it less amenable to distribution across global, multilingual markets (Freeman 2015: 19). The gender politics of Eighties teen movies contributes to a sense in which 'they did things differently then', while their distinct lack of glamour corresponds to Hughes's taste for the undramatic and suburban (Smith 2016: 232). As the analysis will demonstrate, it is Olive's belief that the Eighties provides a better space in which to be a teenage girl that structures her desire to return to, and later to embody, the mores of the decade.

The Eighties is not the only nostalgic construct evoked in *Easy A*. Certainly, the film's highly allusive qualities can be seen themselves to evoke the Hollywood teen movie of the 1990s, most obviously *Clueless*.[24] Like many a 1990s teen movie, *Easy A* is a highly knowing literary adaptation of its source text and demonstrates an understanding of its positioning within a series of other, previous adaptations of *The Scarlet Letter*.[25] Not only are Olive's class studying the book, but she also recommends the 1926 adaptation starring Lillian Gish over the more recent, yet ill-conceived Roland Joffé reworking. Furthermore, framed as a live webcast that aims to correct the rumours that have been circulating about Olive so that she can reclaim her own identity, *Easy A* itself reflects the retrospective structure of Hawthorne's novel. This case study will demonstrate how the film's allusivity, which is aligned conventionally with the nostalgia mode, can be seen to possess the affectivity more often associated with the nostalgia mood. Further, I will show that the evocation of the gender relations of the past highlights the complexities and contradictions of contemporary postfeminist femininity.

The Performing Postfeminist Subject

The opening scenes of *Easy A* quickly establish the film's location in Ojai, a small town on the northern fringes of Los Angeles. Notably, the film's locale is given equal priority with its generic positioning as part of the high school teen movie. Fleeting establishing shots prior to the opening credits convey two distinct filmic legacies. The first two shots position the film in unremarkable suburbia; a long shot depicts Ojai's wide main street, while a second shows a road sign welcoming drivers to the town, which is seen to count only 8,202 residents. The suburbia evoked by these shots recalls the typical setting of the high school teen movie, one that underscores the conventionality and typicality of its inhabitants. The narrative depicted in such a place, the film implies, could be replicated in any other middle-class American suburb.

Two further shots locate the film specifically in California. In this case we are presented with a long shot of a large orangery whose trees are in full fruit, before cutting to a shot of a flag pole on which the Star-spangled Banner and California's state flag wave in the breeze. The contrast in the evocation of suburban ordinariness and this comparatively exotic, Californian location is significant to the film's nostalgia for the Eighties, and for the articulation of sexuality as performance. Certainly, John Hughes's teen movies are prominently associated with the suburbs of Chicago, and by extension, with the stodgy quotidian of America's Midwest. Conversely, *Easy A* insists on the film's geographical proximity to Los Angeles, and by extension, to the glamour and artifice of Hollywood. The film can thus be seen to take place in an arena that combines suburbia – the teen movie's conventional milieu – with a setting that calls attention to the construction of gender and sexuality as a performance. It is in this environment not only that Olive will masquerade as sexually active, but that members of the evangelical Christian abstinence group will prove to have been less chaste than their solemn vows attest.

Despite Olive's articulate introductory voiceover, she claims that she is 'invisible' and anonymous at her high school. As the camera glides through the disparate clutches of students arriving at school, it focuses on a group of girls, seemingly led by a tall blonde wearing sunglasses. The positioning of the camera, as it tracks backward to follow the girls' path, invites the audience to infer that one of these girls may be the face behind Olive's voice-over. However, they merely walk into Olive's path, oblivious to having tripped her, leaving her papers in disarray. The character's poise and verbal dexterity, bolstered by Emma Stone's star power, is thereby contrasted with Olive's ungainliness. In *Easy A*, Olive makes an equation between her virginity – or at least, the disinterest with which she is regarded among her male classmates – and her lack of social currency.

It is Olive's lack of social capital at the beginning of the film that leads her not to correct her friend Rhi's (Aly Michalka) and other students' belief that she has indeed had sex with a community college student. Arriving at school the following day, Olive is far from ignored, but the object of both awe and intrigue as other students stop to let her pass. She also becomes the focus of Marianne's (Amanda Bynes) 'pledge club', an evangelical Christian abstinence group who make it their business to have Olive 'repent' of her supposed sins. This group's fetishisation of virginity and 'purity' are constructed as an alternative reaction to the majority of students' focus on acquiring sexual knowledge (if not actually having sex). Their earnest piety, combined with the number of their members who have had to repeat several years of their high school education ('because He wanted it that way'), present the pledge club as ridiculous and simple-minded. Nonetheless, in portraying their misguided zealotry, which gradually bleeds out into the high school cohort, *Easy A* conveys the extent to which the puritanical fervour expressed in Hawthorne's novel continues to this day. The contemporary postfeminist climate is shown to be a highly contradictory one for teenage girls to navigate; while, as discussed in the previous chapter, girls' social capital is shown to be bound up in their attractiveness to the opposite sex, actual – or indeed, perceived – promiscuity is shown to be detrimental to Olive's social status. Consequently, the film exposes the very narrowness of the permissible expression of female sexuality in postfeminist culture.

Easy A is clear throughout the film that Olive's claims to sexual experience are entirely fictitious. Conversely, it emerges that one of the members of the pledge club, Micah (Cam Gigandet) is engaged in a sexual relationship with a married teacher (Lisa Kudrow). Neither the pledge group's chastity nor Olive's supposed promiscuity can be readily verified by others, yet both claims are unquestioningly believed by their peers. Jeffers McDonald observes the difficulty – if not the impossibility – of representing virginity, a seemingly private, internal quality, in such a visual medium as film (Jeffers McDonald 2010: 2). Prior to 1968, when the Production Code held sway in Hollywood, express discussions of virginity were in any case prohibited.[26] Consequently, film-makers learned to refer to it obliquely, relying on audiences to make inferences from coded language and visual clues, such as costume. In *Easy A* it is the very lack of verifiable evidence that allows Olive, as well as Micah, to construct their own sexual identities through rumour and performance.

Easy A calls into question the ways in which performance and costume in particular can be used as a means of reading sexuality on screen. While Micah presents himself as a devout member of the group, vigorously singing hymns with the other pledge club members, Olive uses clothing as a means of advertising her newly acquired sexuality. Frustrated at the speed with which she is dubbed a 'dirty skank' even by her closest friends, Olive determines to create a costume that will provide an exaggerated spectacle of sexuality. As she states, 'I'm going to be the dirtiest skank they've ever seen.' The scene in which Olive creates this costume strongly recalls the longer sequence in which Andie creates her prom dress in *Pretty in Pink*. In that film, the equivalent scene shows Andie using the two dresses available to her to carve out a space in which her own particular construction of femininity can find voice. In contrast to that relatively harmonious process, in which Andie is shown concentrating on her creative efforts, in *Easy A* this is a scene of frustration and anger in which Olive angrily grunts as she tears through seams and bites through thread. While both scenes portray the creativity offered by costume, it is only in *Easy A* that the endeavour is born principally from anger.

The scene's soundtrack, a cover version of Joan Jett's 'Bad Reputation' recorded by contemporary pop-punk band the Dollyrots, underscores Olive's sense of anger. Originally released in 1981, the song is significant to the film's construction of nostalgia and its negotiation with female sexuality. The song's lyrics proudly state that the singer doesn't 'give a damn about my reputation/ you're living in the past it's a new generation'. In this, 'Bad Reputation' rejects the label traditionally applied to women who eschew patriarchal norms of a demure, female sexuality, most obviously through promiscuity. Furthermore, while the Dollyrots' sugary cover version seems to dampen the anger of the

Figure 5.6 Olive (Emma Stone) creates a spectacle of sexuality.

original song, the rage and defiance of its lyrics remain. The fury articulated by the song and expressed in Olive's behaviour substantially differs from the film's representation of a knowing, affect-free postfeminism. Gill's recent account of feminism's emergence in popular culture observes that women are increasingly required to engage in 'affect policing', wherein the expression of righteous anger is to be denied in favour of a flimsy, content-free (yet media-friendly) manifestation of feminism (Gill 2016: 618). Implied in this scene, then, is a nostalgia for the unalloyed anger of second-wave feminism, which, in the face of the evident sexual double standards that remain, is shown still to be required in the present.

Olive wears the resulting costume – what she terms her 'whore couture' – to school the next day. This outfit consists of a black corset emblazoned with a letter 'A' to signal her self-consciously taboo positioning, which is then worn over tight black trousers. This change in costume is accompanied by a performance of sexuality. Greeting Rhi's boyfriend, Anson (Jake Sandvig), Olive puts on a breathy, seductive voice, stating 'Hello, handsome', which has the desired effect. Her costume and performance strongly resemble those of Sandy at the conclusion of *Grease*, a character who, like Olive, is virginal, yet engages in a performance of sexuality. In *Grease*, Sandy's gestures to the Pink Ladies indicated her unease with this sexual identity, while the setting at the carnival signalled that her transformation was almost certainly a temporary one. In *Easy A*, too, Olive's hyperbolic sexuality is shown to be a performance. In the cafeteria she spies an opportunity to enact her sexual persona, putting a spoon in her mouth in a manner that clearly arouses the boys immediately behind her. However, on seeing Mr Griffith (Thomas Hayden Church) on her other side, Olive abruptly stops the performance and adopts a more relaxed pose.

Depicting Olive's sexual identity as distinct from her ordinary personality, *Easy A* presents a doubling of her characterisation, which proves later to be problematic for her prospective romance with Todd (Penn Badgley). As Katherine Farrimond notes, the film stages a contrast between Olive's sense of her own sexual identity and that which exists in the minds of her peers (Farrimond 2013: 49). This disjunction is manifested in Olive's increasing alienation from herself. When she is handed a detention, she notes that it was her 'slutty alter-ego' who committed the offense, but she who must endure the punishment. What is more, Farrimond argues that *Easy A* exposes the disingenuous promise of postfeminism that it is through ostentatious displays such as these that women can control their sexuality (Farrimond 2013: 53–4). However, as she observes, the illusion that sexuality is fully within an individual woman's remit does not take into account wider power relations. That Olive lacks control is apparent in her encounter with the slovenly Evan (Jameson Moss), who remarks that he 'doesn't need [Olive's] permission' in order to claim that the pair had had sex. *Easy A* can therefore be seen to demonstrate the contradictory landscape presented by postfeminism: one that valorises controlled displays of sexuality and sexual knowledge, but is positively puritanical about actual instances of women supposedly instigating sex. These seeming difficulties in carving out a sexual identity are what prompt Olive's nostalgia for the Eighties teen movie, with its apparently less complicated, more chivalrous sexual politics.

'Don't you forget about me': Allusivity and Nostalgia

In *Easy A*, the nostalgia mood and the nostalgia mode are usefully combined to create a powerful affective dimension that acknowledges both the impossibility of accessing the past and, conversely, the possibility of briefly participating in a particularly resonant cultural moment. It is significant that what prompts Olive's nostalgia for the Eighties is the contemporary sexual politics of the male students at Ojai high school. Retreating briefly from recounting the many deceptions that have led to her positioning as a sexual pariah, Olive's webcast features a series of brief clips from a number of Eighties teen movies, over which the following voiceover is overlaid.

> 'Whatever happened to chivalry? Did it only exist in Eighties movies? I want John Cusack holding a boom-box outside my window. I want to ride off on a lawnmower with Patrick Dempsey. I want Jake from *Sixteen Candles* waiting outside the church for me. I want Judd Nelson thrusting

his fist in the air because he knows he got me just once. I want my life to be like an eighties movie.'

This voiceover and the corresponding images reference *Say Anything* (Cameron Crowe, 1989), *Can't Buy Me Love* (Steve Rash, 1987), *Sixteen Candles*, *The Breakfast Club* and *Ferris Bueller's Day Off*, which is presented for its musical number. With the exception of *Sixteen Candles*, all of these films centre on male characters who, though cheeky, are portrayed as sexually innocent. The gestures to which Olive refers are particularly telling. Having her life 'directed by John Hughes' appears to involve her engaging in ostentatious courtship rituals in which the female partner is the grateful recipient of male affection, however dubious the circumstances in which it is bestowed.

What is desired, then, is the male partner of the Eighties teen movie. The male students at Ojai high school seem generally self-involved; more interested in bolstering their reputations as promiscuous than engaging in real relationships. In contrast, the male characters of Olive's montage are monogamous, loving and committed to their seemingly chaste relationships. While the desire for a chivalric partner might demonstrate Olive's wish to relinquish the limited control that she has, thereby aligning her with the gender roles of the past, what is actually desired here is the characters' emotional vulnerability and capacity to display their love to their girlfriends. The individualistic properties of postfeminism are particularly relevant here. As Negra discusses, many examples of postfeminist media depict women actively choosing to retreat from public life, and by extension from the range of opportunities that have become available as a result of feminist activism.[27] Such a retreat, however, being framed as an active choice, is portrayed in a positive light. In the context of postfeminism, which claims that gender equality has already been achieved, there is no requirement for the personal to be political, as was oft-claimed by second-wave feminist activists.

In addition to its many allusions to the Eighties teen movie, *Easy A* makes reference to a number of other cultural texts that, while incidental to the film's overall narrative, nevertheless work to demonstrate its high levels of reflexivity. As well as the film's many references to *The Scarlet Letter* and that book's subsequent adaptations, other references in the film work to position *Easy A* as a highly knowing teen movie in the model of *Clueless*. In its casting of Malcolm McDowell as the school's principal, for instance, *Easy A* nods to his much earlier role as the chief hell-raiser of *If . . .* (Lindsay Anderson, 1968).[28] Further, the names of two contemporary comedy writers, Phil Lord and Chris Miller, provide the names of two of Olive's customers. What is more, when Marianne unexpectedly befriends Olive, a cover version of 'We Go Together', plays over a montage of scenes depicting their brief friendship. That this song is the final number of *Grease*, in which Danny and Sandy join the other Rydell students in a celebration of community, provides an ironic commentary on the obvious incompatibility of Marianne and Olive.

For Roberta Garrett, reference-spotting in films, such as that seen in the previous paragraph, remains principally associated with a masculine cinephile elite (Garrett 2007: 28). This, she argues, emerged from the film-school generation of Hollywood directors who, in the 1970s, acquired a reverence for classical Hollywood and new European movements alike, resulting in self-conscious cinematic techniques that privileged a select cognoscenti (Garrett 2007: 29). In contrast, *Easy A* demonstrates the ways in which the conventionally masculine forms of allusionism may be taken up in order both to valorise mainstream forms of culture (traditionally, as Garrett notes, associated with the feminine (2007: 29)) and to express a female character's particular dissatisfaction with the complexities and contradictions in the construction of female sexuality under postfeminism. What *Easy A* achieves, then, is a rejection of the contradictions of postfeminism, while remaining within the knowing, referential modes associated with postfeminist media (Gill 2005).

The complex affect wrought by *Easy A* is elucidated by Grainge's distinction between the nostalgia mood and the nostalgia mode. While the former, he argues, consists in the emotional longing for the past, the latter refers to its manifestations in culture, a return to the past that is only effected through a loose evocation of pastness (Grainge, 2000). Certainly, Olive desires to return to a simulacrum of gender roles in the past. However, this is not simply a representation of past forms. Rather, in Olive's webcast, which frames the film's narrative, we can see a way in which the nostalgia mood and the nostalgia mode might converge. Indeed, Olive's very evocation of the nostalgia mood is seen to occur through her use of the camera, through which she is able to splice footage from her favourite teen movies. Consequently, *Easy A* demonstrates how the nostalgia mood might inflect the nostalgia mode to create a particularly evocative, albeit brief, return to the past.

The end of the film portrays Olive indulging in the chivalric possibilities of her much-loved teen movies. Ending her webcast with the assertion that her sexuality is her 'own damn business', her attention is drawn to the window from which Todd (Penn Badgley) can be seen holding up two small speakers, from which Simple Minds' 'Don't You Forget About Me' can be heard. While the gesture is taken from *Say Anything*, the music is taken from the concluding scenes of *The Breakfast Club*. As Olive runs down to see him, Todd tells her that he has borrowed a lawnmower, on which he invites her to ride so that they might re-enact the ending of *Can't Buy Me Love*. The pair leave the scene with their left fists raised, further evoking Judd Nelson's closing scene in *The Breakfast Club*. All of these references were namechecked in Olive's webcast earlier in the film. Throughout this scene, both Todd and Olive are highly knowing about the gestures in which they are participating. Although

NOSTALGIA, POSTFEMINISM AND THE TEEN MOVIE

Figure 5.7 Olive (Emma Stone) and Todd (Penn Badgley) re-create moments from Eighties teen movies.

the cinematography apes the angles and shot-scales used in the original films, Todd notes the ways in which the scene does not quite measure up, as he laments, 'It's not quite a boom box,' and later, 'I borrowed this from a neighbour,' in reference to the lawnmower. While in their original Eighties films these were portrayed as spontaneous, romantic gestures that did not require such commentary, in *Easy A* the moment depends on Todd having seen Olive's webcast, and it has clearly required some preparation. This is therefore a highly engineered scene in which Todd invites Olive to participate in a cultural moment, rather than in a romantic gesture.

That romance must now be conducted in a series of references to earlier cultural works is apparent in another film in which Emma Stone, the star of *Easy A*, later featured. In *Crazy Stupid Love* her character, Hannah, encounters Jacob (Ryan Gosling), whose 'big move', she discovers, is to perform the lift choreography of *Dirty Dancing*. In a manner that recalls *Easy A*, Jacob assumes that Hannah, like all his previous partners, will be a fan of *Dirty Dancing*, and that participating in the dance will endear him to her. As I have argued elsewhere, the use of this particular move from *Dirty Dancing* not only evokes the central positioning of the female character in that scene, but also the eroticised submission in which she participates (2014: 74). Similarly, in *Easy A*, Olive is both within and outside of the romantic gestures in which she participates; her cultural knowledge enables her to enjoy the cultural moment as evidence that Todd has watched the webcast and is attentive to her tastes. However, her knowledge that this has been planned undermines the lo-fi spontaneity of the original moment.

In portraying Olive's participation in these scenes *Easy A* presents the possibility that it might, in part, be possible to return to the past, but it is never possible to fully recapture the innocence of those past eras. As Hutcheon observes, postmodern art does not provide the possibility of returning to the past outside of textual means (2010). Nonetheless, it is surely significant that Olive is able literally to embody this nostalgic scene in a way that calls attention to the sexual disparities of the 1980s, and also embraces the positive elements of the present. While the chapter began with the claim that nostalgia was an impossible desire to turn back the clock, *Easy A* shows that, to some extent, a return to the past is possible.

Conclusion

These three case studies have demonstrated the complex politics of the nostalgic teen movie. As such, this chapter as a whole effectively refutes those who would regard looking back to the past as a regressive mode of retreating from the complexities of the present. What is more, close analysis of *American Graffiti* in particular has successfully disputed Jameson's claim that the film constitutes little more than blank parody which obscures our access to the past. In fact, while the film is shown to offer a selective portrayal of the teenagers growing up in Modesto (not least in its epilogue, which disregards even the principal female players), *American Graffiti* is shown filmically to recognise this. Indeed, the film invites the viewer to question the means through which a selective idealisation of the Fifties takes place.

Postfeminism presents a contradictory view that, since its aims have been achieved, feminism is now surplus to requirements, while at the same time demonstrating its continued necessity. While presenting itself as a modern phenomenon in which women are now highly knowing about gender equality, postfeminism nevertheless advocates the freedom to choose the retrograde roles from which women once sought liberation. It is in this framework of looking backward and forward at once that postfeminism shares common ground with the nostalgic teen movie. Certainly, within the diegeses, the characters are looking forward to the future, with the audience's retrospective gaze injecting a note of hope or caution. The postfeminist perspective has enabled us to perceive the gaps and fissures in the construction of gender relations in the past.

A significant factor that links all three films is the construction of a diegetic audience whose mass – and inaccurate – opinion has consequences for the film's presentation of popular memory. In *American Graffiti*, onlookers at the hop are distanced from Laurie and Steve, such that they only see a couple sharing a loving embrace. However, the film audience's position closer to the action enables us to see that Laurie is crying, while Steve is doing his best to extricate himself from the relationship. The film thus shows how popular, yet mistaken, memories of a single incident come to be constructed. *Dirty Dancing* too featured a number of diegetic audiences. At the Sheldrake, the audience applauds as they watch Johnny and Baby run through their rather stilted routine. Yet the camera's position allows us to hear Johnny's terse instructions, and to witness Baby's hesitation and unease when she realises that she does not feel confident to perform the lift at the performance's conclusion. Similarly, *Easy A* shows that the reputation that has built up around Olive's single untruth is entirely false. All three of these films convey the ease with which an incorrect interpretation can become retrospectively galvanised as the defining view of a particular event. It is in the portrayal of this very process that the very instability of our access to the past is shown.

The analysis of *Easy A* and to a lesser extent of *Dirty Dancing* has shown that the teen movie, one that has been identified as a refracted representation of a film-maker's past, can itself function as an object of nostalgia. There is now an industry that has built up around *Dirty Dancing*, in retro screenings, stage shows and a reported remake, that seems principally defined by its positioning as a 1980s film rather than as a representation of the early 1960s. In turn, *Easy A* has shown the way in which the Eighties teen movie has become a fetishised object of nostalgia, an embodiment of idealised adolescence. With the well-documented trend for retro, and with fewer teen movies that conform to the mould established by Hughes in the present day, this trend may yet continue.[29] As the following chapter will demonstrate, the contemporary Hollywood teen movie is one that largely looks forward, rather than back, often to a dystopian future. This is a teen movie that is often pre-sold, by virtue of its literary past, as a series of popular 'Young Adult' novels, and aspires to become a lucrative multi-episode franchise. The teen movie's recent positioning as a blockbuster has also led to a further development – the construction of the posthuman teenager, which sees the teenager's encounter with the Other.

Notes

1. Davis refers to *American Graffiti* here, as well as to *The Last Picture Show* (Peter Bogdanovich, 1971) and *Happy Days* (ABC, 1974–84).
2. Since 1985, the year in which *Pride* is set, a number of changes in the law have occurred, including the equalisation of the age of consent (1997), legislation for civil partnerships (2005) and same-sex marriage (2013).
3. As if to cement the positioning of *Dirty Dancing* as an object of nostalgia, the film has recently been the subject of an 'immersive' screening experience run by the Secret Cinema. The website invites the viewer to a recreation of Max Kellerman's resort. See <http://www.secretcinema.org/tickets/dirtydancing> (last accessed 17 August 2016).
4. The term 'Generation X' draws from Douglas Coupland's 1991 novel *Generation X: Tales for an Accelerated Culture*, and is said to constitute those born roughly between 1960 and 1975.
5. For Christine Sprengler, Kennedy's death marks the end of the Fifties, the nostalgic construct brought about in part by the mythologising efforts of the 1950s itself and

reignited in the 1970s and 1980s. It is to be distinguished from the 1950s, which denotes the decade between 1950 and 1959 as it was really experienced (Sprengler 2009: 64).
6. For examples of this description, see Shary (2014), p. 10; Shary (2005), pp. 44–7; Speed (1998), pp. 23–4.
7. That *American Graffiti* anticipates and looks forward to the forthcoming counter-cultural movements of the 1960s is indicated by the inclusion of these movements in the film's sequel. Set in 1965, *More American Graffiti* (L. Norton, 1979) portrays the film's characters participating in mass protests.
8. I am thinking in particular of the work of Andrea Dworkin and Catherine MacKinnon in this regard.
9. Many authors describe these positions as signifying an elite status, among them Roz Kaveney (2006), p. 85.
10. The film suggests that Curt is in exile as a draft dodger, since would-be conscripts were not pardoned until 1977.
11. The Prince Charles Cinema's 'Sing-along Dirty Dancing' event promises: 'It's the Summer of 1963; it's college boys versus dancing hunks; it's one of the best loved movies of all time and, yes, there is a guy as great as your dad. Join Baby and Johnny in a fun-filled screening of the 1987 dance classic where YOU are the stars of the show' <https://www.princecharlescinema.com/events/sing-a-long-a-dirty-dancing/> (last accessed 25 September 2016).
12 Claire Molloy (2013) discusses *Dirty Dancing* as a nostalgia text for the 1980s.
13. See Box Office Mojo: *Dirty Dancing*, <http://www.boxofficemojo.com/movies/?page=main&id=dirtydancing.htm> (last accessed 30 March 2017).
14. *Dirty Dancing: Havana Nights* (Guy Ferland, 2004).
15. For further discussion of the many spin-off texts inspired by *Dirty Dancing*, see Tzioumakis, 'Introduction' (2013).
16. See Billboard for further information on their chart position, and the decline in their fortunes as the 1960s went on: <http://www.billboard.com/artist/408695/four-seasons/chart> (last accessed 30 March 2017).
17. Penny's full instructions, 'On the dance floor, he's the boss, if nowhere else,' hint that such patriarchal dominance is being eroded in other spheres of life.
18. Jeffers McDonald (2013, p. 53) observes that Penny prevents Baby from practising this dance with her father, arguing that *Dirty Dancing* stages a switch in Baby's affections from her father to a more appropriate partner outside of her family.
19. Arguably, Marjorie Houseman would have been an ideal reader for Friedan's *Feminine Mystique*, published in February 1963.
20. In the USA, abortion was legalised in 1973 by the Supreme Court decision Roe vs. Wade, in which judges ruled that existing state legislation banning the procedure was unconstitutional since it denied women their 'fundamental right to privacy'. See Boyer (2006), p. 3.
21. This concept was also discussed in relation to *Grease* in Chapter 3.
22. Tim McNelis (2013) identifies a number of other anachronistic songs in *Dirty Dancing*, each of which has a particular function.
23. For Michele Schreiber (2014), this is a central concern of what she describes as the 'postfeminist romance narrative'.
24. For further examples of the allusive 1990s teen movie, see Chapter 4's discussion of *She's All That*.
25. The film refers in particular to *The Scarlet Letter* (Victor Sjöström, 1926), starring Lillian Gish, and is derisive of Roland Joffé's 1995 adaptation of the film, featuring Demi Moore.

26. Films discussing virginity were not entirely absent prior to 1968. We might think of *Tea and Sympathy* (Vincente Minnelli, 1956) in which a teenage boy loses his virginity to an older, married woman.
27. See Negra (2009), particularly pp. 15–46.
28. A similar casting joke can be found in *Election* (Alexander Payne, 2000), in which Matthew Broderick, formerly the cheeky lead of *Ferris Bueller's Day Off* (John Hughes, 1986), is cast as an uptight teacher.
29. In this we might also consider parodic films such as *Scream* (Wes Craven, 1996), *High School High* (Hart Bochner, 1996), *Scary Movie* (Keenan Ivory Wayans, 2000) and *Wet Hot American Summer* (David Wain, 2001). There have since been many more films that remade or revised 1980s texts, as seen in *Love Don't Cost a Thing* (Troy Bryer, 2003), *Sex Drive* (Sean Anders, 2008), *Fame* (Kevin Tancharoen, 2009), *Night of the Demons* (Adam Gierasch, 2009), *The Karate Kid* (Harald Zwart, 2010), *A Nightmare on Elm Street* (Samuel Bayer, 2010), *Footloose* (Craig Brewer, 2011), *Bad Kids Go to Hell* (Matthew Spradlin, 2012), *Red Dawn* (Dan Bradley, 2012), *21 Jump Street* (Phil Lord, Chris Miller, 2012), *Endless Love* (Shana Feste, 2013) and *Me and Earl and the Dying Girl* (Alfonso Gomez-Rejon, 2015). Consequently, we might consider the Eighties as a privileged object of nostalgia.

6. BECOMING OTHER: THE POSTHUMAN AND THE TEEN MOVIE

In 1999, N. Katherine Hayles argued that 'we are all posthuman now' (xv) owing to our daily interactions with intelligent machines. If moral panics about the time teenagers spend with screen media are to be believed, then present-day adolescents may have evolved into another life form entirely.[1] Hayles's conception of the posthuman is tinged with concern for the future; the very notion of human consciousness merged with computers calls up an association with the monstrous. As will become apparent, the question of the monstrous is a significant one for the analysis of the teen movie, particularly given the history of teenagers themselves as liminal figures removed from the more clearly defined identities of child or adult. However, William Brown observes that, like many a 'post', the posthuman should not be conceived as an identity that is wholly removed from the human, but rather a viewpoint that offers a perspective on the contingent position of humans in the world (Brown 2009: 72). The posthuman, then, offers a critical distance from human subjectivity, which allows us to perceive the white, male, Eurocentric assumptions that continue to underpin not only the conception of the human, but the tenets of liberal humanism.

Previous chapters have concerned themselves with the construction of gender and class in the teen movie, and have focused in particular on characters' complex negotiation with the norms governing viable gender and class identities. This analysis has encompassed those who fall firmly within the boundaries of the normative, such as Zack, the high-achieving football team captain of *She's All That*. In contrast, *American Graffiti* provided the example of John, whose position as the town's leading drag racer was compromised by the temporal and physical fact of his ageing, such that he now finds himself at a remove from the prevailing cultural norms. These questions of gender, class and ageing are certainly significant vectors of identity. This chapter aims to augment these considerations with an analysis of how the teenager in the Hollywood teen movie works to trouble the category of the human. As discussed, considering the genre as a sexual coming-of-age narrative constructs the teenager as a liminal figure on the threshold of assuming adulthood. It is in this in-between period, during which the teenager holds neither childhood or adult identities, that the possibility of disrupting the norms that constitute the human may reside.

The question of the human – seemingly a given from which other concerns stem – is far from an obvious one. As discussed in Chapter 3, Judith Butler makes the connection between the necessity of recognition to count as a viable subject, and 'being human' (Butler 2004: 3). As might be expected, Butler's designation of the human is by no means straightforward: she observes that within the category of the human, 'certain humans are recognised as less than human . . . [and] certain humans are not recognised as humans at all' (Butler 2004: 2). It is this understanding that illuminates her work on the ethics of grief, *Frames of War*, in which Butler analyses the tendency of the Western news media to dehumanise those whose lives are lost in contemporary American conflicts. Her aim to expand the norms of recognition so as to incorporate many more people into the embrace of the 'fully human' nevertheless maintains a tacit anthropocentrism. In contrast to the sections that have preceded it, this chapter aims to explore the construction of identity in teen movies in which characters encounter, and often become, the non-human. In doing so, the aim will be to examine the critical distance of which will elucidate the construction of the human, and the tenuous place of teenagers within that category.

Butler's continued advocacy of the human attests to the continued pull of liberal humanism. For Rosi Braidotti, this consists principally of a belief in the notion of the autonomous self, and 'faith in the unique, self-regulating and universally moral powers of human reason' (Braidotti 2013: 13). These tenets of liberal humanism, themselves eighteenth- and nineteenth-century reifications of the ideals of the Italian Renaissance, provide the philosophical underpinning of legal and political frameworks across much of Europe and the United States. Yet Braidotti also observes the divisions enacted by these seemingly benign assumptions, most obviously the construction of Europe as the bedrock of political reason (Braidotti 2013: 15). To be anything other than European is to be constructed as Other, which incurs some measure of pejoration. For Braidotti, it is the disjunction between the grandiose rhetoric of universalism and self-determination, and the considerably narrower range of those who are to be included in that vision, that reveals the latent oppressions of liberal humanism. To be sure, the human evoked in liberal humanism is always already understood as Man, and a masculine, white, heterosexual, urbanised and educated man at that (Braidotti 2013: 65). While evoked in the service of hope and aspiration, liberal humanism also underlies the worst excesses of European colonial ambition.

In the place of these Eurocentric, male ideals at the core of liberal humanism, Braidotti proposes *zoe*, or life-force, which captures companion species, technological others and even the hazy prospect of life after death. While liberal humanism assumes the autonomy of its self-governing subject, Braidotti's formulation follows Deleuze and Guattari's attentiveness to relations of interdependence between humans and other beings (1980). What is envisaged is a continuum between the human and these other forms as a means of displacing anthropocentrism (Braidotti 2013: 66). The posthuman therefore presents an opportunity to expose the contingency of the 'human' as it is constructed under liberal humanism, to explore the interdependencies of the human with other forms of life, and to theorise new identities that are distinct from such cultural baggage.

Braidotti's optimistic approach to the posthuman owes much to the work of Donna Haraway, whose 1991 publication, *A Manifesto for Cyborgs*, has been central to the elaboration of critical posthumanism. A combination of 'cybernetic' and 'organism', the cyborg consists in an interplay between the technological – and therefore the constructed – and the organic, which is supposedly untouched by culture. Haraway's theorisation is a liberating one, in which the cyborg is figured as a model of a subject free from the constraints of binary gender difference, of social class, or indeed of ethnic or national distinction. Haraway uses the concept of the cyborg as a means to describe the subjectivity of identities that do not sit easily in such pre-defined categories. She argues, for instance, that women of colour are cyborgs, since they are not considered fully women, while the conception of people of colour as a whole remains a masculinised one (Haraway 2003: 34). The cyborg is thus found in the interstices between animals and humans, humans and machines, and the physical and non-physical (Haraway 2003: 8–11). Despite the apparent threat to the integrity of the subject, Haraway is insistent that there is no possibility of a return to an Edenic, 'natural' realm. Now that the 'natural' and the 'constructed' are irrevocably bound up together, the radical potential of the possibilities afforded as a result must be explored.

Although Haraway presents the cyborg as a phenomenon to be welcomed, it is science fiction cinema – whose worlds and creatures are startling for their similarity to, as much as their distinction from, those we know – with which the cyborg has hitherto been principally associated (Haraway 2003: 8; Hassler-Forest 2015: 70). As many have observed, analogy is the key *modus operandi* of science fiction, through which parallels may be drawn between our present circumstances and those portrayed on screen. Consequently, the cyborg embodies contemporary anxieties about interactions between technology and the human in 1980s films such as *The Terminator* (James Cameron, 1984) and *Blade Runner* (Ridley Scott, 1982), in which the lines between robot, human and replicant are horrifyingly indistinct. In contrast, although it is rarely associated with the cyborg or indeed with the posthuman, I argue that the liminality of adolescence, in which characters defy existing categories and forge new identities, makes the teen movie particularly apposite for an analysis informed by a posthumanist appreciation of the contingency and partiality of the human. As Jeffrey A. Brown observes, the contemporary superhero blockbuster maintains an 'obsessional focus' on the process of the ordinary protagonist becoming a superhero, suggesting a cultural preoccupation with these porous boundaries between the human and the non-human, on which the teen movie can shed some light (Brown 2016: 134).

The broad perspective wrought by the conception of the posthuman as one that provides a critical perspective on the human necessitates an equally expansive series of representations in the case studies examined here. Accordingly, this chapter analyses *Spider-Man* (Sam Raimi, 2002), a film in which a teenage boy is transformed into a creature that combines certain physical attributes of the spider with the cognitive abilities and appearance of a man. Conversely, in *Twilight* (Catherine Hardwicke, 2008), the main character, Bella (Kristen Stewart), falls in love with a vampire, with whom she pleads – unsuccessfully at this stage – to be transformed into one of his kind. Lastly, *Chronicle* (Josh Trank, 2012) features a teenager filming his gradual acquisition of destructive telekinetic powers. These short synopses already indicate the films' differences in focus and approach. However, the consistent focus on characters that are uncharismatic, if not ostracised by their peers, suggests that the conception of the 'human' is one that feels remote to many subjects.

This century in particular has seen the Hollywood teen movie offer multiple constructions of the posthuman. When revising *Generation Multiplex* for its second edition in 2014, Shary notes that it was the section on fantasy and the supernatural – prime arenas for the exploration of the posthuman – that required the most radical expansion (Shary 2014: xiv). For Shary, the current predominance of the fantasy-themed teen movie owes much to the popularity of the British franchise *Harry Potter* (2001–11), whose bespectacled protagonist is called from the quotidian 'Muggle' world to attend Hogwarts school of witchcraft and wizardry (Shary 2014: 208). Throughout his time at the school, Harry is seen to move between the human and non-human worlds as he comes to realise his potential as a wizard. Shary further suggests that the popularity of the fantasy teen movie can readily be explained by the teen audience's taste for the melodramatic. Teenagers, he argues, find in these narratives an exaggerated reflection of their rather more everyday concerns (Shary 2014: 218).

The high budgets and extensive marketing of such films in recent years suggests that Hollywood is confident in continued teen interest in the fantasy narrative.

The recent deluge of adaptations of fantasy young-adult novels that lack the pedigree or fan base of J.K. Rowling's work surely owes much to the success of the *Harry Potter* films.[2] Yet the possibilities offered by increasing developments in digital cinema techniques to create 'impossible bodies in fantastical situations' should not go unremarked (Purse 2013: 57). For William Brown, the increased prevalence of computer-generated imagery and motion capture constitute a posthumanist cinema (2009: 70). Significantly, this posthumanist cinema does not negate the principles of what might be termed humanist cinema. Indeed, Brown is keen to emphasise that the use of digital techniques is typically in the service of making impossible movements and camera angles seem possible, such that these new techniques can be said to be used in the service of realism (Brown 2009: 71). What's more, even though digital film negates the need for conventional editing using a cut, the terminology itself hailing from an era in which one took a pair of scissors to the celluloid in question, this type of editing is still found in films that strongly rely on digital techniques. Brown proposes that the combination of new and older practices found in this posthumanist cinema suggests a wish to hide its radical potential to disrupt established film-making methods (Brown 2009: 78). In other words, digital cinema presents a masquerade of humanist verisimilitude to its audience.

Yet to argue that the posthumanist teen movie is solely a twenty-first-century phenomenon would be a mistake. Shary is certainly correct that the current prevailing trend in teen cinema is towards the fantastical. However, the 1950s also saw a number of teen movies that featured characters transformed into a variety of monstrous figures, including *I Was a Teenage Werewolf* (Gene Fowler, 1957), *Blood of Dracula* (Herbert L. Strock, 1957) and *I Was a Teenage Frankenstein* (Herbert L. Strock, 1957). Released by American International Pictures (AIP) in quick succession, these low-budget films were marketed to teenagers following the wave of juvenile delinquency films, such as *Rebel Without a Cause*, which largely courted an adult audience (Miller and Von Riper 2015: 131). While the juvenile delinquency films presented the teenager as an unfathomable, figurative monster, the AIP films made the monstrosity of adolescence literal in portraying their transformations into various supernatural creatures. Both film cycles suggest that the on-screen teenager holds a privileged position in relation to monstrosity, a contention that chimes with Jeffrey Jerome Cohen's seminal 'Seven Theses of the Monster', in which he argues that it is the sense of category crisis, 'disturbing hybrids whose externally incoherent bodies resist attempts to include them in any systematic structure', that is at the heart of the monstrous (Cohen 1996: 6). As discussed in previous chapters, the teenager has been seen to be a figure that evades easy categorisation, which lends itself well to a positioning as Other, or indeed as monstrous. The liminality of the teenager demonstrates that teenage characters constitute representations of a subjectivity in flux. Through close textual analysis informed by theories of the posthuman, I will demonstrate that on-screen representations of teenagers are uniquely placed to interrogate what is at stake in the delimitations of the human.

Spider-Man (Sam Raimi, 2002)

With its focus on the origins of its eponymous hero, Sam Raimi's *Spider-Man* set the template for the past decade of superhero films, and, following the success of *X-Men* (Bryan Singer, 2000) before it, contributed to the establishment of Marvel's now burgeoning 'cinematic universe'. McAllister, Gordon and Jancovich draw attention to the status of the comic superhero adaptation as a 'tentpole' of a Hollywood film studio's annual release schedule; that is, as a high-profile film with the economic potential to single-handedly boost a studio's financial profile for the year (McAllister, Gordon and Jancovich 2006: 108). Despite the relatively niche positioning of the Marvel and DC comics themselves (which together constitute 70% of the market)[3], the heroes who feature in them are recognised around the world, which facilitates marketing film adaptations in their name across a number of geographical territories. What is more, these materials not only attract the apocryphal nineteen-year-old male, whose custom is much sought by canny studios (Betrock 1986), but, in their evocation of heroes created in the middle of the twentieth century, assert a nostalgic pull for older audiences too (McAllister, Gordon and Jancovich 2006: 110). Although the definition of the blockbuster remains contested (Krämer 1998; King 2002), *Spider-Man's* outsized budget, cross-media marketing, focus on spectacle and a simple, high-concept narrative surely position the film as one of its number. As Marvel hoped, *Spider-Man* was hugely successful, recouping $821m worldwide from its hefty $139m production budget,[4] and remains one of the highest-grossing films of all time. Inevitably, it spawned two sequels, *Spider-Man 2* (Sam Raimi, 2004) and *Spider-Man 3* (Sam Raimi, 2007).[5] The film is therefore distinct from the majority of Hollywood teen movies, which possess considerably lower budgets and production values.

For Dan Hassler-Forest, the superhero is the posthuman *par excellence* – an outsider, vigilante figure whose unearthly powers shine a light on the bodily vulnerability of the human (Hassler-Forest 2015: 66). While typically assuming an outwardly human appearance, the superhero finds themselves at a threshold between the human and the non-human in a manner that demonstrates the limits of human capability. Such hybridity is especially apparent in the hyphenated title of *Spider-Man*, which indicates that our hero neither fully inhabits the identity of spider, nor of man. The posthuman elements of the superhero film extend to the computer-generated imagery used in its production. Stan

Lee's 1960s comic books, from which the film was adapted, comprised handdrawn, primary-coloured illustrations, with speech and thought bubbles to convey interaction with, or interiority from, other characters. This type of aesthetic style was strikingly conveyed in Robert Rodriguez's *Sin City* (2005), which took up the two-dimensional visual style and colour scheme from Frank Miller's comic creation. However, whereas Rodriguez's comic-book aesthetic creates a sense of distance between the audience and the on-screen action, Raimi's *Spider-Man* co-opts digital techniques in order to create the impression that the seemingly impossible events shown on screen actually take place in contemporary New York City. Just as the Spandex-clad hero must blend into the background in his own daily life, *Spider-Man* is a film that disguises its own alterity.

Yet among superhero films, *Spider-Man* remains an outlier. Unlike the majority of its counterparts, which detail the struggles of adult superheros, *Spider-Man* tells of the transformation of its ordinary teen protagonist into a superhero. Brown observes that comic-book adaptations are particularly concerned with how the superhero came into being in the first place, whether transported from outer space (Superman), constructed from technological know-how (Iron Man) or, as is the case with *Spider-Man*, bitten by a genetically-modified spider (Brown 2016: 135). Arguably, then, the focus on a teenager, whose identity is seen to possess an element of the monstrous and whose identity is in any case regarded as always already in flux, is an apt one.

Problematising the superhero film's claim to the posthuman is the formulaic plot, which pits our hero against an adversary of similar abilities and skill set, though invariably with a more nefarious and destructive worldview. In *Spider-Man* this adversary is supplied by Norman Osborn (Willem Dafoe), whose zeal for profit and scientific discovery prompts him to ignore his advisors and test out his prototype technology on himself. As Norman becomes ever more destructive and violent, Peter (Tobey Maguire) is moved to save New York from its aggressor, prompting its citizens to praise, essentially, the humanitarianism of the Spandex-clad hero. The posthuman superhero, then, continues to comply with the ethical framework of the human complicating her/his claim to be a construction of the posthuman (Hassler-Forest 2015: 72). As the analysis will demonstrate, *Spider-Man* holds an ambivalent relationship with the human; while his physical abilities go beyond the parameters of human possibility, Spider-Man nevertheless continues to uphold human ideals as his own. The first half of the film is saturated with the tropes of the Hollywood teen movie that we have encountered elsewhere, including the school bus, the cafeteria, the school lockers and high school graduation itself. Martin Flanagan argues that *Spider-Man* possesses a dual address, since despite the teen appeal inherent in the film's high school topography, *Spider-Man* resolutely avoids any overt references to the popular culture of 2002. As a result, he claims, the world of Raimi's film is constructed as timeless (Flanagan 2004: 148).[6] In the analysis, it will be important to consider how these two distinct gazes upon the action are mobilised by the film's teen-oriented narrative.

Transforming the Nerd

Spider-Man stages the transformation of Peter Parker (Tobey Maguire) into a half-man/half-spider superhero. However, it should be noted from the outset that Peter is not merely an ordinary teenager, but a nerd – that is, an image of inadequate masculinity. For Shary, Anthony Michael Hall's character, Brian, in *The Breakfast Club*, provides the archetype of the ungainly male nerd (Shary 2014: 39). In this he quotes film critic David Denby's description of the character, who, with his 'pale skin, pale-blue eyes and almost milky blonde hair' is 'almost translucent' (Denby quoted in Shary 2014: 39). The nerd's weedy physicality suggests a limited interest in the conventionally manly arena of sports, while his disinterest in personal grooming marks him as boyish and virginal. Significantly, it is with this nerdish masculinity that superhero culture itself is associated, an observation that Umberto Eco has linked with a fantasy of super-masculinisation that is otherwise beyond the grasp of these young men (Eco, 1972).

Further to Peter's nerdish characterisation, he is depicted as working class. Even when transformed into his vigilante alter ego, Peter remains in his low-paid job as a photographer, living in a small house in Queens with his Aunt May (Rosemary Harris). Peter's working-class positioning contrasts with the billionaire lifestyles of other superheroes such as Bruce Wayne (Batman) and Tony Stark (Iron Man), who are able single-handedly to fund and build new gadgets for their arsenal of weapons, and speaks to Spider-Man's status as an aspirational fantasy figure.[7] As will be discussed later in the analysis, Peter's next-door neighbour and later love interest, Mary-Jane (Kirsten Dunst), is also depicted as working class.

The opening scenes of *Spider-Man* establish Peter's lack of corporeality, and affirm that the narrative is constructed from his personal perspective. Peter's voice-over positions him as the film's master of ceremonies, guiding the action presented to us on screen, and it is in this way that the film is able temporarily to deceive the audience as to who the prospective Spider-Man may be. Peter's voice-over, which signals a visually absent presence (see Kozloff 1989), introduces the opening scene on a school bus. As Peter claims, 'This is a story about a girl,' the camera is trained on Mary-Jane, whom the audience correctly deduces to be the girl at the centre of the story. However, the spectator incorrectly infers that her companion – in fact, the boorish Flash Thompson (Joe Manganiello) – is Peter. The camera movement embodies the spectator's confusion, moving to another student hungrily scoffing doughnuts in the row in

Figure 6.1   Peter Parker (Tobey Maguire) is positioned outside the high school community.

front of the pair, before Peter states 'nope, not me either'. This rather delayed introduction defies the audience's expectations that the camera placement inside the school bus means that the speaker is sure to be one of its passengers. Rather, Peter is placed literally outside the school community, as only his hand on the outside of the vehicle as he begs the driver to stop registers his presence, while the voice-over confirms, 'That's me.' Only when Mary-Jane asks the driver to stop, more out of pity than in friendship, is Peter able to board. With his slight frame, short stature, undistinguished clothing, glasses and lack of friends, Peter certainly seems to fit the bill of the archetypal nerd, one that makes his later physical transformation all the more apparent.

Shary observes that male nerds are punished for their conventionality and compliance with authority. 'Cool', with its stance of passive disrespect, is instead the preferred attitude, having become a norm of teen masculinity (Pountain and Robins 2000: 19). Female nerd characters are another matter entirely. As was observed in *She's All That*, it was Laney's very lack of conventionality, and therefore her resistance to complying with the norms of teen femininity, which demonstrated her nerdishness and with it, her undesirability.[8] While Laney is undistinguished academically and known principally for her politically-inspired art, Peter is portrayed as possessing an aptitude for science. As was underscored in Chapter 4, the importance of academic education provided by the high school is dwarfed by that of physical attractiveness and conformity to hegemonic ideals of gender. Peter's unremarkable, functional clothing can therefore be seen as part of his prioritisation of the rational, scientific mind – the foundations of which lie in the tenets of liberal humanism – as much as it does with his economic circumstances that might preclude zanier purchases.

Along with his classmates, Peter is taken on a field trip to Columbia University's science department, where the guide is eager to show the students their recent developments in genetically modified organisms, notably spiders.[9] As if to emphasise the cutting-edge scientific endeavour under way at the lab, its walls display moving images of double helix structures with sections added and removed to emphasise the scientists' mastery over the complexity of this foundational biological substance. As the researcher explains to the largely underwhelmed group of high school students, scientists at this lab have selected spider species that possess particular properties, such as the ability to jump long distances or a particularly effective web structure, in order to create the ultimate in its class. In this way, the researchers demonstrate their absolute superiority and the anthropocentrism of their endeavour. The spiders they have created are monstrous, and have no purpose other than those that serve the lab.

It is the spider combining the very best aspects of other successful arachnids that has escaped from the careless researchers, and that bites an unsuspecting Peter on the hand. The shot scale amplifies the impact of what might have appeared a routine incident, providing an extreme close-up of the spider's pincers at the moment of their contact with Peter's skin. The importance of this moment is underscored by the film's sound design, too, as the spider bite makes an unexpectedly loud noise on impact, at which point the film cuts to a medium shot of Peter rubbing his hand while the spider scuttles out of view.

The resulting large red and blue bruise and swelling speaks to the unnatural process Peter is undergoing. Later, when Peter takes shelter in his bedroom as the transformation occurs, we see images seemingly inside his body, in which spiders crawl around our hero's nervous system, while new red and blue sections of DNA are added to his existing grey double helix. This scientific imagery recalls similar sequences used in the American crime series *CSI* (CBS 2000–15), in which the discovery of genetic material – however minute – enables the investigators to uncover the perpetrators of various crimes. These images, which imply the use of a microscope, are seen to have a privileged relation with the truth such that a genetic match with a suspect is seen to constitute definitive proof that the person in question committed the crime. The use of such imagery demonstrates that a fundamental, unalterable change has taken place within Peter, one that is later shown to have more obviously spectacular outward manifestations.

It is true that the film emphasises the serendipity of Peter's encounter with the spider, an aspect that foregrounds his difference from Norman Osborn, whose destructive alter ego, the Green Goblin, is born of his greed. Yet it is telling that Peter does not seek the advice of his guardians Aunt May and Uncle Ben (Cliff Robertson) following his bite, suggesting that he is curious to observe the outcome of his encounter with the spider. Retreating to his bedroom, a space that, as Flanagan notes, provides a site in which teenagers forge their identities alone, an increasing gulf is already apparent between Peter and his guardians through the use of *mise-en-scène* (Flanagan 2004: 158). The small house's communal areas are adorned with floral wallpaper and filled with natural light, while numerous houseplants demonstrate an attempt to bring nature into the house itself. These prints are echoed in Aunt May's floral apron and blouse, emphasising her alignment with the home environment. For his part, Uncle Ben's plaid shirt and jeans signify his role as a labourer who works outside the home, a position from which he has been dislodged owing to his ignorance of computers. In contrast to the interiors elsewhere, Peter's bedroom features no such floral tributes to the natural world. Rather presciently, the bedroom wallpaper is blue – a colour not often seen in nature – and bears a thin, grey web pattern. Reflecting the character's interest in science, the walls bear a poster of Einstein, while science equipment is spread across his desk. Even at this early stage in his transformation the film draws attention not only to the differences between Peter and his guardians, but to a division in the worlds they represent. While Aunt May and Uncle Ben remain firmly associated with the world of the past, Peter's experiences and encounters lead him into a different ontological space.

The Limits of Alterity

Changes in Peter's physique and cognitive abilities occur largely off-screen, with only vivid dreams and a disturbed sleep registering the substantial transformation that has occurred overnight. Rather, he wakes up feeling refreshed, and only gradually becomes aware of his newly acquired powers throughout his day at school. The first indications of the transformation that has occurred are shown in point-of-view shots as Peter raises and lowers his glasses, in the discovery that these encumbrances now blur, rather than enhance, his vision. Discarding them, he looks in the mirror to observe that his formerly flabby physique is now rippling with muscles. Satisfied, he leaps down the stairs to see his guardians, who tellingly equate his quick recovery from the illness he claimed the previous evening with 'hormones', the bellwether of adolescent transformation. However, as this section demonstrates, there are notable limits to changes that can be ascribed to Peter's adolescence, which have consequences for the character's cultural intelligibility.

Arguably, *Spider-Man* stages the limits of alterity, and it is in the high school, the site of the socialisation of American youth, where these limits are established. As is typical of the function of the high school in the teen movie, it is the 'informal' spaces apparently governed by the students themselves – the cafeteria and the corridor – that provide the places of contestation. In the cafeteria, Peter is shown eating his lunch alone, demonstrating his positioning as a friendless outsider who already falls short of the norms of teen masculinity. As he spots Mary-Jane, walking briskly and obliviously in his direction, the film cuts between Peter's open-mouthed gaze, and a low-angle shot of Mary-Jane, from his perspective. As she approaches him, her movement appears to slow down, demonstrating the camera's continued alignment with Peter and constructing Mary-Jane as a passive object of his desiring gaze. His reverie is broken by a quick cut to spilled liquid on the patch of floor in Mary-Jane's path. Since the camera has hitherto followed Peter's perspective, the shot of the spilled water represents a sudden switch in his attention, from which he can gauge how to catch Mary-Jane as she falls and reunite her with her tray of food. This is Peter's first encounter with his 'Spidey-sense': enhanced cognitive abilities that allow him to predict the movements of others, which Mary-Jane admiringly attributes to his 'great reflexes' as she falls into his waiting arms.

In contrast, Peter's fight with Flash Thompson demonstrates abilities that are not so easily explained away. Still in the canteen, Peter is bemused to find a fork mysteriously affixed to the palm of his hand. Attempting to dislodge it, he inadvertently emits his web string onto another student's tray, which is then accidently whipped behind him to hit none other than Mary-Jane's boyfriend, Flash Thompson. Even though Peter quickly leaves the scene, Flash is easily able to discern the culprit and heads in pursuit. With Peter's back to Flash his Spidey senses come to his aid, as close-up, slow-motion footage of a drop of liquid leaving a straw, which then disrupts a fly's trajectory, indicate that Flash is on the point of throwing a punch at his head. The camera alternates between the perspective of the crowd who have assembled around the pair and who see Peter effortlessly dodging Flash's blows, and Peter's own perspective, in slow-motion. This latter perspective sees Peter's bemusement at the ease with which he is able to evade what seem to him to be extremely slow assaults. Finally, Peter punches Flash with a blow that definitively ends the fight. Maguire's wide-eyed expression as his arm remains outstretched emphasises Peter's confusion, fear and exhilaration at the outcome.

The contrasting reception to these two events must be understood in relation to Peter's characterisation as a nerd. When Mary-Jane compliments his quick thinking, he grins silently at her until, uncomfortable, she leaves the scene. Peter's social awkwardness here corresponds with his nerdish positioning, and allows Mary-Jane perhaps to attribute his 'reflexes' to the cognitive abilities he has acquired through his scientific skills. In contrast, Peter's fighting skills are totally out of character for the nerd, which is further demonstrated by his unnaturally outstretched arm at the fight's conclusion. Rather than being congratulated for retaliating so effectively, he is derided as a 'freak' by his classmates. *Spider-Man* can therefore be seen to demonstrate how particular divisions within the category of the human present limits to the acceptable possibilities of alterity.

While the high school is shown to be a highly regulatory environment in which difference is suspect, wrestling provides a space in which Peter can use his powers anonymously, away from the scrutiny of his classmates. Further, he is attracted by the $3,000 prize offered to anyone prepared to take on the incumbent wrestler in a three-minute bout. Unlike boxing, whose amateur ranks are replete with similar inducements, wrestling possesses a theatrical dimension, with participants fighting under the guise of fanciful pseudonyms – in Peter's case, as the 'Human Spider', a name that safely contains his abilities as part of his wrestling persona. Conspicuous because of his youth and slight frame, Peter is goaded by the other wrestlers, the cheerleaders and the bloodthirsty audience alike. The other wrestler is presented as animal-like, bearing minimal clothing, long hair and a beard, and caged with the sole purpose of fighting. For him, too, the film implies, wrestling provides a space to air his animalistic aggression. The wrestling arena indicates to Peter the importance of costume and identity in making his vigilante an acceptable part of New York City's populace. While such difference would not be tolerated in his identity as Peter Parker, his costuming and visible hybridity conversely code him as Other, yet conversely, culturally intelligible.

For all that Peter's alter-ego, Spider-Man, can be seen to trouble existing divisions between the human and the animal world, it is nevertheless significant that heteronormativity and Peter's desire for Mary-Jane is never disrupted in the film. As Peter's voiceover declares in the opening scenes, 'This is a story about a girl.' Indeed, the representations of gender and of romance remain largely traditional ones. While Aunt May is a nurturing, maternal figure, Mary-Jane is Peter's love interest, who herself possesses little agency and must be repeatedly rescued by Spider-Man. For Joseph Walderzak she constitutes the archetypal 'damsel in distress', both a prize for the hero and a construct of romantic fantasy (Walderzak 2016: 48). Wielding only limited agency, and needing to be rescued on multiple occasions, Walderzak argues that Mary-Jane's characterisation is part of the construction of *Spider-Man* itself as nostalgic.[10]

While the backstreets of New York City provide an anonymous shelter for Peter to develop and practise his powers, they constitute a site of danger for Mary-Jane. No sooner does Peter take his leave than she is accosted by a group of men who are intent on raping her. Having rescued her, the scene in which Spider-Man and Mary-Jane kiss is one in which the full potential of the posthuman can be realised. Spider-Man is depicted hanging upside down, held up by his web, while Mary-Jane stands immediately in front of him, such that she is level with his face. There is a hyperbolic aspect to the scene, with Mary-Jane's rain-soaked hair and vest, while the Spandex-clad hero hangs passively as she uncovers his mouth to kiss him. Unusually, this moment is orchestrated by Mary-Jane, who accepts the alterity of Spider-Man and his desire not to

Figure 6.2 Spider-Man (Tobey Maguire) and Mary-Jane (Kirsten Dunst) kiss.

reveal his identity. That it is she who leads this moment defies the conventional logic of the romance narrative that, in the frequent rescue scenes, the film has hitherto followed, wherein the female of the pair is subjugated to the strengths of the masculine partner.

Despite the possibilities presented by the romance between Spider-Man and Mary-Jane, the end of the film sees her preference for Peter Parker. Furthermore, he rejects her affections, preferring instead to remain her protector. The end of the film can therefore be regarded as a conservative one in terms of its representation of the posthuman, since Peter's refusal of the romance with Mary-Jane can be seen to deny the possibilities of miscegenation between the human and the non-human. With the film prioritising the protection of the people of New York City, *Spider-Man* can be regarded as upholding the primacy of the human, as Hassler-Forest suggests (2015).

Masculinities in Confrontation

As a teen movie, *Spider-Man* stages not only Peter Parker's transformation into a spider, but also into a man. Certainly, this is Uncle Ben's central point, when he reminds Peter that 'the man you're becoming now is the man you're going to be for the rest of your life'. The construction of masculinity, then, provides the backdrop to Spider-Man's narrative, not least his inevitable confrontation with his adversary, the Green Goblin. As this section demonstrates, the contrasts between Spider-Man and the Green Goblin, and further, between Norman Osborn and Uncle Ben, illuminate the film's construction of the posthuman.

Just as Spider-Man provides Peter's masculine ideal, so too does the Green Goblin constitute an extension of Norman's will. During much of the film

Norman is a benevolent presence in Peter's life, observing with interest his scientific capabilities. Nonetheless, the contrasting manner in which the two characters acquire their powers demonstrate their distinct relationships with the posthuman. Under pressure at his business, Oscorp Industries, to progress with a pioneering technology that remains stuck in the prototype phase, Norman takes the drastic decision to trial the technology on himself. His acquisition of superpowers is both instigated by him, implying rational control, yet also subtly out of his control, since he kills his colleague, Dr Strom (Ron Perkins) without being aware of it, and only gradually comes to realise the extent of his powers. The image of Norman and his demonic mirror image is an affecting one that demonstrates the radical splitting of his subjectivity. This, then, is the literal collapse of rational, individualised subjectivity, the key tenet on which liberal humanism rests. The mindless destruction of the Green Goblin is therefore connected with Norman's greed and his overweening desire for mastery of his nascent technology.

In contrast, Peter acquires his powers by chance and must learn how to deploy his instincts to wield them usefully. Having got into trouble deploying his web accidentally in the school cafeteria, Peter takes to the streets of New York, where Marvel comics' wry sensibility is in evidence, since Peter's earnest orders to 'Go, web, go!' do not work. Close-ups of Peter's hand and wrist in a variety of gestures, accompanied by his increasingly frustrated commands, do not work. Instead, it is only when he orients his hand in an instinctive fashion that the web emits from his wrist. These inhuman powers can therefore be seen to defy the rationality and will – the hallmarks of liberal humanism – of his earlier orders and actions.

For Richard Kaplan, Peter is beset by surrogate father figures (Kaplan 2011: 298). Early in the film, Peter is angry at Uncle Ben for 'trying to be [his] father', while Norman later claims Peter as his son, remarking, 'You've been like a brother to Harry, and that makes you family.' The contrasting figures represented by Uncle Ben and Norman speak to the construction of masculinity that is valorised in the film. For his part, the metallic surfaces and sharp angles of the Green Goblin echo those of Willem Dafoe's gaunt face. Susan Jeffords memorably associates the 'hard body' of action heroes in the 1980s and 1990s with the Reagan administration (Jeffords 1994). While it is problematic to connect Hollywood cinema with a particular political ideology, it is significant that Norman's capitalist zeal, destruction and self-made identity – the components of hard masculinity – correspond to the ideas espoused during the Reagan era.

Conversely, Uncle Ben constitutes a figure of 'soft' masculinity. Unlike that of Norman, his is a doughy face, 'so soft, it's almost feminine' (Kaplan 2011: 299). While he advises Peter on how to conduct oneself as a man, this is a role that, according to the conventional grammar of the film, he is failing to perform. Wearing the typical garb of the working man, he is put out to discover that his skills are gradually being superseded by computers and machines. Nonetheless, Spider-Man's eventual victory and the visual similarity between Cliff Robertson, the actor who plays Uncle Ben, and Tobey Maguire, combine to create the impression that it is this responsible, unglamorous vision of masculinity that ultimately triumphs, rather than the cyborg vision of financial and technological hubris that the Green Goblin embodies. *Spider-Man* ultimately stages the limits, as well as the dizzying potentials, of the posthuman.

Twilight (Catherine Hardwicke, 2008)

Comprising five films released between 2008 and 2012, the Twilight Saga was one of the most lucrative film franchises in history, and certainly one of the most commercially successful representations of vampires on screen.[11] Adapted from Stephanie Meyer's four novels (the last of which, following the mould established by the Harry Potter films, was divided into two parts), the series tells of Bella Swan (Kristen Stewart), who, having moved to the bleak small town of Forks, Washington, becomes attracted to mysterious vampire Edward Cullen (Robert Pattinson) while she is also being pursued by Jacob (Taylor Lautner). While later films take a greater interest in Jacob's Native American family, who, it turns out, are also werewolves, Catherine Hardwicke's 2008 teen melodrama is principally invested in the taboo relationship between a human, Bella, and Edward, a vampire. For Michael Hauskeller, the vampire is 'postmortal', both alive and dead at the same time, yet can never perish entirely (Hauskeller 2015: 206). The vampire can therefore be seen to trouble the boundaries between living and dead, recalling the liminality of the teenager, who is neither wholly child nor adult. In this context, it is significant that the teen film has in recent years tended to construct the vampire not as monstrous, as it is frequently depicted, but as desirable.[12] In addition to *Twilight* we might think of the Swedish film *Let the Right One In* (Tomas Alfredson, 2008), which depicts the friendship between a human boy and a girl who turns out to be a vampire. This case study will therefore assess how the conventions of the teen movie in particular inflect the portrayal of this human/vampire romance.

Braidotti's conception of the posthuman espouses *zoe* or life-force as a means of displacing the centrality of the human. For Braidotti, death is a precondition of existence since knowledge of one's temporality is the principal driving force of human life (Braidotti 2013: 131). Conversely, her contention that *zoe* is beyond the physical life of any individual subject means that *zoe* transcends death. The vampires portrayed in *Twilight* can be seen to provide an example of *zoe*'s enduring power. If, following Deleuze, *zoe* consists in a 'creative synthesis of flows . . . of perpetual becoming' (Braidotti 2013: 129), then Edward Cullen presents a particularly apposite vision of life after death.

Although born in 1901, his body is forever held in its seventeen-year-old incarnation, always a year short of graduating from high school. To maintain this illusion the Cullens have a peripatetic existence, moving between towns every few years. Edward therefore constitutes a figure that remains unmapped in existing conceptions of adolescence, a teenager whose coming of age can never be fully realised.

For Ananya Mukherjea, the male vampire constitutes the ideal male partner for the contemporary postfeminist teen girl, since they embody a number of contradictory gender roles from multiple eras, ages and subcultures (Mukherjea 2011: 3). For many of *Twilight*'s teenage female fans, she argues, Edward satisfies their desire for a traditional gentleman figure who, in contrast to the teenage boys they encounter ordinarily, will not pressure them sexually (Mukherjea 2011: 3). Because of their advanced age, which contrasts with their ever-youthful appearance, male vampires often possess old-fashioned ideals. Yet their shape-shifting vampirism is shown to extend itself to their understanding of how to move with the times, as a result of which they are able endlessly to evolve with the mores of the contemporary age as well. Both youthful and old, experienced and virginal, wealthy and vulnerable, Edward is constituted as the ideal partner for Bella.

Nonetheless, Milly Williamson finds herself troubled by Edward's stern self-control and patterns of behaviour – such as the seemingly unintended physical harm that he inflicts on Bella – that indicate an abusive relationship between the pair (Williamson 2014: 87). Williamson, though, is loath to cede ground to commentators who are quick to dismiss the legions of young female fans that the series has acquired. She quotes wiseacre film journalists who bemoan the vampire's descent from Murnau's nightmarish *Nosferatu* to glittering teen pin-up (Jeffries, quoted in Williamson 2014: 85). Taking a closer look, Williamson finds that with Bella acting as the audience's surrogate, the narrative motivation throughout the series consists solely in passionate love, one that operates in defiance of the rational obstacles placed in the couple's path. It is this narrative motivation that allows the still relatively powerless teenage girl to assume a position of stardom within her own life story (Williamson 2014: 88). In contrast to the 1980s 'fantasies of achievement' (McRobbie 1991), *Twilight* presents a world in which passionate desire can single one out from the crowd.

The Posthuman Teenage Girl

The lush rural landscape of Forks, Washington in which *Twilight* takes place stands in marked contrast to the sunny Californian locales common to the 1990s teen movie, and to the subdued glamour of the New York streetscapes that provided the backdrop to *Spider-Man*. Perhaps most importantly for

Bella, the damp, temperate climate is particularly distinct from the arid climes of Phoenix, Arizona, from where she has arrived to live with her father. Hardwicke's cinematography is attentive to the variations of green that permeate the small town's surroundings. Certainly, the focus on the fecund potency of the woods that surround the small town reminds us of the many life forms that are supported there. Yet the green tinge that haunts the film's footage also underscores the strangeness of this place. As the analysis will demonstrate, while the film ostensibly presents a conventional high school romance narrative that culminates in the prom, the unusual setting draws attention to its differences from the tropes of the school film, which, as I demonstrate, have consequences for the film's construction of the posthuman.

The analysis of *Spider-Man* observed that Peter Parker constituted an archetypal nerd whose lack of physicality was apparent in the character's introduction through voiceover. In *Twilight*, too, Bella is introduced through voiceover, as she states somewhat cryptically, 'I'd never given much thought to how I might die . . . but dying in the place of someone you love seems like a pretty good way to go.' Bella's first words indicate an implicit belief in the persistence of *zoe* after death, since her statement implies a transition rather than a definitive end point. Since Bella will eventually be transformed into a vampire, and thereby killed in her human form, her statement is an apt one. The film's use of voiceover as the audience takes in the densely wooded landscape certainly serves to ground the narrative as being recounted from Bella's own perspective. While Peter's voiceover granted the character a presence in a scene from which he was otherwise absent, Bella's voiceover draws attention to her bodily vulnerability by evoking the very possibility of death.

The voiceover follows Meyer's first-person narration in recounting the events of *Twilight* from Bella's perspective. In this, the film is placed squarely in the tradition of the female gothic narrative. Both Catherine Spooner (2006) and Estella Tincknell (2009) identify an increased interest in female-oriented gothic narratives since the 1990s. Certainly, gothic-themed films have featured female characters some decades previously, for instance, *The Exorcist* (William Friedkin, 1973); *Carrie* (Brian De Palma, 1976); *Halloween* (John Carpenter, 1978) and *A Nightmare on Elm Street* (Wes Craven, 1984), to provide but a few examples. However, Spooner observes a distinct division between these films of the 1970s and 1980s, and those released since 1990. While female teenagers in the gothic films of earlier decades were depicted as overwhelmed by the forces they faced, those of the 1990s and beyond show their female characters taking control over these supernatural beings (Spooner 2006: 102). The exemplar here of course is the television series *Buffy the Vampire Slayer* (Fox, 1997–2003),[13] whose eponymous character (Sarah Michelle Gellar) is charged with saving the world from a scourge of vampires. While Bella does not herself possess supernatural powers, the narrative is propelled principally by her determination to discover more about, and integrate with, the vampires.

Bella, however, is distinct from the models of femininity previously established in these gothic narratives. Carol Clover's seminal analysis of the 1980s slasher film draws attention to the androgyny of the film's lone survivor, the 'final girl' (1992). Perhaps best exemplified by Laurie (Jamie Lee Curtis), the babysitter in *Halloween*, the final girl is noted not only for her honesty, integrity and virginity but also for her resourcefulness and cunning, thereby combining feminine and masculine qualities in a single figure (Clover 1992: 39). Buffy, meanwhile, presents a contradiction, as a figure of idealised, middle-class femininity who bears echoes of the final girl in her role as a slayer (Brown 2011: 191). In contrast to these representations of exceptional teen girlhood, Bella is conspicuous for her very ordinariness, neither particularly academic nor a homecoming queen in waiting. Instead she is presented as hesitant, unassuming and gawky. While the teen female protagonist has long provided a cypher for an encounter with alterity, it is typically the exceptional rather than the ordinary girl who is tasked with such an encounter.

Bella's instantiation of both the ordinary and the feminine moves the presentation of the female gothic seen in *Twilight* towards the traditionally 'female' genres of the melodrama and the romance. Scenes depicting Bella getting to grips with her life in a new part of the country as she rebuilds her relationship with her taciturn father certainly work to place *Twilight* within the frame of reference of melodrama, one that explains the film's unusual presentation of the high school. As was observed in Chapter 4, starting at a new school provokes considerable anxiety in the high school film. Indeed, it forms the basis of the entire plot of *Mean Girls*, as home-schooled Cady struggles to acclimatise to the cut-throat world of the American high school. In contrast, Bella settles into Forks High School uncannily easily, as she is swiftly integrated into Jessica's (Anna Kendrick) group of friends. *Twilight*, then, is at a remove from

Figure 6.3 Bella (Kristen Stewart) swiftly finds friends at Forks High School.

the school film While the film is happy to employ sites such as the cafeteria and the prom in the service of the narrative, it is clear that its attentions are directed elsewhere.

Anne-Helen Petersen draws attention to the film's 'amateurishness' in her examination of adult female fans of the *Twilight* saga (2012: 13). She notes, for instance, that the Cullens' make-up is slathered on, with clear tide marks showing the actors' real skin colour. Observing that *Twilight* allows viewers to reconnect with their teenage selves, Petersen locates the appeal of a film and book series that, she believes, ought to be below the notice of its otherwise discerning feminist fanbase. There is a sense, then, that the experience of overwrought emotion is critical to the evocation of the female teenage experience. Certainly, in contrast to many Hollywood teen movies of its period, which have become highly knowing and self-reflexive, *Twilight* remains unusually earnest, even heavy-handed, in its portrayal of the growing romance between Bella and Edward. An example of these tendencies occurs when Jessica introduces Bella to the Cullens at the high school cafeteria. As discussed in relation to *Mean Girls*, the figure of a more experienced student describing the school's social ecosystem to its latest *ingénue* is a commonplace one, typically handled humorously. However, in *Twilight* the event is staged to privilege the glamour of the Cullens in their white and grey outfits and strikingly dark eyes and hair, and the intensity of the gaze between Edward and Bella, which foregrounds the possibility of romance between them. The focus on the teenage girl's desires therefore orients the narrative away from the comedic delineation of teen archetypes, and towards the prioritisation of romantic desire.

Further invocations of the romance film are apparent when Edward and Bella meet for the first time in their biology class. As Bella turns to see Edward, now allocated as her lab partner, a fan behind her blows her long, wavy hair, such that she now presents a hyperbolic vision of feminine desirability. As the film cuts to Edward, though, we see the fan flutter up a piece of paper on his desk, conveying a sudden, unexpected interest. However, Edward's gestures signify disgust, as he puts his hand over his mouth, seemingly gagging at her presence. He then nudges the tapeworm specimen on the desk towards her, keeping his body oriented away from Bella as though wary of any inadvertent contact between them. Remaining silent throughout the class, Edward walks abruptly out of the door a split second before the bell signals the end of the session. So acute is his apparent distaste for Bella that she is prompted to check her hair for any unwanted odours.

Jeffers McDonald notes that the partners' initial dislike of one another is a common feature of the romance narrative, wherein the extent of their hatred is seen to mask the attributes they share (Jeffers McDonald 2012: 45). Consequently, the use of tropes from the romance narrative allows for the prospect of the relationship between a human and a vampire appearing a desirable outcome.

Discovering the Sparkling Other

Bernard Beck's contention that the female protagonists of recent vampire tales should be regarded as 'intergroup pioneers in establishing contact with these "alien" creatures' counters those who would regard Bella as the unwitting participant in a controlling and abusive relationship (Beck 2011: 92). This is not to say that there are not troubling aspects to Edward and Bella's coupledom, in which the latter is never on an entirely equal footing. Many such elements emerge in this and the next sections of the chapter. However, with a focus on the posthuman and resulting adolescent encounters with alterity, it is notable that it has been teenage girls – so recently acknowledged both as a potentially lucrative demographic, and as somewhat distinct from a film-making imaginary that continues to privilege the male – who have sought out the supernatural in the ways that Beck describes.

Bella gradually learns that Edward's apparent distaste for her is in fact a suppression of his desires. Her blood, he claims, is irresistible to him, his 'own personal brand of heroin', as he puts it. While he, in common with the other members of his clan, has learned to subsist on the blood of animals, there remains a latent desire for human blood, the vampire's instinctive choice. Edward's characterisation, then, establishes his rational control of his more predatory instincts, aligning him with the liberal humanist vision of the self-governing subject. However, he does demonstrate the extent of his powers to Bella in a sequence that both shows off his capabilities and aims to warn her off a relationship with him. Edward is keen to stress his positioning as a predator to Bella, stating 'as if you could outrun me', before flying off into the trees, and 'as if you could fight me off', when he uproots a tree. Nonetheless, his show of strength does not diminish Bella's desire for the vampire.

It is significant that this scene occurs in the midst of a luscious forest, in which Edward's balletic displays of speed and strength are framed in panning long shots that emphasise the breadth of the space. The camera takes in the tall trees letting in shafts of sunlight, as well as the mosses that cover the tree barks, ferns and other flora at the base of the trees. The camera is attentive to the many shades of green in the forest, which adds to the sense that the forest is teeming with life. With Bella and Edward's pale faces tinged with the green filter that characterises much of the film, the scene demonstrates the extent of the life that exists beyond the human. In this context, and in Bella's accepting gaze, Edward becomes merely another form of life to be understood, rather than feared. The parallelism generated by the forest's surroundings is emphasised as the pair lie together on the forest floor, staring into one another's eyes, while the camera encircles them from above. As a result, the characters become merely another two creatures in the forest, such that the taboo element of the relationship between human and vampire is elided.

As part of a bid to dissuade Bella from any further association with him, Edward shows her how his skin appears in sunlight. Her research into the occult portrayed the vampire as monstrous, prompting the audience to imagine that Edward's appearance in daylight will be similarly hideous. Conventional folklore holds that exposure to sunlight has deadly consequences for vampires (see Abbott 2009). However, the Cullens' avoidance of the sun is ascribed to the family's concern for their human neighbours. As Edward claims, 'they wouldn't know what to think'. Moving into the sunlight, Edward's skin appears to shimmer, sparkling 'like diamonds', to use Bella's description. Her encounter with alterity, then, is not horrifying, but attractive – one that provides a further aspect to Edward's desirability.

That Edward's skin reflects light is a significant deviation from the conventional representations of the vampire as a creature that thrives only in darkness. As a result, I argue that the vampires' sparkling surface in *Twilight* demonstrates the film's attentiveness not only to the ambiguities of sparkle in postfeminist media targeting girls, but also to the feminisation of the vampire in *Twilight*, as well as drawing attention to the vampire as a figure of whiteness and self-control. To unpick the first point, I draw from Mary Celeste Kearney's observation that sparkle and glitter are prevalent in contemporary media aimed at girls. Indeed, Kearney argues that sparkle 'vies with pink as the primary signifier of youthful femininity' (Kearney 2015: 263). The connection that Kearney identifies between glitter and girlhood chimes with Lisa Bode's assessment of the (largely unfavourable) critical coverage received by the films, which notes that *Twilight* offends (largely male) horror genre purists (Bode 2010: 708). Consequently, Edward's sparkling skin is instrumental in demonstrating his positioning as an object of desire for a teenage girl, whose romantic desire drives the narrative here.

Kearney is attentive to the multifaceted meanings produced by such sparkle and luminosity, following Moseley in her contention that in the frequent equation between glamour and magic, female power is conceived as a shimmering, ephemeral surface phenomenon (Moseley 2002: 408–9; Kearney 2015: 268). Kearney also cites *Twilight* as an example in which 'environmental sparkle' in the lovers' private spaces, such as the forest, confers sexual agency on its female protagonist. Yet her taxonomy of sparkle does not explore the meanings produced by Edward's sparkling skin. He, too, understands the power of surface, arguing that Bella is only taken with his 'camouflage ... everything about me is designed to draw you in'. While he is feminised in his depiction as an object, as Bella gazes in wonder at his sparkling skin, Edward's luminosity is not part of his glamorous packaging, but a symptom of his vampiric alterity.

Indeed, his repeated assertions of his predatory speed and strength work to re-establish his mastery and contain his feminisation.[14]

Edward's luminosity can be further connected with Dyer's theorisation of whiteness (1997) and with it, the Western associations of whiteness with knowledge, power and goodness. It is no accident that the philosophical ideas that underpin liberal humanism were established in a period known as the Enlightenment. Vampires are known for their pallor, demonstrating their embodiment, and threat, of death (Dyer 1997: 222). The paleness of Bella is also remarked upon in the film, as her new friends are surprised to discover that she, despite coming from the sunny climes of Arizona, has no hint of a tan. Edward's skin, though, is described as being 'like marble', an extreme whiteness and hardness that speaks to the rigidity of his self-control. In *Twilight*, then, the vampire is a figure of glamour, old-fashioned, gentlemanly values and wealth – yet also of death, attesting to Dyer's contention that the vampire constitutes 'what whiteness aspires to and also fears' (1997: 222).

Edward's vampirism and pallor demonstrate his embodiment of an extreme whiteness in which rationality, control and the spectre of death feature prominently. *Twilight* sets up a dialectic in which these 'white' traits are constructed in opposition to the non-white Quileute tribe, who are deemed animalistic and unrefined by comparison. Tellingly, Jacob's surname is Black, underscoring his representation of the non-white. As the series progresses, Jacob is increasingly characterised by spectacles of emotionality, which contrast to the rationality and control displayed by the Cullens.[15] A further binary is also established between what Edward believes to be Bella's recklessness in her desire for him, and the restrictions he places on his own cravings for her. Consequently, there is a tension in presenting the teenage girl as a vehicle for encountering alterity in the film, and the values upheld by the film, which continue to be those of the white, masculine and upper-class; implicitly those of liberal humanism.

Ethics and Responsibility

Throughout *Twilight* much is made of the fact that the Cullens, in defiance of conventional vampiric mores, do not consume human blood. Instead, under the aegis of their patriarch, Carlisle Cullen (Peter Facinelli), the vampires have learned to content themselves with drinking only the blood of animals. So conscious is Carlisle of his tentative position in Forks that he has forged an agreement with the Quileute werewolves, stating that the vampires will not trespass their land and the Quileute in turn will not harm the human population. In both cases, neither party is to reveal the other's vampiric or lycanthropic traits. Consequently, the people of Forks largely uphold Carlisle not only as a respected physician, who may well be in demand in more glamorous locales, but also as a seemingly prolific foster parent. Under Carlisle's stewardship the

Cullens have assumed a protective role over the human population, which demonstrates humans' vulnerability and dependence on the non-human.

Derrida's consideration of the 'wholly other they call animal' – the very essence of alterity – elucidates the critical perspective on the human enacted in *Twilight* (Derrida 2002: 383). Contemplating a cat's gaze on his naked body, Derrida considers how his body might be regarded as meat to the animal, thereby illustrating the anthropocentrism of the perspective that conventionally regards animals as subject to the whims of humankind. Indeed, Derrida argues that the relationship between humans and animals is typically one of subjection, since animals lack the language to demand changes in their treatment, which if applied to other humans, would amount to nothing less than genocide (Derrida 2002: 389). Instead it is the capacity for suffering, not dissimilar to Braidotti's advocacy of *zoe*, which ought to be of primary consideration. Unlike humanist accounts, the ability to suffer does not depend on one's capacity for reason and intellect. Derrida's account of animality draws attention to the intellectual blindness in human relationships with animals, and to how, as the cat views the human body as a source of meat, the animality of humans themselves might be understood.

As Edward reveals his relationship with Bella to his family, she is increasingly positioned in ways that demonstrate her animality from the perspective of the vampire. Braidotti calls on Jorge Luis Borges's typology of human–animal relationships, which groups animals into three distinct types: 'those we watch television with, those we eat and those we are scared of' (Borges in Braidotti 2013: 68). Though wry in intent, Borges's categorisation can assist in determining how Bella's relationship with the other Cullens might be conceptualised. Certainly, as Edward has been at pains to point out, Bella remains prey for all vampires, despite the family's pact not to drink human blood. Even in this context, though, members of the family, notably Jasper (Jackson Rathbone) and Alice (Ashley Greene), comment favourably on the scent of Bella's blood, which Edward has likewise found so irresistible. Perceiving her thus, the viewer is reminded that for the vampires Bella falls into the second category of animal life, namely those we eat. Anthropocentric notions of physical attractiveness are consequently displaced in favour of discernment of qualities that we, as human viewers, cannot comprehend. While Meyer describes Bella's appearance and personality as unremarkable, the vampires confer other aspects of attractiveness which are not grounded in conventional human criteria.

Yet Bella also serves as what Haraway terms a companion species, when she is invited to join the vampires while they play baseball. In contrast to the typical norms of this summer pastime, the Cullens play the sport only when they are sure that there will be a storm, which not only ensures that humans are unlikely to disturb them but also that the sounds of the storm will mask the extraordinary noises produced as the vampires hit the ball far into the distance, only for another to swoop and catch the player out. Bella's role here is simply to watch and keep careful score. Here, she becomes an animal with whom one might watch television, charged simply with being a passive presence for its master while they enjoy the activities that interest them. While the Cullens' positioning remains constant, as temporarily tamed predators, that of the human morphs in order to serve the vampires' purpose.

The vampires have been presented thus far as a homogenous group. However, when the baseball game is interrupted by a nomadic troupe of vampires with a feral appearance, it is clear that the Cullens comprise only one particular instantiation of the creature. The group comprised of James (Cam Giganet), Victoria (Rachelle Lefevre) and Laurent (Edi Gathegi) reinstate Bella as legitimate prey, as James leeringly remarks, 'I see you brought a snack.' The Cullens are positioned as aristocratic in the film by virtue of their wealth, their presentation as a family and the impressive lineage that family possesses, apparent when Bella notices an old oil painting in which Carlisle features prominently. In contrast, this other group of vampires appears to exist outside of the boundaries and covenants that the Cullens have established with the local community. While the Cullens are shown to perceive their responsibility for those that lack their predatory capacity, James's vampire clan continues to live in accordance with their instincts and feed from the blood of humans. This is an existence outside the Cullens' self-prescribed responsibility for the other. Following Derrida, then, it is these vampires that constitute the wholly Other of the human, and whose key players are killed by the end of the film.

The inevitable clash that ensues between the two groups sees Bella hospitalised when James throws her to the ground. Having saved her, the end of the film sees Edward calling at her father's house to accompany Bella to the high school prom. Waiting for Bella, Edward and her father sit opposite one another silently, allowing the viewer to contrast Edward's vampiric pallor and rectitude with the father's more casual posture as they both wait for Bella. The film then cuts to a close-up of Bella's plaster cast as she walks down the stairs, before finally panning up her body to reveal the dress that she intends to wear for the prom. This sequence closely resembles the equivalent scene in *She's All That*, in which the characters wait to see Laney's made-over appearance for the first time. In that film the scene's importance was signalled by Mackenzie's announcement of Laney's entrance, the use of a non-diegetic soundtrack, and previous scenes that portrayed the labour of her transformation. In contrast, Bella's entrance receives no prior introduction, her walk down the stairs takes place in silence, and her choice of dress was borrowed at the last minute from a friend. Whereas close-ups of Laney's feet showed that she was wearing stilettos, here Bella wears an ungainly plaster cast on one foot and a trainer on the other. While the former was seen to acquiesce to the norms of hegemonic

THE POSTHUMAN AND THE TEEN MOVIE

Figure 6.4 Bella's (Kristen Stewart) entrance recalls the makeover scenes of *She's All That*.

femininity, Bella's footwear, and the gendered ambivalence of the grey leggings beneath her dress, demonstrate her distance from this construction.

Bella's distaste for the prom is signalled earlier in the film, foretelling her later distance from the event. While Alice and Jessica excitedly try on prom dresses in a local shop, Bella stares out of the window absent-mindedly and leaves with Edward at the first opportunity. At the event itself Bella is reluctant to enter the dance hall, while Edward primly reminds her that 'prom is an important rite of passage' which, like so many others before her, she must simply tolerate. The prom scenes' difference from the majority of the film is indicated through shot scale. Earlier in the film, close framing on Bella and Edward portrayed their growing desire and fascination for one another. Further, as our understanding of Edward's situation develops, the audience is able to scrutinise his face for evidence of the conflict between his desires and his self-control. In contrast, scenes at the prom are depicted in long shot, inviting the audience to share the pair's critical distance from the events. Their interactions with other students are limited, only waving at Alice and Jessica from across the hall, while Bella recoils from one student's clumsy attempt to engage her in a dance. Unlike other films in which the prom features, which emphasise its primary importance, *Twilight* depicts the event as small and meaningless.

As the pair leave the event to dance in the bandstand, Bella demonstrates that she has developed a critical perspective on the human, such that she now wants to become a vampire. While Edward objects, stating that to transform her into a vampire would be to kill her, Bella argues that 'I'm dying every day,' echoing Braidotti's contention that death constitutes a precondition of life itself (Braidotti 2013: 132). In other films we have seen how the prom is intended, as Edward claims, to be an important rite of passage that celebrates heteronormative, sexual coming of age. Certainly, Bella and Edward's slow dance conforms to expected behaviour at the prom. However, Bella declares that she is ready to become a vampire 'right now', acquiescing to what turns out only to be a tender kiss on her neck. In this, she conveys her refusal to grow into an adult, and therefore the formative purpose of the prom. As Bella states that she won't 'give in', and that her decision has definitively been made, the film is shown to valorise her perspective. In *Twilight*, then, the teenage girl is both an embodiment and an agent of the posthuman.

CHRONICLE (JOSH TRANK, 2012)

Of the three films discussed in this chapter, *Chronicle* comes closest to Hayles's vision of the posthuman, wherein human subjectivity has become embroiled with those of surrounding machines (Hayles 1999: xv). As this analysis will demonstrate, Andrew's (Dane DeHaan) decision to document everything that happens to him using his video camera begins a series of processes that cause the displacement of his subjectivity, first becoming intertwined with that of his camera, before he (and the camera) acquires still greater powers. Nonetheless, in this book's last case study, there are echoes of the family melodrama in the mould of *Rebel Without a Cause*, the film with which this book began. Jim Stark's misunderstood, alienated adolescence is reflected in Andrew's social unease and loathing for his father, Richard (Michael Kelly).[16] *Chronicle* also draws from Nicholas Ray's teenage classic in portraying his family's woes as stemming (albeit indirectly) from a thwarted masculinity. As a firefighter who is no longer able to work as a result of an injury, Richard is depicted as a failed patriarch who subsists in an abusive, alcoholic stupor from the money he received in compensation. In turn, Andrew's mother, Karen (Bo Petersen) is frail and dying. She, then, is an individual who requires, rather than provides, care. Living within a crumbling family unit, and with few friends at school, Andrew is portrayed as a vulnerable, lonely character.

Despite these echoes of the family melodrama, *Chronicle* resists easy classification. The encounter with a mysterious object located underground that grants Andrew, Matt (Alex Russell) and Steve (Michael B. Jordan) telekinetic powers positions the film in the science fiction genre, although its location there is diminished by the teenagers' incuriosity about the source of their powers.[17] Instead, the characters are principally interested in developing their new telekinetic abilities in the simple adolescent pleasures of blowing wind up cheerleaders' skirts, or causing confusion in a supermarket by having products fly off the shelves and hitting unsuspecting grocery shoppers. Consequently, the film's classification as a low-budget offshoot of the superhero blockbuster emerges as a more apt characterisation. Indeed, the characters' inadvertent discovery of their powers and their subsequent practice likens *Chronicle* to similar scenes in which Peter Parker gets to grips with his new powers in *Spider-Man*.

In contrast to the superhero film, though, *Chronicle* can be seen to portray the consequences of an absence of the morality and responsibility that were at the heart of Raimi's film. Rather than save the people of New York from the destruction of their city, Andrew comes to perpetuate such mindless destruction in his guise as an 'apex predator'.

The instantiation of the posthuman in *Chronicle* emerges most obviously in the integration of Andrew's subjectivity with his camera. The film has erroneously been deemed an example of the 'found-footage' genre; that is, films that create a conceit in which the footage the audience is watching has been acquired in the wake of some extraordinary events.[18] A notable recent example of such a film is *Cloverfield* (Dan Trachtenberg, 2008), which opens with an official-looking title card which states that the film to follow is 'classified material' obtained from a digital SD card that was fortuitously recovered following an extra-terrestrial attack. This extra-textual baggage, which deems the film 'evidence', alongside its knowingly amateurish aesthetic, work to grant the events of *Cloverfield* a spurious realism. In the case of *Chronicle*, too, the use of the handheld camera grounds the film's more far-fetched narrative elements with a semblance of the ordinary, and by extension, the real. In its integration of perspectives that are beyond the possible scope of Andrew's camera, I will demonstrate that the film's integration of human and machine subjects is far more complex than is implied by its critical positioning as a found-footage film.

Chronicle secured positive reviews for its 'fresh' approach to the material, with Peter Bradshaw of the *Guardian* praising the film's unusual camera angles and range of movement (Bradshaw 2012). Perhaps because of its low-key release and its cast and film-making personnel being comprised largely of unknowns,[19] the film secures only a modest mention in Shary's revised *Generation Multiplex*, seemingly making it a minor work in the teen movie genre. However, with hindsight, it is now possible to perceive the film as a significant precursor to recent teen horror films *Unfriended* (Levan Gabriadze, 2014) and *Friend Request* (Simon Verhoeven, 2016), in which teenage subjectivities being enmeshed with technology is a given that is taken up to supernatural effect. *Chronicle*, then, is a significant example of the recent posthuman teen movie.

Aspects of the posthuman are explored both in the teens' acquisition of their powers, and later, in the exploration of Andrew's (a)morality. In his aimless destruction of 'lesser' beings, he is shown to foreground the latent hypocrisy of humans' treatment of animals and, indeed, of each other. *Chronicle* portrays Andrew, a lonely working-class teenager who is frequently set upon by his bullying father and has few social ties outside of his cousin, Matt. After a party that Andrew begrudgingly attends, Matt and class president Steve come across a mysterious underground object that grants them powers. However, as

Andrew hones his powers to a greater extent than the other two teenagers, his urge for destruction and violence prove an overwhelming force against which Matt and Steve's worthier intentions are powerless. An analysis of *Chronicle* from a posthuman perspective promises to interrogate the ways in which the film complicates and undermines the primacy of the human.

Teen with a Movie Camera

Undoubtedly the most formally striking aspect of *Chronicle* is the positioning of the camera within the diegesis, which occurs as a result of Andrew's decision to 'film everything from here on out'. The film's 'chronicle' is therefore ostensibly one of his life, told from his own perspective. As a consequence of the film's amateur aesthetics and diegetic reference to the camera, I have noted that a range of commentators have referred to *Chronicle* as a 'found-footage' film (Bradshaw 2012; Robey 2012; Heller-Nicholas 2014). Common to these critics is a sense in which, by the time of *Chronicle*'s release in 2012, the technique has become a 'gimmicky' one (Robey 2012) whose ability to disrupt the audience's relationship with the truth has long since waned. A key antecedent here, of course, is *The Blair Witch Project* (Daniel Myrnick, Eduardo Sanchez, 1999), whose affect was derived not only from the shakily viewed action on screen, but also extra-textual baggage purporting that its footage had been serendipitously tracked down in the wake of some supernatural phenomenon.

In contrast to those who regard *Chronicle* as aping these filming practices, Celia Lam describes the film's aesthetics in terms of Lev Manovich's conceptualisation of 'DV (digital video) realism' (2001). That is, the 'raw, gritty and

Figure 6.5   Teen with a movie camera.

occasionally grainy imagery associated with consumer grade handheld video cameras', with a movement that demonstrates the presence of its human operator (Lam 2014: 84). As Lam points out, although the majority of the film's footage is ostensibly filmed using Andrew's Canon XL1 Mini DV camera, which is shown within the diegesis, there are a number of scenes that adopt other perspectives, particularly that of high school vlogger Casey (Ashley Hinshaw) and those of the CCTV cameras of the various buildings that Andrew goes on to destroy (Lam 2014: 88). There is, furthermore, no dramatic conceit stating how the footage was indeed 'found'. As a result, *Chronicle* does not possess the distancing aspect of the found-footage narrative, wherein the film is positioned as a narrative of events in the past. Rather, the story is placed in the present, and with insight from a posthuman perspective, can be seen to stage the gradual rapprochement between Andrew's subjectivity and his camera.

The film opens with a view of the camera, which is positioned on a tripod facing the bedroom door, on which a full-length mirror allows us to take in the set-up. As Andrew kneels immediately behind the camera his face and body merge with the mechanics of the camera, already foretelling its alignment with his subjectivity. On the other side of the door, Andrew's father is heard drunkenly demanding entrance into his son's bedroom, the sounds of which subside when he hears that the interaction is being filmed. Consequently, the camera is shown to have a protective role for Andrew, one that is implicitly recalled in the later footage filmed from surveillance cameras, which are fitted with the aim of safeguarding their occupants. The use of the camera as a defensive mechanism also echoes its use in the much-emulated *Paranormal Activity* (Oren Peli, 2009), whose doomed protagonists naïvely declare that 'we'll film it all, and we'll be fine'. The characters of *Chronicle* and *Paranormal Activity* alike understand the camera's privileged relationship with the truth, which, they believe, will later secure them the assistance they need to change their situations. As I shall demonstrate, the presentation of reality in *Chronicle* is not a straightforward one, which complicates the audience's sympathies with Andrew.

Andrew and the camera are increasingly integrated as his day progresses. When characters appear, their eyeline flickers between the camera's lens and into a space immediately above the lens, where we assume Andrew can be found, holding the camera. As Andrew introduces his surroundings to the camera – 'this is my mom', 'this is my school', 'this is my street' – the audience is given to question, as his mother does, 'who's the audience' for his film project. While his mother speaks directly into the camera, this is not an instance of direct address as Tom Brown describes it (2012), wherein a character looks directly out of the diegesis to the non-diegetic viewer. Rather, it is clear that she is looking at her son through the camera's lens. In portraying Andrew's express intent to present the facts of his own life, seemingly for his own benefit, *Chronicle* is distinct from other examples of the found-footage film.

For Lam, the camera serves throughout much of the film as Andrew's emotional doppelgänger, such that the movements of the camera – be they still and floating, or darting wildly out of his control – can be seen to stand in for his state of mind (Lam 2014: 88). Scenes at the high school reinforce the equation made between Andrew and his camera. Although his popular cousin Matt drives him to school, their association ends at the school gates, such that Andrew spends most of the day alone with his camera. Walking through the school corridors, the camera's lens takes in the students' scornful glares as Andrew describes the scene. His descriptions can be seen to possess two key functions in the narrative. In the first place, the undramatic content of the scenes he describes establishes the film's verisimilitude, which later scenes will call into question. Of more significance, though, is the way in which Andrew's narration draws attention to the film's sound design, which presents the immediacy of his voice in contrast to the other, naturalistic sounds heard around the school. In accordance with the film's DV realist aesthetic, the audio is enslaved to the film's visual content, abruptly changing in volume and immediacy in tandem with changes in the images shown. In contrast, Andrew's voice remains immediate in these scenes, demonstrating the equation between the scenes shown and his own subjectivity.

Other characters' actions in scenes at the school show the extent to which Andrew's subjectivity, and in particular his emotional state, is tied in with his camera. When he sits on the bleachers 'where I eat my lunch', Andrew places the camera immediately behind him so that it can share his perspective (and free up his hands so he can eat). The resulting wide shot depicts a group of cheerleaders practising their routine in the far-left hand side of the frame. The perspective that we see through the camera's lens shows that they are not the object of Andrew's focus. Nevertheless, one of the cheerleaders objects to his presence, remarking that his filming is 'super-creepy'. Despite his denials, the cheerleader remains convinced that the camera serves as a vehicle for Andrew's voyeuristic tendencies. That Andrew and his camera are considered one and the same is made further apparent when he encounters a group of bullies within the school itself. This group not only mock Andrew, but his 'lame 2004' camera as well. When he is knocked to the ground, so too is the camera, conveniently still recording, as it is tossed among the group before being glided across the floor to its rightful owner. The abuse that he receives is thus reflected in the treatment of the camera, and the resulting physical force perceived by the audience.

When Andrew is bullied and his camera is taken away from him, it is clear that it is his emotional state, rather than his physicality that is aligned with the camera. Consequently, the camera not only facilitates the portrayal of, but in fact instantiates, what he wants to represent of his experience. As discussed, the banality of Andrew's story, combined with DV realist film techniques, serve to ground the narrative in the world of the real. This, we are led to believe, is an authentic account of a lonely, bullied teenager's life, thereby securing the audience's sympathy with DeHaan's awkward male lead, who will eventually become the film's antagonist. Yet elements of the footage draw attention to possibilities of its manipulation, and therefore call into question Andrew's account of the miseries of his school and home life as they are presented here. When he and Matt drive to school, there is a jump cut when Matt goofily sings along with the car radio. What is more, on a number of occasions, we see Andrew watching the footage back using a laptop, scenes that demonstrate at least the possibility of manipulating the apparently raw footage with which we are presented. A question is raised here as to the possibility of omissions in the day, which might make Andrew's later behaviour towards the community considerably less sympathetic.[20] Even before the teenager acquires supernatural powers, Andrew is presented as a cyborg, a teenager whose consciousness has merged with that of his camera.

Coming of Age in *Chronicle*

The beginning of the film portrays Andrew as lonely and vulnerable. Inclined to introspection, he has few friends and, as has been observed, engages with others primarily through his camera. All this changes when he reluctantly attends a party with Matt, where, with Steve, he discovers a mysterious crystalline object underground. Andrew's sexual coming of age is therefore refracted through his and his friends' acquisition of supernatural powers as a result of contact with this object. As discussed at the beginning of this chapter, a number of films have framed teenagers' gradual attainment of adult sexual identities as monstrous, owing to the liminality that teenagers embody. Conversely, in *Chronicle*, it is Andrew's virginity that is shown to underpin his monstrous destruction.

Given the connections made between teenagers' monstrous transformations and puberty (Klein 2011), it is significant that this mystery object is implicitly coded as female. It is no accident that it is precisely a cavern to which Matt and Steve excitedly lead Andrew, so that he can film their discovery. Andrew's shaky camerawork as the group run towards the cave foregrounds the disorientation he experiences, which is then transferred to the viewer. Steve, Matt and finally Andrew enter the cave, and find themselves in a deep network of subterranean tunnels. Barbara Creed's description of the monstrous womb as one that is characterised by dark, unknowable spaces and networks of tunnels certainly chimes with the presentation of this cave in *Chronicle* (Creed 2012: 43–6). Observing that the abject, monstrous womb is most often found in the horror film, Creed proposes that it is fear of the womb's generative power, combined with its raw assertion of sexual difference, which lies at the root of its uncanny potential to compel and disgust in equal measure (Creed 2012: 43–6). At the nexus of the cave's tunnels sits a translucent crystalline structure through which it is possible to see a network of arteries and branches, complicating its positioning as either organic or constructed. The object's disruptive potential is demonstrated in its ability to affect organic matter, such as the droplet of water that remains suspended from the tip of Steve's nose, and Andrew's digital camera, through which disturbances in the visual and audio feed are registered.

The teenagers' encounter with the monstrous feminine complicates their construction of gender and their sexual coming-of-age narrative. Following an abrupt cut that appears to signal their ejection from the cave, Andrew, Matt and Steve are shown in a rather more ordinary milieu, showing off their new powers for the camera as they experiment with controlling the trajectory of a ball in mid-air. Even at this early stage Andrew is shown to be the strongest of the three, able to make the baseball hover at his eye level. His strength in comparison to the other two characters calls to be read in terms of his virginity. When the teenagers entered the caves, they did so in order of their level of sexual experience, such that Steve entered first, followed by Matt, and lastly Andrew. In contrast, as the three show off their powers to one another, Steve is shown to be the least competent of the group. It seems that the teenagers' acquisition of sexual identity is inversely proportionate to their ability to develop these supernatural abilities.

Pete Falconer rightly points out that virginity cannot verifiably be discerned from outward appearances. And yet, he argues, virginity often finds expression through costuming that suggests childlikeness and, given the historical significance of female virginity in particular, the 'closedness' of bodies (Falconer 2010: 134). The critical instability of the concept is indicated by the elision between being a virgin and simply 'looking like one' (Falconer 2010: 134). In *Chronicle*, Andrew's virginity is claimed through overt referencing of the fact, his introversion and his costuming. What is more, while Matt and Steve both wear considerably more 'adult' clothing, Andrew is consistently found in jeans and a zipped-up hooded sweatshirt. Combined with his small stature, his zipped sweatshirt (with which he is even identified by Steve) closes him off from the world around him and cements the character's positioning as virginal. Andrew's virginal potency, when positioned alongside his troublesome home life and loneliness at school, recalls the woes of Carrie (Sissy Spacek), the 'terrifying and terrified' teenager of Brian de Palma's 1976 film of the same name (Sobchack 1986: 73). Carrie's powers first become apparent soon after her first menstrual period, which occurs in the communal showers at school. In *Chronicle* that incident of female coming of age is invoked in its three male characters, as the object at the centre of the caves elicits nosebleeds from Matt, Steve and Andrew. Consequently, although Shelley Stamp is surely correct that Carrie's monstrousness stems in part from her sexual difference from a presumed male norm of aggression (Stamp 1991: 36), it is striking that the nosebleed – a cypher for the menstrual period – signifies the bond between these male teenagers. When, later in the film, Matt's nose begins to bleed, he intuitively understands that 'Andrew's in trouble.' The monstrous cyborg identities that disrupt the centrality of the human in *Chronicle* are also seen to undermine the heteronormative gender distinction that continues to structure human experience.

Andrew's missed opportunity to lose his virginity demonstrates his monstrousness. At a party, Matt and Steve operate the camera while Andrew is pursued by Monica (Anna Wood), who is impressed by the magic show he has staged earlier that evening. When Andrew and Monica enter a bedroom, Steve is keen to build up the moment, excitedly declaring 'Behind this very door, my boy Andrew is becoming a man!' Yet almost immediately afterwards Monica quickly emerges from the room, calling Andrew a 'freak', while he is left with vomit on his suit jacket lapels. Like Carrie, Andrew, too, is 'uninitiated in the world of sex [and so] belongs in the world of violence' (Falconer 2010: 133). Falconer draws attention to the importance placed on virginity in the horror film, and observes the significant parallel between Clover's final girl and her monstrous antagonist. As discussed, Clover constructs the final girl as sexually reluctant, particularly in comparison to her peers, while the psycho killer is also depicted as sexually inexperienced.[21] In the horror film, then, it appears that virginity both destabilises gender distinction, as Clover observes in the case of the final girl, and as a consequence, confers monstrosity if retained too long. In contrast to teen horror films in which it is the liminality of puberty that is depicted as monstrous, *Chronicle* portrays the elongation of virginity and, by extension, childhood, as the rightful location of the monstrous. As we will see in the final section of the case study, it is in part Andrew's childlike abnegation of responsibility to those around him that causes him to perpetuate the mindless destruction with which the film concludes.

An 'Apex Predator'

In analysing *Twilight*, I argued that the vampires' perception of the human characters as prey was a posthuman one, since it provided a critical perspective on humanity's unspoken dominance as a species. As *Chronicle* progresses Andrew becomes increasingly alienated from his friends, and interested only in furthering his own powers. When this draws him into conflict with Steve, who points out his hubris, Andrew fights with and kills the class president. Throughout the film, Andrew has become used to levitating the camera into various positions such that he can be seen as though from the position of another character. As a result, the camera's movement comes to be an index of Andrew's emotional state; swooping smoothly when he feels ebullient, while his volatility is signalled through jerky movements. In one scene, Andrew stares into the camera to state that 'a lion doesn't feel guilty when it kills a deer', appearing to imply that the absence of remorse in this scenario is the 'natural' way of things. The film's destructive concluding scenes portray Andrew's ever-increasing distance from the human. However, I demonstrate that the camera, once a vehicle for representing Andrew's perspective on his experience, comes to be aligned with other characters and perspectives that continue to uphold the centrality of the human.

Andrew's mother's increased frailty brings about his transformation into the self-styled 'apex predator'. When attempting to acquire the medication she requires, he discovers that his father has been unable to pay the pharmacist, who will now no longer dispense the drugs. Seeking upwards of $700, Andrew holds up a nearby petrol station, opening the cash register himself and using his powers to pour the cash directly into his bag. He is able briefly to abscond with the money before the petrol station employee pursues and shoots at him with a shotgun, which, being in a petrol station, causes a large explosion. Tellingly, this latter scene, in which Andrew attempts to leave the scene of the robbery, is filmed from the perspective of the garage's CCTV camera rather than his own camera, which continues to accompany his movements. Such cameras are commonly held to observe objectively the details of the incidents they record. Indeed, we are no longer positioned alongside Andrew, but are encouraged to view him at an impartial distance, as a spectacle with which we have only a limited involvement. As Lam notes, the resulting distance created by this alternative positioning diminishes the empathy that Andrew's camera once commanded (Lam 2014: 96).

Andrew's violence reaches its zenith at the hospital where he is treated for injuries sustained at the petrol station. Lying in a hospital bed, he learns that his mother has died at the very moment when he was committing the robbery. Viewed from Andrew's own levitating camera, we see his father issuing splenetic invectives over the worthlessness of his son, at which point Andrew unexpectedly grabs his arm. Assuming control, he destroys the room, and with it, his own camera. Consequently, the film cuts such that these actions are now portrayed from the point of view of the hospital's own surveillance footage. These cameras, which are used frequently in the film's closing scenes, decrease the audience's well-established empathy with Andrew's vulnerability and loneliness. Once again, the audience is encouraged to view the scene as though from the perspective of an objective bystander. In the absence of Andrew's own camera, it is now that of Casey through which we principally view the remaining scenes. Matt, whom Casey most often films, is a far more conventional

Figure 6.6   Andrew (Dane DeHaan) is filmed by onlookers.

teenager than either Andrew or Steve, being neither exceptional (like Steve) nor alienated (like Andrew). Matt can therefore be seen to represent an ordinary human perspective with which the audience can readily identify.

Matt's perspective as an embodiment of humanity and ordinariness, as well as the perspectives of fearful onlookers, brings the film to a close. As our view of Andrew is increasingly supplied by CCTV footage of the buildings he mindlessly destroys, our empathy with his emotional state, as a character whose mother has just died, is diminished in favour of an objectified spectacle of destruction. Perhaps the most telling episode of his objectification occurs when Andrew circles the Seattle Space Needle. When the occupants instinctively grab their smartphones to record the bizarre spectacle of a floating teenager in a hospital gown, he breaks the windows of the restaurant in order to summon these devices to him, such that they, and their voyeuristic lenses, surround his levitating body. The film then fleetingly cuts between these onlookers' various devices so that we see Andrew from a number of different angles. In contrast to the long takes associated with Andrew's use of his own camera, which conferred a sense of intimacy between camera and operator, these are merely short glimpses through the lenses of the spectators' devices, demonstrating their voyeuristic lack of emotional investment with the scene (Lam 2014: 94). Unlike Matt, Andrew now appears to be entirely transformed beyond the realm of the human emotional experience.

Now that Andrew is depicted as beyond the scope of the human and our perspectives are lodged with Matt, it is only a matter of time before the latter kills Andrew. In so doing, Matt can be seen to uphold the primacy of the human, even as he himself possesses powers that render him distinct from most. Nonetheless, the film's closing scenes see him carrying out the wish expressed by himself, Steve and Andrew, namely to travel around the world. Accordingly, Matt films the moment of his arrival in Tibet, addressing the camera *as though it were* his friend. As Matt leaves the camera in the midst of the Himalayas, *Chronicle* presents the possibility that Andrew's subjectivity, once integrated with the camera, is now embodied by it. The film can be seen to chart the transformation from human to posthuman.

Conclusion

This book has demonstrated that the teenager is engaged in a process of becoming, while this chapter has specifically addressed the question of what exactly the teenager may become in this process. Certainly, as has been observed both in this chapter and elsewhere, the teenager has been perceived as something other than fully human. In contrast to the relative stability offered by the identities of childhood and adulthood, the teenager's liminality brings with it the spectre of monstrousness.

This chapter has explored the possible identities that teenagers might assume, all of which move the characters beyond the conventional capacities of the human. In *Spider-Man* Peter assumes the identity represented by the film's hybrid title. Neither fully spider nor man, the character strives both to assimilate himself into human society and to carve out a position outside it, as an ally of the human population with the ability to save them from other, darker forces at work. While Peter's transformation into Spider-Man is accidental, occurring due to an escaped spider at the lab, in *Twilight* Bella is determined to become a vampire, and in so doing to renounce her humanity. The film frames her steadfastness as exemplifying the strength of her love for Edward, although she does not become a vampire in this particular film. *Chronicle* sees a return to the serendipitous transformation that occurred in *Spider-Man*. Yet Andrew deliberately works on his skills, eventually rejecting the friendship offered by Matt and Steve in favour of mindless destruction.

It is striking that while the three films see the characters coming to terms with their positioning as somewhat other than human, they nevertheless do so in the frame of reference offered by humanism. Indeed, considerations of ethics, responsibility and self-control are all brought to the fore, even when, as in Andrew's case, characters choose to disregard them. In all the films analysed here, posthuman characters are divided into distinct types; those who continue to adhere to the norms of humanism, and those who reject them. Thus Peter Parker/Spider-Man is pitted against Norman Osborn/the Green Goblin, while *Twilight* sees the Cullens, who subsist on roadkill, deflect the more predatory, nomadic tribe of vampires who are passing through the area. Finally, while Andrew finds destructive potential in his telekinetic powers, the film (and his camera) effectively abandon him for Matt, who finds a simple joy in his ability to fly around the world. In all cases, it is the character more sympathetic to the humanistic worldview who ultimately prevails.

Yet in their very existence these posthuman characters demonstrate the contingency of the human and, in turn, of humanism. The potency of Spider-Man, in comparison to the weedy Peter Parker and the weak masses of New York City, demonstrates the vulnerability of the human population to aggressors that are arguably of their own making, being produced by genetic modifications at the forefront of science. Similarly, in *Twilight*, the vampires regard humans as prey and provide alternative criteria for attractiveness, where the scent of blood trumps the focus on physical appearance that dominates discussions of idealised femininity in the Hollywood teen movie. *Chronicle* provides no explanation for the source of the teenagers' powers. Yet the film speaks to concerns voiced in the popular media about the enmeshment of teenagers' lives with the devices that connect them to one another. That it is the teenager that provides the locus of such concerns as to the continued viability of the human is doubtless significant. It speaks not only to the perennial othering of teenagers that has been so central to the construction of adolescence on screen, but also to increasing concerns for the viability of the human race into the future.

Notes

1. See CNN's recent piece on the discovery that American teenagers spend nine hours per day with screen media: <http://edition.cnn.com/2015/11/03/health/teens-tweens-media-screen-use-report> (last accessed 30 March 2017).
2. I am thinking in particular of the *Divergent* (2014–) and *Maze Runner* (2014–) series.
3. McAllister, Gordon and Jancovich report that, at the time of writing, Marvel represented 37 per cent of the total comic book market to DC Comics' 33 per cent (2006: 108).
4. Figures taken from Box Office Mojo: <http://www.boxofficemojo.com/movies/?id=spiderman.htm> (last accessed 30 March 2017).
5. As if to demonstrate the endless fascination with Peter Parker's metamorphosis into his superhero counterpart, 2012 saw the reboot of the franchise, this time with Andrew Garfield as the eponymous hero in *The Amazing Spider-Man* (Marc Webb, 2012).
6. The aversion to 2002 in particular, particularly in the context of the destruction of New York City, might also be attributed to the then-recent terrorist attack on the World Trade Center in September 2001. Indeed, the film's advance posters in the late summer of 2001 saw Spider-Man between the Twin Towers of the World Trade Center. Following the terrorist attacks, these posters were banned.
7. As if to emphasise the relative realism of Spider-Man as a hero whom working-class male teenagers might aspire to emulate, the characters of *Kick-Ass* (Matthew Vaughn, 2010) and *Scott Pilgrim vs. the World* (Edgar Wright, 2010) see nerdish teenage boys aspire – and fail – to become superheroes.
8. For Shary, Laney is 'nerdly', an ungainly descriptor that fits her lack of poise. See Shary (2002b).
9. Significantly, this is a change from Stan Lee's original comic books, in which Peter is said to be transformed by a bite from a radioactive spider. This change from the

original series is doubtless a way of updating the story, to replace the scientific fears of the 1960s with those of the recent present, where the potential to create new, genetically-modified organisms is still only just being realised. Genetic modification has featured in a number of Hollywood films, typically with disastrous results. The reference to genetically modified creatures speaks to an unease about the increasing capabilities of science.

10. In the later Spider-Man films, Gwen Stacey (Emma Stone) becomes Spidey's love interest, a character with far greater agency than Mary-Jane here.
11. Worldwide box-office figures attest to their success: *Twilight*: $393,618,788; *Twilight New Moon*: $709,711,008; *Twilight Eclipse*: $698,491,347; *Twilight Breaking Dawn Part 1*: $712,205, 856; *Twilight Breaking Dawn Part 2*: $829,746,820. Figures available at <http://www.boxofficemojo.com/search/?q=twilight> (last accessed 30 March 2017).
12. Milly Williamson argues that this tendency in fact dates back to the early Victorian period. It was only in the later Victorian period, epitomised by *Dracula*, that vampires began to be portrayed more negatively. See Williamson (2014), p. 73.
13. *Buffy the Vampire Slayer* (Fran Rubel Kuzui, 1992) was originally released as a film, and was also written by later showrunner Joss Whedon.
14. Steven Cohan's work, referenced in the previous chapter in relation to *Dirty Dancing*, provides an important touchstone here.
15. In the following film, *New Moon*, Bella is taken aback to see that Sam Ulley (Chaske Spencer), one of the tribe's members, has 'lost control' and drastically scarred his fiancée Sarah (Tinsel Korey) during an argument.
16. As if to emphasise the parallel, DeHaan has since gone on to play a fictionalised version of Dean in *Life* (Anton Corbijn, 2015).
17. Notably, the film's closing scene sees Matt promising to discover more about the substance that granted their powers. However, the focus of the film is on further honing their abilities.
18. *Chronicle* is deemed an example of the found-footage film in multiple reviews of the film (e.g. Bradshaw, 2012; Robey, 2012) and indeed in critical literature on the found-footage film itself (Heller-Nicholas, 2014).
19. Nonetheless, many reviewers mention in passing that that the screenplay for *Chronicle* was written by Max Landis, son of John Landis, the director of *American Werewolf in London* (1981) and *Animal House* (1978).
20. The possibility that Andrew manipulates his own footage is mirrored in the treatment to which the film-makers subjected *Chronicle* itself. Certainly, the film was shot using 35mm stock, yet was treated to give the footage the texture of amateur footage (Lam 2014, p. 89).
21. We might consider here the figure of Norman Bates in *Psycho* (Alfred Hitchcock, 1960) and his later 'heirs', such as Michael Myers in *Halloween* or Jason Voorhees of *Friday the 13th* (Sean S. Cunningham, 1980).

7 CONCLUSION: NOT ANOTHER TEEN MOVIE?

Released in 2001, *Not Another Teen Movie* (Joel Gallen, 2001) was released to a public that had become familiar to the point of exhaustion with the genre's conventions. Along with other similarly-titled spoof films, including *Scary Movie* (Keenan Ivory Wayans, 2000), *Date Movie* (Aaron Selzer, 2006) and *Dance Flick* (Damien Dante Wayans, 2009), *Not Another Teen Movie* was intended as disposable fare that would capitalise on the vitality of teen movies in the 1990s whose popularity reached well beyond their intended youth audience. *Not Another Teen Movie* is a pastiche – both in the sense of a knowing imitation, and as an indiscriminate mish-mash of the teen movie's typical attributes (Dyer 2007). Thus, the film is set at John Hughes High, in tribute to the veteran director, and the plot is loosely modelled on the makeover narrative of *She's All That* while also incorporating elements from other recent teen movies.

The humour of *Not Another Teen Movie* could not be accused of subtlety. The principal character's transformation consists solely of removing her glasses, reminding the audience of Wood's claim that Rachel Leigh Cook, who plays Laney in *She's All That*, was 'obviously attractive from the start' (Wood 2003: 325). And while *Not Another Teen Movie* has a point in highlighting the genre's widespread neglect of people of colour, this political stand is likewise made with broad, slapstick comedy that obscures the validity of its otherwise worthy argument. Nonetheless, the film's purpose is to demonstrate the ease with which the widely accepted conventions of the high school teen movie can be made ridiculous. Some elements of the genre undoubtedly possess a latent element of the absurd, not least the lavish house parties found throughout the teen genre, which are seemingly thrown at the spur of the moment and contain little sense of consequence when the family home is destroyed. Nonetheless, *Not Another Teen Movie* takes advantage of widespread knowledge of the genre's tropes, an awareness that reached beyond its immediate, teenage audience. As I demonstrate, given youth culture's current lack of visibility, this type of knowing pastiche may no longer be possible.

The house party motif mentioned above provides a moment where the portrayal of everyday adolescence encounters Hollywood glamour. As I have shown throughout, such instances of indeterminacy and liminality are the teen movie's most potent defining factors. The films analysed in this book have consisted principally of sexual coming-of-age narratives; the movement and negotiation between child and adult identities is the genre's central concern. The first case study, *Rebel Without a Cause,* saw that new forms of masculine stardom, propelled by the popularity of the Method style of acting, gave voice to a generation of young men who perceived themselves at a distance from the contemporary norms of adult masculinity. It is for this reason that Jim Stark is so preoccupied by ideas of honour and the question of what, exactly, you have to do to be a man. The character is therefore distraught to discover that even his father, who outwardly conforms to the 1950s ideals of respectable masculinity, cannot live up to the model that Jim holds in his mind. While Jim was an outsider seeking affiliation with Buzz, the analysis of *Grease* showed that even Danny Zuko, a popular gang leader, is beset with anxiety. Through attention to Travolta's movements and gesture, the acuity of Danny's malaise was observed as he transitions through different masculine social roles. Whether characters are outsiders or insiders, then, the teen movie shows that the various norms that govern the construction of adult identity are far from easily assumed.

The central concerns portrayed in *Rebel* and *Grease* – of recognising the constituent elements of normative identity, and observing that one falls short of those expectations – have been apparent throughout this book. It should be noted that such an understanding has been enabled by attention to the details of teen movies' aesthetic, which has been eluded in previous scholarship. What is also evident is that this discrepancy provokes one of two reactions: either a character seeks to fulfil those norms, or, knowing that their identity flouts convention in any case, they seek to defy them still further. Where characters strive to bridge the gap between their own identities and the ideal is most obviously portrayed in the makeover, which promises to move its participant from their current, often abject, positioning, into another that is more desirable. In Chapter 4, where this idea was principally encountered, the urge for transformation was often brought into focus by the high school prom, which was portrayed as a space in which adherence to norms of gender and class was strenuously enforced.

CONCLUSION

Yet the desire to assimilate normative ideals was not confined to Chapter 4. Nor, as I shall observe, was the journey to the normative examined even in those case studies an entirely uncomplicated one. To return to the construction of youth rebel masculinity, Jim Stark was shown to crave a masculine ideal that was coming to be contested by the mid-1950s. A similar struggle is depicted in *American Graffiti*, in which the audience's retrospective position on the action allows us to see the futility of Terry's attempts to pose in Steve's car, and of Laurie's desperation to remain in her unfulfilling relationship. However, it is John's characterisation that portrays the extent to which the norms of masculinity have irretrievably changed. This is shown not only through John's literal displacement by Bob Falfa, as Modesto's leading drag racer, with 'the bitchinest car in the valley', but also through his tastes, which are those of an older generation of teenagers. *American Graffiti* provides the most potent demonstration that cultural intelligibility can never be taken for granted. Even when that position has provisionally been achieved, the physical ageing of the body, combined with wider sociocultural changes, means not only that the norms governing intelligibility change over time, but also that the body signifies those norms differently, as it also changes.

The opposing reaction brought on by the chasm between one's own identity and a fictionalised ideal is to reject those very ideals. In *Heathers*, J.D. provides a significant example of a character who refuses the normative. Christian Slater's multiple performance references to similarly iconoclastic characters played by Jack Nicholson and Clint Eastwood demonstrate J.D.'s absolute rejection of the values embodied by the high school. In *Heathers*, J.D.'s decision to take his own life is unsurprising. However, this urge for self-destruction emerges as an unlikely tie between him and Bella of *Twilight*. Whereas J.D. is fuelled solely by nihilism, Bella's patient determination to become a vampire and live perpetually with Edward stems from the certainty of her love for him. As Edward patiently explains, though, becoming a vampire will mean that her life as a human will be over; neither living nor dead, she will become a monstrous vision of postmortality, the consequences of which Edward continues to endure. In turn, while the ending of *Chronicle* sees Andrew's demise, his aim is not self-destruction, but to become something that is wholly beyond the normative construction of the human. In the purge of characters who provide the most radical challenge to the norms of identity can be seen the machinations of ideology. If, as Thomas Schatz argues, Hollywood genre cinema is a space of ritualistic repetition (1981), then the dissolution of dissenting figures must be perceived as a corrective to these deviations from the normative. The consequences of failing to adhere to these norms – or to refuse their call entirely – are brutal indeed.

Nonetheless, close attention to the aesthetic detail of these key examples of the teen movie have revealed that the refusal of, or acquiescence to, the norms of gender, class and the human are not nearly so clear-cut as these brief summaries might appear to indicate. In *Pretty in Pink*, for instance, we see that Andie does wish to attend the prom, and perhaps later, to inhabit the affluent suburbs that 'richies' Benny, Steff and Blane take for granted. When she creates a pink dress to attend the prom from which she would otherwise be excluded, her transformation might have been perceived within the framework of fitting in. However, as the case study observed, Andie's positioning is far more ambiguous than this trajectory might imply; throughout the film, she has been shown subtly undermining the middle-class gender norms inhabited by her classmates. What is more, her dress itself is a converse to the traditional hourglass-shaped style that celebrates heteronormative coming of age. Equally, both *Mean Girls* and *Easy A* portray the impossibility of adhering to the ideal of postfeminist femininity, which is sexy, yet carefully controlled, and not overtly sexual. In *Spider-Man*, too, Peter Parker must find a way to blend his hybrid identity into the fabric of contemporary New York City. Ironically, he finds that it is in the mask of a Spandex-clad alter ego that he can manage his radical alterity. This book has shown that attention to the films' aesthetics reveals how the norms of identity are negotiated in the teen movie.

These textual analyses were informed by theoretical perspectives, which further elucidated the constriction of identity portrayed in the films. Butler's theorisation of gender as performative, for instance, enabled us to see the characters' entanglement in a series of norms to which they are required to adhere, yet which do not adequately encompass the complexity of their subjectivity. Butler's principal insight is that heteronormative gender is neither natural nor inevitable, but is an ephemeral construct constantly being made and remade on the surface of the body. In Chapter 4, the perspective accrued from a reading informed by Butler's theorisation of gender was accompanied by one that understands social class, to be similarly constructed. As a result, we were able to observe how the norms that govern idealised femininity are always already connected to its positioning as a classed construct, which specifically excludes working-class women.

Chapters 4 and 5 were also informed by postfeminism. For Gill, postfeminism is not a critical perspective, but a phenomenon that itself requires analysis (2005). There are merits to this approach, not least the opportunity it affords to observe trends in particular types of postfeminist media, and more recently, for post-postfeminist media, across time (Gill 2016). Nonetheless, I have shown that an understanding of the contradictory impulses of postfeminism, which both acknowledges and repudiates feminism, can be used as a lens that allows us to identify how characters negotiate the construction of identity in the teen movie. In Chapter 5, a postfeminist appreciation of how gender roles have changed over time was significant to the analyses performed there. Thus, it is with hindsight that we can perceive the hypocrisies and injustices of

Dirty Dancing, and, with the conclusion of *American Graffiti* that affirms the young women's relative unimportance, open up a space for the articulation of second-wave feminism. Looking forward to the future and back to the past in a single gesture, postfeminism elucidates how gendered behaviour and, perhaps crucially, the acceptability of certain gendered practices have altered over time.

Finally, recent work on the posthuman, which seeks to bring a critical perspective on humans' partial and contingent place in the world, has shed light on the teenager's encounter with the non-human, and the construction of the teenager themselves as posthuman. In *Twilight* we observed how the vampires both have the capacity to discern attractiveness in a manner that differs from conventional human modes, and in turn, to perceive humans as ineffective prey. The results of the perspective that humans are a vulnerable, barely distinguishable mass are shown to spectacular effect in *Spider-Man* and *Chronicle* alike, as American cityscapes are swiftly devastated around the conflict between the hero and his adversary. Teenagers, of course, lend themselves easily to the construction of the posthuman, since, being beyond the scope of childhood yet not fully adults, their liminality is easily transposed to the monstrous.

That teenagers possess an element of the monstrous has been apparent in their uneasy relationship with the adults around them, and in their representation in other forms of the media. Certainly, as my earlier delimitation of the teen movie makes clear, teenagers' struggle for autonomy within parental constraints is one of the genre's significant defining factors. Further, as the history of the teen movie shows, teenagers have consistently been 'othered' by adults, be it through various moral panics or in a conscious avoidance of particular spaces and cultural practices associated with them. Nonetheless, one unintended consequence of this widespread ephebiphobia, or fear of teenagers, has been the consolidation of the identity of the teenager itself as one that is known, viable and recognisable. In turn, this recognition contributed to the establishment of the teen movie – as well as, of course, those cycles that capitalised on the fear generated by the existence of teenagers themselves.

To return to *Not Another Teen Movie*, it appears that such an understanding of the teenager, and of the cinematic form with which teenagers are most associated, was still in play in 2001, such that it was possible to create a viable spoof of its conventions. However, writing in 2016, film critic Charlie Lyne observed that 'youth culture has never been so easy to ignore', now that it is hidden among increasingly niche social media and esoteric video streaming sites (Lyne 2016: n.p.).[1] When youths congregated at the drive-in cinema in the middle of the twentieth century and listened to what was then regarded as subversive music, they were highly visible and were therefore better understood as a specific, definable group. It is perhaps no coincidence that the generation most associated with these practices, the baby boomers, have arguably had the most privileged coming of age of any generation before or since. In contrast, the popular culture consumed by the teenagers of today is more indistinct, but also doubtless more diffuse and diverse than ever before, characterised by multiple media channels received on multiple devices, with little regard for media specificity.[2] While the online streaming firm Netflix has recently taken to creating films that specifically target teenagers, these are unlikely to be discovered serendipitously by those of older generations.[3]

This is not to say that there are now no teen movies. Rather, that we seem to be in the midst of a cyclical nadir in their production. As Shary observes, the genre's history has seen waves of successful production, such as that which provides the source texts for *Not Another Teen Movie*, while other years have seen waning interest in the genre (2014: 12). In contrast, 2017 finds the teen movie in a rather different situation. Certainly, the high audiences seen for teen-oriented sci-fi blockbuster films, epitomised by the *Hunger Games* franchise (2012–15), appears to be fading. Consider the muted enthusiasm for the *Divergent* series, the last instalment of which (*Ascendant*, Lee Toland Krieger, 2017) will be a TV movie without a theatrical release.[4] Nonetheless, the American indie market has in recent years provided an intriguing alternative to those offered by Hollywood. Films such as *Boyhood* (Richard Linklater, 2014) and *The Edge of Seventeen* (Kelly Fremon Craig, 2016) have been critically acclaimed for their poignancy. Likewise, low-budget horror films such as *Friend Request* and *It Follows* (David Robert Mitchell, 2015) show that teen sexuality remains a rich seam for makers of horror films.

As if to indicate the continued interest in the teen movie, yet a distrust of the teen audience to attend the cinema in sufficient numbers, a further trend has seen adult characters return to their former high school. While *Romy and Michele's High School Reunion* (Mike Birkin, 1997) provides an evident precursor, central to this recent wave of films has been *21 Jump Street* (Phil Lord, Christopher Miller, 2012). A remake of the eponymous 1980s television series, which starred a young Johnny Depp, the film possesses abundant cross-generational appeal. *21 Jump Street* centres on two young police officers who are assigned to infiltrate a drug ring at a local high school. In contrast to their actual adolescent experiences, Schmidt (Jonah Hill) finds that his nerdish characteristics are a hit with contemporary high school students, while Jenko (Channing Tatum), the former captain of the football team – precisely the figure of hegemonic teen masculinity that has hitherto been idealised – is sidelined. *21 Jump Street* holds up for question the assumptions made about the construction of idealised gender in the Hollywood teen movie. In a similarly idealised corrective, *Central Intelligence* (Rawson Marshall Thurber, 2016) sees former class president Calvin Joyner (Kevin Hart) languishing in a run-of-the-mill accountancy role, while formerly overweight class pariah Bob Stone (Dwayne Johnson) has blossomed into a body-building CIA agent.[5] While cross-generational appeal has long been a key ingredient in many Hollywood teen movies, these roles see adults reprising the roles formerly reserved for their younger counterparts.

These latter two examples suggest that adulthood does not spell the end of the processes of becoming. However, this book has shown the particular complexity and indeterminacy of the Hollywood teen movie's construction of identity. That these issues are now being more frequently explored outside of the Hollywood system shows that there is potential for still further aspects to be explored in relation to adolescence and contemporary, transnational cinema. Nonetheless, for Hollywood studios seeking reliable returns, the youth audience increasingly looks like a risky investment. With films now addressing a youthful yet adult audience, this book ends in the hope that *Not Another Teen Movie* remains an ill-conceived spoof, rather than a prediction.

Notes

1. Charlie Lyne is also a film-maker in his own right, having created *Beyond Clueless* (Charlie Lyne, 2014), a documentary in homage to the teen genre.
2. The BBC's 2016 decision to make its youth channel, BBC Three, online only, can be viewed in this context.
3. See for instance *XOXO* (Christopher Louie, 2016).
4. In addition to the *Divergent* series, we might also think of the declining interest in the *Maze Runner* films (2014–). Other recent Hollywood misfires include *The Host* (Andrew Niccol, 2013), *Ender's Game* (Gavin Hood, 2013), *The Giver* (Phillip Noyce, 2014), *Vampire Academy* (Mark Waters, 2014), *The Seventh Son* (Sergei Bodrov, 2014) and *Tomorrowland* (Brad Bird, 2015). Despite many of these films sharing many of the traits of *The Hunger Games* – not least a charismatic teen fighting against an authoritarian regime – they failed to chime with a contemporary teen audience sated with such fare.
5. In the vein of adults revising their high school lives, we could also consider *Grown Ups* (Dennis Dugan, 2010), *Grown Ups 2* (Dennis Dugan, 2013), *Smosh: The Movie* (Alex Winter, 2015) and *The Do-Over* (Steven Brill, 2016).

BIBLIOGRAPHY

Abbott, S. (2009), *Celluloid Vampires: Life After Death in the Modern World*, Austin: University of Texas Press.
Allen, K., I. Tyler and S. De Benedictis (2014), 'Thinking with "White Dee": The Gender Politics of "Austerity Porn"', *Sociological Research Online*, 19: 3, <http://www.socresonline.org.uk/19/3/2.html> (last accessed 30 March 2017).
Altman, R. (1987a), *The American Film Musical*, Bloomington: Indiana University Press.
Altman, R. [1987b] (2002), 'The American Film Musical as Dual-Focus Narrative', in S. Cohan (ed.), *Hollywood Musicals: The Film Reader*, London: Routledge, pp. 48–62.
Altman, R. [1987c] (2003), 'A Semantic/Syntactic Approach to Film Genre', in B. K. Grant (ed.), *Film Genre III*, Austin: University of Texas Press, pp. 27–41.
Anderson, P. L., and M. N. Hansen (2011), 'Class and Cultural Capital – the Case of Class Inequality in Educational Performance', *European Sociological Review*, 27: 1, 1–15.
Anonymous (1923), 'Climbing Everest is Work for Supermen', *The New York Times*, 18 March, <http://graphics8.nytimes.com/packages/pdf/arts/mallory1923.pdf> (last accessed 30 March 2017).
Arnett, J. J., and H. Cravens (2006), 'G. Stanley Hall's *Adolescence*: A Centennial Reappraisal', *History of Psychology*, 9: 3, 165–71.
Austin, J. L. (1962a), *How To Do Things with Words*, 2nd edn, Cambridge, MA: Harvard University Press.
Austin, J. L. [1962b] (2000), 'Performative Utterances', in R. J. Stainton (ed.), *Perspectives in the Philosophy of Language: A Concise Anthology*, Peterborough, ON: Broadview Press, pp. 239–52.
Babington, B., and P. W. Evans (1985), *Blue Skies and Silver Linings: Aspects of the Hollywood Musical*, Manchester: Manchester University Press.

Bailey, S., and J. Hay (2006), 'Cinema and the Premises of Youth: Teen Films and their Sites in the 1980s and 1990s', in S. Neale (ed.), *Genre and Contemporary Hollywood*, London: BFI Publishing, pp. 218–32.

Baron, C., and S. M. Carnicke (2008), *Reframing Screen Performance*, Ann Arbor: University of Michigan Press.

Beck, B. (2011), 'Fearless Vampire Kissers: Bloodsuckers We Love in Twilight, True Blood and Others', *Multicultural Perspectives*, 13: 2, pp. 90–2.

Berger, J. (1972), *Ways of Seeing*, London: Penguin.

Bernstein, J. (1997), *Pretty in Pink: The Golden Age of Teenage Movies*, New York: St Martin's Press.

Best, A. L. (2000), *Prom Night: Youth, Schools and Popular Culture*, London: Routledge.

Betrock, A. (1986), *I Was a Teenage Juvenile Delinquent Rock'N'Roll Horror Beach Party Movie Book: A Complete Guide to the Teen Exploitation Film, 1954–1969*, New York: St Martin's Press.

Biltereyst, D. (2007), 'American Juvenile Delinquency Movies and the European Censors: The Cross-Cultural Reception of *The Wild One*, *Blackboard Jungle* and *Rebel Without a Cause*', in T. Shary and A. Seibel (eds), *Youth Culture in Global Cinema*, Austin: University of Texas Press, pp. 9–26.

Bingham, D. (1994), *Acting Male: Masculinities in the Films of James Stewart, Jack Nicholson and Clint Eastwood*, New Brunswick, NJ: Rutgers University Press.

Bleach, A. C. (2010), 'Postfeminist Cliques? Class, Postfeminism, and the Molly Ringwald-John Hughes Films', *Cinema Journal*, 49, No. 3, pp. 24–44.

Bode, L. (2010), 'Transitional Tastes: Teen girls and genre in the critical reception of *Twilight*', *Continuum: Journal of Media and Cultural Studies*, 24: 5, 707–19.

Bolton, L., and J. Lobalzo-Wright (eds) (2016), *Lasting Screen Stars: Images that Fade and Personas that Endure*, Basingstoke: Palgrave Macmillan.

Bourdieu, P. (1986a), *Distinction: A Social Critique of the Judgement of Taste*, trans. Richard Nice, London: Routledge.

Bourdieu, P. [1986b] (2011), 'The Forms of Capital', in I. Szeman and T. Kaporey (eds), *Cultural Theory: An Anthology*, Oxford: Wiley-Blackwell, pp. 81–93.

Bourdieu, P. (1998), *Language and Symbolic Power*, Cambridge, MA: Harvard University Press.

Box Office Mojo (2012a), 'Worldwide gross for *Dirty Dancing*', <http://www.boxofficemojo.com/movies?id=dirtydancing.htm> (last accessed 30 March 2017).

Box Office Mojo (2012b), 'Worldwide gross for *The Twilight Saga: Breaking Dawn Part Two*', <http://www.boxofficemojo.com/movies/?id=breakingdawn2.htm> (last accessed 30 March 2017).

Boyer, P. S. (2006), *The Oxford Companion to United States History*, Oxford: Oxford University Press.

Bradshaw, P. (2012), '*Chronicle*: Review', *The Guardian*, 2 February 2012, <https://www.theguardian.com/film/2012/feb/02/chronicle-film-review> (last accessed 30 March 2017).

Brady, A., and T. Schirato (2011), *Understanding Judith Butler*, London: Routledge.

Braidotti, R. (2013). *The Posthuman*, Cambridge: Polity Press.

Brammer, R. (2009), 'Left of Centre: Teen Life, Love and Pain in the Films of John Hughes', *Screen Education*, 56, pp. 22–8.

Brickman, B. (2012), *New American Teenagers: A Lost Generation of Youth in 1970s Film*, New York: Continuum.

Brook, T. (1999), 'Teen power storms US box office', BBC America, 5 March 1999, <http://news.bbc.co.uk/1/hi/special_report/1999/03/99/tom_brook/290955.stm> (last accessed 30 March 2017).

Brown, J. A. (2011), *Dangerous Curves: Action Heroines, Gender, Fetishism and Popular Culture*, Jackson: University Press of Mississippi.

Brown, J. A. (2016), 'Superhero Film Parody and Hegemonic Masculinity', *Quarterly Review of Film and Video*, 33: 2, pp. 133–50.

Brown, T. (2012), *Breaking the Fourth Wall: Direct Address in the Cinema*, Edinburgh: Edinburgh University Press.

Brown, W. (2009), 'Man Without a Movie Camera: Towards a Posthumanist Cinema?', in W. Buckland (ed.), *Film Theory and Contemporary Hollywood Movies*, London: Routledge, pp. 66–84.

Bruzzi, S. (2011), '"It will be a magnificent obsession": femininity, desire, and the New Look in 1950s Hollywood melodrama', in A. Munich, *Fashion in Film: New Directions in National Cinemas*, Bloomington: Indiana University Press, pp. 160–80.

Buckland, W. (ed.) (2009), *Film Theory and Contemporary Hollywood Movies*, London: Routledge.

Butler, J. (1990), *Gender Trouble: Feminism and the Subversion of Identity*, London: Routledge.

Butler, J. (1993), *Bodies That Matter: On the Discursive Limits of Sex*, London: Routledge.

Butler, J. (2004), *Undoing Gender*, London: Routledge.

Butler, J. (2005), *Giving an Account of Oneself*, New York: Fordham University Press.

Butler, J. (2006), *Precarious Life: The Power of Mourning and Violence*, London: Verso.

Butler, J. (2010), *Frames of War: When Is Life Grievable?*, London: Verso.

Butler, J. G. (ed.) (1991), *Star Texts: Image and Performance in Film and Television*, Detroit: Wayne State University Press.

Clover, C. J. (1992), *Men, Women and Chainsaws: Gender in the Modern Horror Film*, Princeton: Princeton University Press.

Cohan, S. (1993), 'Feminising the Song-and-Dance Man: Fred Astaire and the Spectacle of Masculinity in the Hollywood Musical', in S. Cohan and I. R. Hark (eds), *Screening the Male: Exploring Masculinities in Hollywood Cinema*, London: Routledge, pp. 46–69.

Cohan, S. (1997), *Masked Men: Masculinity and the Movies in the Fifties*, Bloomington: Indiana University Press.

Cohan, S. (ed.) (2002), *Hollywood Musicals: The Film Reader*, London: Routledge.

Cohan, S., and I. R. Hark (eds) (1993), *Screening the Male: Exploring Masculinities in Hollywood Cinema*, London: Routledge.

Cohen, J. (1996), *Monster Theory: Reading Culture*, Minneapolis: University of Minnesota Press.

Conrich, I. (ed.) (2009), *Horror Zone: The Cultural Experience of Contemporary Horror Cinema*, London: I. B. Tauris.

Considine, D. M. (1985), *The Cinema of Adolescence*, London: McFarland.

Constable, C. (2005), *Thinking in Images: Film Theory, Feminist Philosophy and Marlene Dietrich*, London: BFI Publishing.

Cook, P. (2005), *Screening the Past: Memory and Nostalgia in Cinema*, London: Routledge.

Coupland, D. (1991), *Generation X: Tales from an Accelerated Culture*, London: Abacus.

Creed, B. (1987), 'From Here to Modernity: Feminism and Postmodernism', *Screen*, 28: 2, pp. 47–68.

Creed, B. (2012), *Monstrous Feminine: Film, Feminism, Psychoanalysis*, 2nd edn, London: Routledge.

Crick, N. R., and J. R. Grotpeter (1995), 'Relational Aggression, Gender and Social-Psychological Adjustment', *Child Development*, 66: 3, 710–22.
Cripps, T. (1977), *Slow Fade to Black: The Negro in American Film 1900–1942*, Oxford: Oxford University Press.
Croft, A. (2012), *The Lindsay Lohan Story*, London: Hachette.
Crompton, R. (2008), *Class and Stratification*, 3rd edn, Cambridge: Polity Press.
Curtis, J. M. (1980), 'From *American Graffiti* to *Star Wars*', *Journal of Popular Culture*, 13: 4, 590–601.
Davis, F. (1979), *Yearning for Yesterday: A Sociology of Nostalgia*, New York: Free Press.
Davis, H. H. (2006), '"I was a Teenage Classic": Literary Adaptations in Turn of the Millennium Teen Films', *The Journal of American Culture*, 29: 1, 52–60.
Deleuze, G., and F. Guattari [1980] (2013), *A Thousand Plateaus: Capitalism and Schizophrenia*, London: Bloomsbury.
Derrida, J. (2002), 'The Animal That Therefore I am (More to Follow)', trans. David Wills, *Critical Inquiry*, 8: 2, 369–418.
Desmond, J. C. (ed.) (1997), *Meaning in Motion: New Cultural Studies of Dance*, Durham, NC: Duke University Press.
De Vaney, A. (2002), 'Pretty in Pink? John Hughes Re-inscribes Daddy's Girl in Homes and Schools', in M. Pomerance and F. Gateward (eds), *Sugar, Spice and Everything Nice: Cinemas of Girlhood*, Detroit: Wayne State University Press, pp. 201–16.
Devine, F., M. Savage, J. Scott and R. Crompton (eds) (2005), *Rethinking Class: Culture, Identities and Lifestyle*, Basingstoke: Palgrave Macmillan.
DeWitt, J. (2010), 'Cars and Culture in *American Graffiti*', *American Poetry Review*, 74, 47–50.
Dickinson, K. (2001), 'Pop, Speed and the "MTV Aesthetic" in Recent Teen Films', *Scope*, June 2001, pp. 1–13.
Dika, V. (2003), *Recycled Culture in Contemporary Art and Film: The Uses of Nostalgia*, Cambridge: Cambridge University Press.
Doherty, T. (2002), *Teenagers and Teenpics: The Juvenilization of American Movies in the 1950s*, Philadelphia: Temple University Press.
Driscoll, C. (2011), *Teen Film: A Critical Introduction*, London: Berg.
Driscoll, C. (2014), 'Afterword: Imagine Becoming Someone', in Shary, T. (2014), *Generation Multiplex: The Image of Youth in Contemporary American Cinema*, revised edn, Austin: University of Texas Press, pp. 303–8.
Dwyer, M. D. (2015), *Back to the Fifties: Nostalgia, Hollywood Film and Popular Music of the Seventies and Eighties*, Oxford: Oxford University Press.
Dyer, R. (1979), *Stars*, London: BFI.
Dyer, R. (1986), *Heavenly Bodies: Film Stars and Society*, London: BFI.
Dyer, R. (1992), 'Entertainment and Utopia', in S. Cohan (ed.), *Hollywood Musicals: The Film Reader*, London: Routledge, pp. 19–27.
Dyer, R. (1997), *White*, London: Routledge.
Dyer, R. (2002), *Only Entertainment*, 2nd edn, London: Routledge.
Dyer, R. (2007), *Pastiche*, London: Routledge.
Eco, U. (1972), 'The Myth of Superman', trans. Natalie Chiton, *Diacritics*, 2: 1, 14–22.
Falconer, P. (2010), 'Fresh Meat? Dissecting the Horror Movie Virgin', in T. Jeffers McDonald (ed.), *Virgin Territory*. Detroit: Wayne State University Press, pp. 123–37.
Faludi, S. (1992), *Backlash: The Undeclared War Against Women*, London: Vintage.
Farrimond, K. (2013), 'The Slut that Wasn't: Virginity, (Post)Feminism and Representation in *Easy A*', in J. Gwynne and N. Muller (eds), *Postfeminism and Contemporary Hollywood Cinema*, Basingstoke: Palgrave Macmillan, pp. 44–59.

Feuer, J. (1993), *The Hollywood Musical*, 2nd edn, Bloomington: Indiana University Press.
Feuer, J. (2013), 'Is *Dirty Dancing* a Musical and Why Should it Matter?', in Y. Tzioumakis and S. Lincoln (eds), *The Time of Our Lives: Dirty Dancing and Popular Culture*, Detroit: Wayne State University Press, pp. 59–72.
Flanagan, M. (2004), 'Teen Trajectories in Spider-Man and Ghost World', in I. Gordon, M. Jancovich and M. McCallister (eds), *Film and Comic Books*, Jackson: University of Mississippi Press, pp. 137–59.
Fowler, B. (ed.) (2001), *Reading Bourdieu in Culture and Society*, Oxford: Wiley-Blackwell.
Freeman, H. (2014), 'Why I'd like to be . . . Molly Ringwald in *Pretty in Pink*', *The Guardian*, 21 July, <http://www.theguardian.com/film/filmblog/2014/jul/21/molly-ringwald-pretty-in-pink-role-model> (last accessed 30 March 2017).
Freeman, H. (2015), *Life Moves Pretty Fast: The Lessons We Learned from Eighties Movies*, London: Simon and Schuster.
Freud, S. [1917] (2005), *On Murder, Mourning and Melancholia*, London: Penguin.
Friedan, B. (1963), *The Feminine Mystique*, London: Penguin.
Fussell, P. (1984), *Caste Marks: Style and Status in the USA*, London: Heinemann.
Garrett, R. (2007), *Postmodern Chick Flicks: The Return of the Woman's Film*, Basingstoke: Palgrave Macmillan.
Gelder, K. (2007), *Subcultures: Cultural Histories and Social Practice*, London: Routledge.
Gelder, K., and Thornton, S. (eds) (1997), *The Subcultures Reader*, London: Routledge.
Gibbs, J. (2002), *Mise-en-scène: Film Style and Interpretation*, London: Wallflower.
Gill, R. (2005), 'Postfeminist Media Culture: Elements of a sensibility', *European Journal of Cultural Studies*, 10: 2, 147–66.
Gill, R. (2016), 'Post-Postfeminism? New Feminist Visibilities in Post-Feminist Times', *Feminist Media Studies*, 16: 4, 610–30.
Gilligan, S. (2011), 'Performing Post-Feminist Identities: Gender, Costume and Transformation in Teen Cinema', in M. Waters (ed.), *Women on Screen: Feminism and Femininity in Visual Culture*, Basingstoke: Palgrave Macmillan, pp. 165–82.
Gordon, I., M. Jancovich and M. McCallister (eds) (2004), *Film and Comic Books*, Jackson: University of Mississippi Press.
Grainge, P. (2000), 'Nostalgia and style in retro America: Moods, Modes and Media Recycling', *Journal of American and Comparative Culture*, 23: 1, 27–35.
Grant, B. K. (ed.) (2003), *Film Genre III*, Austin: University of Texas Press.
Gray, T. (2016), 'Oscars nominates all white actors for second year in a row', *Variety*, 14 January 2016, <http://variety.com/2016/biz/news/oscar-nominations-2016-diversity-white-1201674903/> (last accessed 30 March 2017).
Gwynne, J., and N. Muller (eds) (2013), *Postfeminism and Contemporary Hollywood Cinema*, Basingstoke: Palgrave Macmillan.
Hall, G. S. (1904), *Adolescence: its Psychology and its Relations to Physiology, Anthropology, Sociology, Sex, Crime, Religion and Education*, New York: Appleton, Vols 1 and 2.
Halle, D. (1984), 'America's Working Man: Work, Home and Politics Among Blue-Collar Property Owners', in F. Devine, M. Savage, J. Scott and R. Crompton (eds), *Rethinking Class: Culture, Identities and Lifestyle*, Basingstoke: Palgrave Macmillan, pp. 32–48.
Haraway, D. (2003), *The Haraway Reader*, London: Routledge.
Haskell, M. (1974), *From Reverence to Rape: The Treatment of Women in the Movies*, Chicago: University of Chicago Press.
Hassler-Forest, D. (2015), 'Of Iron Men and Green Monsters: Superheroes and Posthumanism', in M. Hauskeller, T. Philbeck and C. Corbonell (eds), *The*

Palgrave Handbook of Posthumanism in Film and Television, Basingstoke: Palgrave Macmillan, pp. 66–76.
Hauskeller, M. (2015), '"Life's a bitch and then you *don't* die": Postmortality in Film and Television', in M. Hauskeller, T. Philbeck and C. Corbonell (eds), *The Palgrave Handbook of Posthumanism in Film and Television*, Basingstoke: Palgrave Macmillan, pp. 205–13.
Hauskeller, M., T. Philbeck and C. Corbonell (eds) (2015), *The Palgrave Handbook of Posthumanism in Film and Television*, Basingstoke: Palgrave Macmillan.
Hayles, N. K. (1999), *How We Became Posthuman: Virtual Bodies in Cybernetics, Literature, and Informatics*, Chicago: University of Chicago Press.
Hebdige, D. (1979), 'Subculture: The Meaning of Style', in K. Gelder and S. Thornton (eds), *The Subcultures Reader*, London: Routledge, pp. 130–44.
Heller-Nicholas, A. (2014), *Found-Footage Horror Films: Fear and the Appearance of Reality*, London: McFarland.
Hill, J., and P. Church-Gibson (eds) (1998), *Film Studies: Critical Approaches*, London: Oxford University Press.
Holmes, S., and S. Redmond (eds) (2006), *Framing Celebrity: New Directions in Celebrity Culture*, London: Routledge.
Hunt, L., S. Lockyer and M. Williamson (eds) (2013), *Screening the Undead: Vampires and Zombies in Film and Television*, London: I. B. Tauris.
Hutcheon, L. (1988), 'Irony, Nostalgia and the Postmodern', <http://www.library.utoronto.ca/utel/criticism/hutchinp.html> (last accessed 30 March 2017).
Hutcheon, L. (2010), *The Politics of Postmodernism*, 2nd edn, London: Routledge.
Jameson, F. (1984), 'Postmodernism, or, The Cultural Logic of Late Capitalism', *New Left Review*, 146, 12–56.
Jameson, F. (1991), *Postmodernism, or, The Cultural Logic of Late Capitalism*, London: Verso.
Jeffers McDonald, T. (ed.) (2010), *Virgin Territory*, Detroit: Wayne State University Press.
Jeffers McDonald, T. (2013), 'Bringing Up Baby: Generic Hybridity in *Dirty Dancing*', in Y. Tzioumakis and S. Lincoln (eds), *The Time of Our Lives: Dirty Dancing and Popular Culture*, Detroit: Wayne State University Press, pp. 43–58.
Jeffords, S. (1994), *Hard Bodies: Hollywood Masculinity in the Reagan Era*, New Brunswick, NJ: Rutgers University Press.
Jordan, C. (2003), *Movies and the Reagan Presidency: Success and Ethics*, Westport, CT: Praeger.
Kael, P. (1973), 'The Current Cinema: *American Graffiti*', *The New Yorker*, 29 October 1973, 53–9.
Kaplan, R. L. (2011), 'Spider-Man in Love: A Psychoanalytic Interpretation', *The Journal of Popular Culture*, 44: 2, 291–313.
Karlyn, K. R. (2011), *Unruly Girls, Unrepentant Mothers: Redefining Feminism on Screen*, Austin: University of Texas Press.
Kaveney, R. (2006), *Teen Films: Reading Teen Film and Television, from Heathers to Veronica Mars*, London: I. B. Tauris.
Kearney, M. C. (2015), 'Sparkle: Luminosity and post-girl power media', *Continuum: Journal of Media and Cultural Studies*, 29: 2, 263–73.
King, B. (1985), 'Articulating Stardom', in J. G. Butler (ed.), *Star Texts: Image and Performance in Film and Television*, Detroit: Wayne State University Press, pp. 125–54.
King, G. (2002), *New Hollywood Cinema: An Introduction*, London: I. B. Tauris.
Klein, A. A. (2011), *American Film Cycles: Reframing Genres, Screening Social Problems and Defining Subcultures*, Austin: University of Texas Press.

Klevan, A. (2005), *Film Performance: From Achievement to Appreciation*, London: Wallflower.
Kosofsky Sedgwick, E. (1985), *Between Men: English Literature and Male Homosocial Desire*, New York: Columbia University Press.
Kozloff, S. (1989), *Invisible Storytellers: Voice-Over Narration in American Fiction Film*, Berkeley: University of California Press.
Krämer, P. (1998), 'Post-Classical Hollywood', in J. Hill and P. Church-Gibson (eds), *Film Studies: Critical Approaches*, London: Oxford University Press, pp. 289–308.
Lam, C. (2014), 'Emotional Realism and Actuality: the Function of Prosumer Aesthetics in Film', *The IAFOR Journal of Media and Communication and Film*, 1: 2, 84–100.
Lee, C. (2010), *Screening Generation X: The Politics and Popular Memory of Youth in Contemporary Cinema*, London: Routledge.
Lewis, J. (1992), *The Road to Romance and Ruin*, London: Routledge.
Lewis, J. (2005), 'Growing up Male in Jim's Mom's World', in J. D. Slocum (ed.), *Rebel Without a Cause: Approaches to a Maverick Masterwork*, New York: State University of New York Press, pp. 89–110.
Lloyd, M. (2007), *Judith Butler: From Norms to Politics*, Cambridge: Polity Press.
Lovell, T. (2001), 'Thinking Feminism with and against Bourdieu', in B. Fowler (ed.), *Reading Bourdieu in Culture and Society*, Oxford: Wiley-Blackwell, pp. 27–48.
Lyne, C. (2016), 'XOXO: how to make a movie for the under-20s', *The Guardian*, 16 September 2016, <https://www.theguardian.com/film/2016/sep/16/xoxo-netflix-edm> (last accessed 30 March 2017).
Marks, L. (2010), *Sexual Chemistry: A History of the Contraceptive Pill*, New Haven: Yale University Press.
Martin, A. (1989), 'The Teen Movie: Why Bother?', *Cinema Papers*, 75: 12, 10–15.
Martin, A. (1994), *Phantasms: The Dreams and Desires at the Heart of Popular Culture*, Melbourne: McPhee Gribble.
Martin, A. (2009), 'Live to Tell: Teen Movies Yesterday and Today', *Lumina*, 2, 6–14.
Mathijs, E., and X. Mendik (eds) (2007), *The Cult Film Reader*, Reading: Open University Press.
McAllister, M. P., I. Gordon and M. Jancovich (2006), 'Art house meets graphic novel, or blockbuster meets superhero comic?: The contradictory relationship between film and comic art', *Journal of Popular Film and Television*, 34: 3, 108–14.
McCann, G. (ed.) (1991), *Rebel Males: Clift, Brando, Dean*, New Brunswick, NJ: Rutgers University Press.
McKelly, J. C. (2005), 'Youth Cinema and the Culture of Rebellion: *Heathers* and the Rebel Archetype', in J. D. Slocum (ed.), *Rebel Without a Cause: Approaches to a Maverick Masterwork*, New York: State University of New York Press, pp. 210–32.
McNelis, T. (2013), 'Dancing in the Nostalgia Factory: Anachronistic Music in *Dirty Dancing*', in Y. Tzioumakis and S. Lincoln (eds), *The Time of Our Lives: Dirty Dancing and Popular Culture*, Detroit: Wayne State University Press, pp. 239–56.
McRobbie, A. (1991), 'Dance Narratives and Fantasies of Achievement', in J. C. Desmond (ed.), *Meaning in Motion: New Cultural Studies of Dance*, Durham, NC: Duke University Press, pp. 207–31.
McRobbie, A. (2004), 'Post-Feminism and Popular Culture', *Feminist Media Studies*, 4: 3, 255–64.
McRobbie, A. (2009), *The Aftermath of Feminism: Gender, Culture and Social Change*, London: Sage.
Miller, C. J., and A. Bowdoin Von Riper (2015), 'Marketing, Monsters and Music: Teensploitation Horror Films', *Journal of American Culture*, 38: 2, 130–41.
Modleski, T. (ed.) (1986), *Studies in Entertainment: Critical Approaches to Mass Culture*, Bloomington: Indiana University Press.

Moi, T. (1991), 'Appropriating Bourdieu: Feminist Theory and Pierre Bourdieu's Sociology of Culture', *New Literary History*, 22: 4, 1017–49.
Molloy, C. (2013), '"It's a feeling, a heartbeat": Nostalgia, Music and Affect in *Dirty Dancing*', in Y. Tzioumakis and S. Lincoln (eds), *The Time of Our Lives: Dirty Dancing and Popular Culture*, Detroit: Wayne State University Press, pp. 223–38.
Morey, A. (ed.) (2012), *Genre, Reception and Adaptation in the Twilight Series*, London: Routledge.
Moseley, R. (2000), 'Makeover Takeover in British Television', *Screen*, 41: 3, 299–314.
Moseley, R. (2002), 'Glamorous Witchcraft: Gender and Magic in Teen Film and Television', *Screen*, 43: 4, 403–22.
Mukherjea, A. (2011), 'My Vampire Boyfriend: Postfeminism, "Perfect" Masculinity, and the Contemporary Appeal of Paranormal Romance', *Studies in Popular Culture*, 33: 2, 1–20.
Munich, A. (ed.) (2011), *Fashion in Film: New Directions in National Cinemas*, Bloomington: Indiana University Press.
Naremore, J. (1988), *Acting in the Cinema*, Berkeley: University of California Press.
Neale, S. (ed.) (2006), *Genre and Contemporary Hollywood*, London: BFI Publishing.
Negra, D. (2009), *What a Girl Wants: Fantasizing the Reclamation of the Self in Postfeminist Culture*, London: Routledge.
Nelson, S. (2016), 'Come together: Overcoming Prejudice in *Pride*', *Screen Education*, 80, 60–7.
Orpen, V. (2003), *Film Editing: The Art of the Expressive*, London: Wallflower.
Peberdy, D. (2011), *Masculinity and Film Performance: Male Angst in Contemporary American Cinema*, Basingstoke: Palgrave Macmillan.
Petersen, A.-H. (2012), 'That teenage feeling: *Twilight*, fantasy and feminist readers', *Feminist Media Studies*, 12: 1, 51–67.
Pomerance, M. (2005), 'Stark Performance', in J. D. Slocum (ed.), *Rebel Without a Cause: Approaches to a Maverick Masterwork*, New York: State University of New York Press, pp. 35–52.
Pomerance, M., and F. Gateward (eds) (2002), *Sugar, Spice and Everything Nice: Cinemas of Girlhood*, Detroit: Wayne State University Press.
Pountain, D., and D. Robins (2000), *Cool Rules: An Anatomy of an Attitude*, London: Reaktion Books.
Projansky, S. (2001), *Watching Rape: Film and Television in Postfeminist Culture*, New York: New York University Press.
Projansky, S. (2014), *Spectacular Girls: Media Fascination and Celebrity Culture*, New York: New York University Press.
Purse, L. (2013), *Digital Imaging in Popular Cinema*, Edinburgh: Edinburgh University Press.
Radner, H. (2013), '*Dirty Dancing*: Feminism, Postfeminism, Neofeminism', in Y. Tzioumakis and S. Lincoln (eds), *The Time of Our Lives: Dirty Dancing and Popular Culture*, Detroit: Wayne State University Press, pp. 131–50.
Rand, A. (1943), *The Fountainhead*, London: Penguin.
Reeves, M. (1978), *Travolta! A Photo Bio*, New York: Jove Books.
Reynolds, S. (2011), *Retromania: Pop Culture's Addiction to its own Past*, London: Faber and Faber.
Richards, O. (2012), 'Pitch Perfect Review', *Empire*, 20 June 2012, <http://www.empireonline.com/movies/pitch-perfect/review/> (last accessed 30 March 2017).
Richardson, N. (2004), 'The Gospel According to Spider-Man', *Journal of Popular Culture*, 37: 4, 694–703.

Ringrose, J. (2006), 'A New Universal Mean Girl: Examining the Discursive Construction and Social Regulation of a new Feminine Pathology', *Feminism and Psychology*, 16: 4, pp. 405–24.
Ringrose, J. (2013), *Postfeminist Education? Girls and the Sexual Politics of Schooling*, London: Routledge.
Rivière, J. (1929), 'Womanliness as a Masquerade', *International Journal of Psychoanalysis*, 10, 303–13.
Roberts, K. (2002), 'The Pleasures and Problems of the Angry Girl', in M. Pomerance and F. Gateward (eds), *Sugar, Spice and Everything Nice: Cinemas of Girlhood*, Detroit: Wayne State University Press, pp. 217–33.
Robey, T. (2012), '*Chronicle* review', *The Telegraph*, 3 February 2012, <http://www.telegraph.co.uk/culture/film/filmreviews/9057707/Chronicle-review.html> (last accessed 30 March 2017).
Rottenberg, C. (2004), 'Salome of the Tenements, the American Dream and Class Performativity', *American Studies*, 45: 1, 65–83.
Salih, S. (2002), *Judith Butler*, London: Routledge.
Sargant, J., S. Tanski and M. Stoolmiller (2012), 'Influence of Motion Picture Rating on Adolescent Response to Movie Smoking', *Pediatrics*, 130: 2, 228–36.
Schatz, T. (1981), *Hollywood Genres: Formulas, Filmmaking and the Studio System*, Austin: University of Texas Press.
Scheibel, W. (2014), 'Bigger than Life: Melodrama, Masculinity and the American Dream', in W. Scheibel and S. Rybin (eds), *Lonely Places, Dangerous Ground: Nicholas Ray in American Cinema*, Albany: State University of New York Press, pp. 177–88.
Scheibel, W., and S. Rybin (eds) (2014), *Lonely Places, Dangerous Ground: Nicholas Ray in American Cinema*, Albany: State University of New York Press.
Schickel, R. (1987), 'Cinema: Teenage Turmoil', *Time*, 14 September, <http://content.time.com/time/magazine/article/0,9171,965450,00.html> (last accessed 30 March 2017).
Schreiber, M. (2014), *American Postfeminist Cinema: Women, Romance and Contemporary Culture*, Edinburgh: Edinburgh University Press.
Scott, J., and D. Leonhardt (2005), 'Class in America: Shadowy Lines that Still Divide', *The New York Times*, 15 May 2005, <http://www.nytimes.com/2005/05/15/national/class/OVERVIEW-FINAL.html?pagewanted=all&_r=0> (last accessed 30 March 2017).
Sender, K., and M. Sullivan (2008), 'Epidemics of will, failures of self-esteem: Responding to fat bodies in *The Biggest Loser* and *What Not to Wear*', *Continuum: Journal of Media and Cultural Studies*, 22: 4, 573–84.
Shary, T. (2002a), *Generation Multiplex: The Image of Youth in Contemporary American Cinema*, 1st edn, Austin: University of Texas Press.
Shary, T. (2002b), 'The Nerdly Girl and her Beautiful Sister', in M. Pomerance and F. Gateward (eds), *Sugar, Spice and Everything Nice: Cinemas of Girlhood*, Detroit: Wayne State University Press, pp. 235–50.
Shary, T. (2005), *Teen Movies: American Youth on Screen*, London: Wallflower Press.
Shary, T. (2011), 'Buying Me Love: 1980s Class-Clash Teen Romances', *Journal of Popular Culture*, 44: 3, 563–82.
Shary, T. (2014), *Generation Multiplex: The Image of Youth in Contemporary American Cinema*, revised edn, Austin: University of Texas Press.
Shary, T., and A. Siebel. (eds) (2007), *Youth Culture in Global Cinema*, Austin: University of Texas Press.
Shaw, G. B. (1914), *Pygmalion*, London: Penguin.
Shumway, D. R. (1999), 'Rock 'n' Roll Soundtracks and the Production of Nostalgia', *Cinema Journal*, 38: 2, 36–51.

Silverman, K. (1986), 'Fragments of a Fashionable Discourse', in T. Modleski (ed.), *Studies in Entertainment: Critical Approaches to Mass Culture*, Bloomington: Indiana University Press, pp. 138–56.

Simmons, J. (2008), 'Violent Youth: the censoring and public reception of *The Wild One* and *Blackboard Jungle*', *Film History: an International Journal*, 20: 3, 381–91.

Skeggs, B. (1997), *Formations of Class and Gender: Becoming Respectable*, London: Sage.

Slocum, J. D. (ed.) (2005), *Rebel Without a Cause: Approaches to a Maverick Masterwork*, New York: State University of New York Press.

Smith, F. (2014), 'Time of my life? The afterlife of *Dirty Dancing* in the contemporary romantic comedy', *The Soundtrack*, 7: 2, 67–78.

Smith, F. (2016), 'Don't You Forget About Me: Molly Ringwald, Nostalgia and Teen Girl Stardom', in L. Bolton and J. Lobalzo-Wright (eds), *Lasting Screen Stars: Images that Fade and Personas that Endure*, Basingstoke: Palgrave Macmillan, pp. 231–43.

Sobchack, V. (1986), 'Child/Alien/Father: Patriarchal Cinema and Generic Exchange', *Camera Obscura*, 15, 7–34.

Speed, L. (1998), '"Tuesday's Gone": The Nostalgic Teen Film', *Journal of Popular Film and Television*, 26: 1, 24–32.

Speed, L. (2000), 'Together in Electric Dreams: Films Revisiting 1980s Youth', *Journal of Popular Film and Television*, 28: 1, 22–9.

Spigel, L. (2013), 'Postfeminist nostalgia for a pre-feminist future', *Screen*, 34: 2, 270–8.

Spooner, C. (2006), *Contemporary Gothic*, London: Reaktion Books.

Spoto, D. (1996), *Rebel: The Life and Legend of James Dean*, London: HarperCollins.

Sprengler, C. (2009), *Screening Nostalgia: Populuxe Props and Technicolor Aesthetics in Contemporary American Film*, London: Berghahn.

Springer, C. (2007), *James Dean Transfigured: The Many Faces of Rebel Iconography*, Austin: University of Texas Press.

Stainton, R. J. (ed.) (2000), *Perspectives in the Philosophy of Language: A Concise Anthology*, Peterborough, ON: Broadview Press.

Stamp, S. (1991), 'Horror, Femininity and Carrie's Monstrous Puberty', *Journal of Film and Video*, 43: 4, 33–44.

Stanislavsky, C. (1936), 'When Acting is an Art', in J. G. Butler (ed.), *Star Texts: Image and Performance in Film and Television*, Detroit: Wayne State University Press, pp. 18–33.

Stewart, S. (1993), *On Longing: Narratives of the Miniature, the Gigantic, the Souvenir, the Collection*, Durham, NC: Duke University Press.

Strasberg, L. (1987), 'A Dream of Passion: The Development of the Method', in J. G. Butler (ed.), *Star Texts: Image and Performance in Film and Television*, Detroit: Wayne State University Press, pp. 42–50.

Studlar, G. (2013), *Precocious Charms: Stars Performing Girlhood in Classical Hollywood Cinema*, Berkeley: University of California Press.

Szeman, I., and T. Kaporey (eds) (2011), *Cultural Theory: An Anthology*, Oxford: Wiley-Blackwell.

Talbot, M. (2002), 'Girls just want to be mean', *The New York Times*, 24 February 2002, <http://www.nytimes.com/2002/02/24/magazine/girls-just-want-to-be-mean.html?pagewanted=all> (last accessed 30 March 2017).

Tasker, Y. (1998), *Working Girls: Gender and Sexuality in Popular Cinema*, London: Routledge.

Thornton, S. (1995), *Club Cultures: Music, Media and Subcultural Capital*, Cambridge: Polity.

Thornton, S. (1997), 'The Social Logic of Subcultural Capital', in K. Gelder and S. Thornton (eds), *The Subcultures Reader*, London: Routledge, pp. 184–92.

Tincknell, E. (2009), 'Feminine boundaries: Adolescence, witchcraft and the supernatural in new gothic cinema and television', in I. Conrich (ed.), *Horror Zone: The Cultural Experience of Contemporary Horror Cinema*, London: I. B. Tauris, pp. 245–58.

Tropiano, S. (2006), *Rebels and Chicks: A History of the Hollywood Teen Movie*, New York: Backstage Books.

Tropiano, S. (2011), *Grease: Music on Film*, Milwaukee: Limelight.

Tzioumakis, Y. (2013), 'Introduction', in Y. Tzioumakis and S. Lincoln (eds), *The Time of Our Lives: Dirty Dancing and Popular Culture*, Detroit: Wayne State University Press, pp. 1–19.

Tzioumakis, Y., and S. Lincoln (eds) (2013), *The Time of Our Lives: Dirty Dancing and Popular Culture*, Detroit: Wayne State University Press.

Walderzak, J. (2016), 'Rebooting the Damsel: the Transformation of the Damsel Archetype in *Spider-Man*, *Superman* and the Batman Films from 1978–2014', *Studies in the Fantastic*, 3, 45–75.

Wallace, K. (2015), 'Teens spend a "mind-boggling" 9 hours a day using media, report says', CNN, 4 November 2015, <http://edition.cnn.com/2015/11/03/health/teens-tweens-media-screen-use-report> (last accessed 30 March 2017).

Waters, M. (ed.) (2011), *Women on Screen: Feminism and Femininity in Visual Culture*, Basingstoke: Palgrave Macmillan.

Wexman, V. W. (2004), 'Masculinity in Crisis: Method Acting in Hollywood', in P. Wojcik (ed.), *Movie Acting: The Film Reader*, London: Routledge, pp. 127–44.

Williamson, M. (2014), 'Let Them All In: The Evolution of the "Sympathetic" Vampire', in L. Hunt, S. Lockyer and M. Williamson (eds), *Screening the Undead: Vampires and Zombies in Film and Television*, London: I. B. Tauris, pp. 71–92.

Wilson, G. M. (1983), *Narration in Light: Studies in Cinematic Point of View*, Baltimore: Johns Hopkins University Press.

Winston-Dixon, W. (2000), '"Fighting, Violence and Everything, That's Always Cool": Teen Films in the 1990s', in W. Winston-Dixon (ed.), *Film Genre 2000: New Critical Essays*, Albany: State University of New York Press, pp. 125–41.

Winston-Dixon, W. (ed.) (2000), *Film Genre 2000: New Critical Essays*, Albany: State University of New York Press.

Wiseman, R. (2002), *Queen Bees & Wannabes: Helping Your Daughter Survive Cliques, Gossip, Boyfriends, and the New Realities of Girl World*, Los Angeles: Three Rivers Press.

Wojcik, P. (ed.) (2004), *Movie Acting: The Film Reader*, London: Routledge.

Wood, R. (2003), *Hollywood from Vietnam to Reagan . . . and Beyond*, New York: Columbia University Press.

Woods, F. (2016), *British Youth Television: Transnational Teens, Industry, Genre*, Basingstoke: Palgrave Macmillan.

Wyatt, D. (2014), 'John Boyega tells Star Wars fans to "get used to" his black Stormtrooper following criticism', *The Independent*, 1 December 2014, <http://www.independent.co.uk/arts-entertainment/films/news/john-boyega-tells-star-wars-fans-to-get-used-to-black-stormtrooper-after-negative-comments-9895316.html> (last accessed 30 March 2017).

Zwarg, C. (2011), '*Easy A*, or Who's Your Daddy?: The Scarlet Letter Once More', *Adaptation*, 4: 2, 219–25.

FILMOGRAPHY

Akira, Katsuhiro Otomo, TMS Entertainment, Japan, 1988.
All About Eve, Joseph L. Mankiewicz, Twentieth Century Fox, USA, 1950.
The Amazing Spider-Man, Marc Webb, Marvel Studios, USA, 2012.
American Graffiti, George Lucas, Universal Pictures, USA, 1973.
American Pie, Greg Weitz, Chris Weitz, Universal Pictures, USA, 1999.
American Werewolf in London, John Landis, Polygram Filmed Entertainment, UK, 1981.
Animal House, John Landis, Universal Pictures, USA, 1978.
Annie, Will Gluck, Sony Pictures, USA, 2014.
L'Arnacoeur, Pascal Chaumeil, Quad Productions, France/Monaco, 2010.
Ascendant, Lee Toland Krieger, Lionsgate, USA, 2017.
Bad Kids Go to Hell, Matthew Spradlin, Bad Kids, USA, 2012.
Bande de Filles, Céline Sciamma, Arte France Cinéma, France, 2014.
Batman, Tim Burton, Warner Brothers, USA, 1989.
Batman Forever, Joel Schumacher, Warner Brothers, USA/UK, 1995.
Beach Party, William Asher, American International Pictures, USA, 1963.
The Beast Within, Philippe Mora, United Artists, USA, 1982.
Beastly, Daniel Barnz, Lionsgate, USA, 2011.
Beautiful Creatures, Richard LaGravenese, Warner Brothers, USA, 2013.
Bend It Like Beckham, Gurinder Chadha, Kintop Pictures, UK/Germany/USA, 2002.
Benefits Street, Channel 4 (2014–).
Beyond Clueless, Charlie Lyne, Kickstarter, UK, 2014.
Biggest Loser, NBC (2008–).
Bill and Ted's Excellent Adventure, Stephen Herek, De Laurentis Entertainment, USA, 1989.
Blackboard Jungle, Richard Brooks, MGM, USA, 1955.
Blade Runner, Ridley Scott, Ladd Company, USA, Hong Kong, UK, 1982.
Blood of Dracula, Herbert L. Strock, American International Pictures, USA, 1957.

Body Snatchers, Abel Ferrara, Warner Brothers, USA, 1993.
Bonnie and Clyde, Arthur Penn, Warner Brothers, USA, 1967.
Boyhood, Richard Linklater, IFC Productions, USA, 2014.
The Breakfast Club, John Hughes, A&M Films, USA, 1985.
Bridesmaids, Paul Feig, Universal Pictures, USA, 2011.
Buffy the Vampire Slayer, Fran Rubel Kuzui, Twentieth Century Fox, USA, 1992.
Buffy the Vampire Slayer, Fox (1997–2003).
Can't Buy Me Love, Steve Rash, Apollo Pictures, USA, 1987.
Carrie, Brian DePalma, United Artists, USA, 1976.
Carrie, Kimberley Peirce, Screen Gems, USA, 2013.
Central Intelligence, Rawson Marshall Thurber, New Line Pictures, USA, 2016.
Cloverfield, Dan Trachtenberg. Paramount Pictures, USA, 2008.
Clueless, Amy Heckerling, Paramount Pictures, USA, 1995.
Crazy Stupid Love, Glenn Ficarra, John Requa, Carousel Productions, USA, 2011.
Crime + Punishment in Suburbia, Rob Schmidt, United Artists, USA, 2000.
Cruel Intentions, Roger Kumble, Columbia Pictures, USA, 1999.
CSI, CBS (2000–15).
Dance of the Dead, Gregg Bishop, Ghosthouse Underground, USA, 2008.
Dance Flick, Damien Dante Wayans, Paramount Pictures, USA, 2009.
Date Movie, Aaron Selzer, New Regency Pictures, USA, 2006.
Dawson's Creek, WB (1998–2003).
Deadly Friend, Wes Craven, Warner Brothers, USA, 1986.
Deal of a Lifetime, Paul Levine, Tomorrow Film Corporation, USA, 1999.
The Diary of a Teenage Girl, Marielle Heller, Caviar Films, USA, 2015.
Diary of the Dead, George A. Romero, Third Rail, USA, 2007.
Dirty Dancing, Emile Ardolino, Great American Films, USA, 1987.
Dirty Dancing: Havana Nights, Guy Ferland, Lionsgate, USA, 2004.
Divergent, Neil Burger, Summit Entertainment, USA, 2014.
Donnie Darko, Richard Kelly, Pandora Cinema, USA, 2001.
The Do-Over, Steven Brill, Happy Madison, USA, 2016.
Dreamgirls, Bill Condon, Paramount Pictures, USA, 2006.
The DUFF, Ari Sandel, CBS Films, USA, 2015.
East of Eden, Elia Kazan, Warner Brothers, USA, 1955.
Easy Rider, Dennis Hopper, Columbia Pictures, USA, 1968.
The Edge of Seventeen, Kelly Fremon Craig, STX Entertainment, USA, 2016.
Election, Alexander Payne, Bona Fide Productions, USA, 1999.
Elephant, Gus van Sant, HBO Films, USA, 2004.
Ender's Game, Gavin Hood, Summit Entertainment, USA, 2013.
Endless Love, Shana Feste, Universal Pictures, USA, 2014.
Everybody Wants Some!! Richard Linklater, Annapurna Pictures, USA, 2016.
The Exorcist, William Friedkin, Warner Brothers, USA, 1973.
Extreme Weight Loss (ABC, 2004–Present).
Fame, Alan Parker, MGM, USA, 1980.
Fame, Kevin Tancharoen, MGM, USA, 2009.
Far from Heaven, Todd Haynes, Focus Features, USA, 2002.
Fast Times at Ridgemont High, Amy Heckerling, Columbia Pictures, USA, 1982.
Ferris Bueller's Day Off, John Hughes, Paramount Pictures, USA, 1986.
A Fistful of Dollars, Sergio Leone, Constantin Film Produktion, Spain/Italy/Germany, 1964.
Five Easy Pieces, Bob Rafelson, Columbia Pictures, USA, 1970.
Flashdance, Adrian Lyne, Paramount Pictures, USA, 1983.
Footloose, Herbert Ross, Paramount Pictures, USA, 1984.

Footloose, Craig Brewer, Paramount Pictures, USA, 2011.
The 40-Year-Old Virgin, Judd Apatow, Universal Pictures, USA, 2005.
Foxfire, Annette Haywood-Carter, Chestnut Hill Productions, USA, 1996.
Freaky Friday, Mark Waters, Walt Disney Pictures, USA, 2003.
Freeway, Matthew Bright, Kushner-Locke Company, USA, 1996.
Friday the 13th, Sean S. Cunningham, Paramount Pictures, USA, 1980.
Friend Request, Simon Verhoeven, Wiedemann & Berg Filmproduktion, Germany, 2016.
G.B.F., Darren Stein, School Pictures, USA, 2013.
Get Over It, Tommy O'Haver, Miramax Entertainment, USA, 2001.
Giant, George Stevens, Warner Brothers, USA, 1956.
Girls Town, Jim McKay, Boomer Pictures, USA, 1996.
The Giver, Phillip Noyce, GEM Entertainment, South Africa/Canada/USA, 2014.
Grease, Randal Kleiser, Paramount Pictures, USA, 1978.
Grown Ups, Dennis Dugan, Columbia Pictures, USA, 2010.
Grown Ups 2, Dennis Dugan, Columbia Pictures, USA, 2013.
Hairspray, Adam Shankman, New Line Pictures, USA/UK, 2007.
Halloween, John Carpenter, Compass International Pictures, USA, 1978.
The Hangover, Todd Phillips, Warner Brothers, USA, 2009.
Happy Days, ABC (1974–84).
Harry Potter and the Chamber of Secrets, Chris Columbus, Warner Brothers, USA/UK, 2002.
Harry Potter and the Deathly Hallows: Part 1, David Yates, Warner Brothers, USA/UK, 2010.
Harry Potter and the Deathly Hallows: Part 2, David Yates, Warner Brothers, USA/UK, 2011.
Harry Potter and the Goblet of Fire, Mike Newell, Warner Brothers, USA/UK, 2005.
Harry Potter and the Half-Blood Prince, David Yates, Warner Brothers, USA/UK, 2009.
Harry Potter and the Order of the Phoenix, David Yates, Warner Brothers, USA/UK, 2007.
Harry Potter and the Philosopher's Stone (UK)/*Harry Potter and the Sorcerer's Stone* (USA), Chris Columbus, Warner Brothers, USA/UK, 2001.
Harry Potter and the Prisoner of Azkaban, Alfonso Cuarón, Warner Brothers, USA/UK, 2004.
Heathers, Michael Lehmann, New World Pictures, USA, 1989.
High Plains Drifter, Clint Eastwood, Universal Pictures, USA, 1973.
High School High, Hart Bochner, TriStar Pictures, USA, 1996.
High School Musical, Kenny Ortega, Walt Disney Pictures, USA, 2006.
High School Musical 2, Kenny Ortega, Walt Disney Pictures, USA, 2007.
High School Musical: Senior Year, Kenny Ortega, Walt Disney Pictures, USA, 2008.
The Host, Andrew Niccol, Chockstone Pictures, USA/Switzerland, 2013.
The Hunger Games, Gary Ross, Lionsgate, USA, 2012.
The Hunger Games: Catching Fire, Francis Lawrence, Lionsgate, USA, 2013.
The Hunger Games: Mockingjay Part 1, Francis Lawrence, Lionsgate, USA, 2014.
The Hunger Games: Mockingjay Part 2, Francis Lawrence, Lionsgate, USA, 2015.
I Know What You Did Last Summer, Jim Gillespie, Columbia Pictures, USA, 1997.
I Still Know What You Did Last Summer, Danny Cannon, Mandalay Entertainment, USA, 1998.
I Was a Teenage Frankenstein, Herbert L Strock, American International Pictures, USA, 1957.
I Was a Teenage Werewolf, Gene Fowler, American International Pictures, USA, 1957.
Idle Hands, Rodman Flender, Columbia Pictures, USA, 1999.

If . . ., Lindsay Anderson, Memorial Enterprises, UK, 1968.
It Follows, David Robert Mitchell, Lighthouse Films, USA 2015.
Jennifer's Body, Karyn Kusama, Twentieth Century Fox, USA, 2009.
Juno, Jason Reitman, Fox Searchlight, USA, 2007.
The Karate Kid, Harald Zwart, Columbia Pictures, USA/China, 2010.
Kick-Ass, Matthew Vaughn, Mary Films, USA/UK, 2010.
Knock on Any Door, Nicholas Ray, Santana Pictures Corporation, USA, 1949.
The Last Picture Show, Peter Bogdanovich, Columbia Pictures, USA, 1971.
Les Misérables, Tom Hooper, Universal Pictures, USA/UK, 2012.
Let Me In, Matt Reeves, Relativity Media, UK/USA, 2010.
Let the Right One In, Tomas Alfredson, Sandrew Metronome, Sweden, 2008.
Life, Anton Corbijn, See-Saw Films, UK/USA, 2015.
Love Is a Many-Splendored Thing, Henry King, Otto Land, Twentieth Century Fox, USA, 1955.
Love Don't Cost a Thing, Troy Byer, Warner Brothers, USA, 2003.
Mad Men, AMC (2007–15).
The Maze Runner, Wes Ball, Twentieth Century Fox, USA, 2014.
Me and Earl and the Dying Girl, Alfonso Gomez-Rejon, Fox Searchlight, USA, 2015.
Mean Girls, Mark Waters, Paramount Pictures, USA/Canada, 2004.
More American Graffiti, Bill L. Norton, Lucasfilm, USA, 1979.
Mustang, Deniz Gamze Erguen, CG Cinéma, France/Germany/Turkey/Qatar, 2015.
Never Been Kissed, Raja Gosnell, USA, 1999.
Night of the Demons, Adam Gierasch, Seven Arts Pictures, USA, 2009.
A Nightmare on Elm Street, Wes Craven, New Line Cinema, USA, 1984.
A Nightmare on Elm Street, Samuel Bayer, New Line Cinema, USA, 2010.
Nosferatu, F. W. Murnau, Jofa-Atelier Berlin-Johannisthal, Germany, 1922.
Not Another Teen Movie, Joel Gallen, Columbia Pictures, USA, 2001.
Now Voyager, Irving Rapper, Warner Brothers, USA, 1942.
O, Tim Blake Nelson, Lionsgate, USA, 2001.
Paranormal Activity, Oren Peli, Solana Films, USA, 2009.
The Parent Trap, Nancy Meyers, Walt Disney Pictures, USA, 1998.
Paris is Burning, Jennie Livingstone, Off White Productions, USA, 1990.
Pitch Perfect, Jason Moore, Brownstone Productions, USA, 2012.
Pitch Perfect 2, Elizabeth Banks, Universal Pictures, USA, 2015.
Pitch Perfect 3, Trish Sie, Universal Pictures, USA, 2017.
Porky's, Bob Clark, Melvin Simon Productions, Canada/USA, 1982.
Powder, Victor Salva, Buena Vista Pictures, USA, 1995.
Pretty in Pink, Howard Deutch, Paramount Pictures, USA, 1986.
Pretty Woman, Garry Marshall, Touchstone Pictures, USA, 1990.
Pride, Matthew Warchus, Pathé Films, UK/France, 2014.
Project Almanac, Dean Israelite, Paramount Pictures, USA, 2015.
Project X, Nima Nourizadeh, Warner Brothers, USA, 2012.
Psycho, Alfred Hitchcock, Shamley Productions, USA, 1960.
Rebel Without a Cause, Nicholas Ray, Warner Brothers, USA, 1955.
Red Dawn, Dan Bradley, FilmDistrict, USA, 2012.
River's Edge, Tim Hunter, Island Pictures, USA, 1986.
Roberta, William A. Seiter, RKO Radio Pictures, USA, 1935.
Rock Around the Clock, Fred Sears, Clover Productions, USA, 1956.
Rogue One: A Star Wars Story, Gareth Edwards, Lucasfilm, USA, 2016.
Romy and Michele's High School Reunion, Mike Birkin, Touchstone Pictures, USA, 1997.
St. Elmo's Fire, Joel Schumacher, Columbia Pictures Corporation, USA, 1985.

Saturday Night Fever, John Badham, Robert Stigwood, USA, 1977.
Say Anything, Cameron Crowe, Gracie Pictures, USA, 1989.
The Scarlet Letter, Victor Sjöström, MGM, USA, 1926.
The Scarlet Letter, Roland Joffé, Allied Stars Ltd., USA, 1995.
Scary Movie, Keenan Ivory Wayans, Dimension Films, USA, 2000.
Scott Pilgrim vs. the World, Edgar Wright, Universal Pictures, USA, UK, Canada, Japan, 2010.
Scream, Wes Craven, Dimension Films, USA, 1996.
The Seventh Son, Sergei Bodrov, Universal Pictures, USA/Canada/UK/China, 2014.
Sex Drive, Sean Anders, Summit Entertainment, USA, 2008.
She's All That, Robert Iscove, Miramax Films, USA, 1999.
The Shining, Stanley Kubrick, Warner Brothers, USA, 1980.
Sin City, Robert Rodriguez, Dimension Films, USA, 2005.
Sixteen Candles, John Hughes, Channel Productions, USA, 1984.
Sleepy Hollow High, Chris Arth, Kevin Summerfield, Scorpio Pictures, USA, 2000.
Smosh: The Movie, Alex Winter, Twentieth Century Fox, USA, 2015.
Society, Brian Yuzna, Re-Animator Productions, USA, 1989.
Spider-Man, Sam Raimi, Marvel Studios, USA, 2002.
Spider-Man 2, Sam Raimi, Marvel Studios, USA, 2004.
Spider-Man 3, Sam Raimi, Marvel Studios, USA, 2007.
Stand by Me, Rob Reiner, Columbia Pictures Corporation, USA, 1986.
Star Wars, George Lucas, Lucasfilm, USA, 1977.
Star Wars: The Empire Strikes Back, George Lucas, Lucasfilm, 1980.
Star Wars: The Force Awakens, JJ Abrams, Lucasfilm, 2015.
Star Wars: Return of the Jedi, George Lucas, Lucasfilm, 1983.
Star Wars Episode I: The Phantom Menace, George Lucas, Lucasfilm, 1999.
Star Wars Episode II: Attack of the Clones, George Lucas, Lucasfilm, 2002.
Star Wars Episode III: Revenge of the Sith, George Lucas, Lucasfilm, 2005.
Superbad, Greg Mottola, Columbia Pictures, USA, 2007.
Tangerine, Sean Baker, Duplass Brothers Productions, USA, 2015.
Tea and Sympathy, Vincente Minnelli, MGM, USA, 1956.
Ten Things I Hate About You, Gil Junger, Touchstone Pictures, USA, 1999.
The Terminator James Cameron, Hemdale, USA/UK, 1984.
The Theory of Everything, James Marsh, Working Title, UK, 2014.
The Trip, Roger Corman, American International Pictures, USA, 1967.
Tomorrowland, Brad Bird, Walt Disney Pictures, USA, 2015.
21 Jump Street, Phil Lord, Christopher Miller, Columbia Pictures, USA, 2012.
Twilight, Catherine Hardwicke, Summit Entertainment, USA, 2008.
The Twilight Saga: Breaking Dawn Part 1, Bill Condon, Summit Entertainment, USA, 2011.
The Twilight Saga: Breaking Dawn Part 2, Bill Condon, Summit Entertainment, USA, 2012.
The Twilight Saga: Eclipse, David Slade, Summit Entertainment, USA, 2010.
The Twilight Saga: New Moon, Chris Weitz, Summit Entertainment, USA, 2009.
Unfriended, Levan Gabriadze, Bazelevs Productions, USA, 2014.
Vampire Academy, Mark Waters, Weinstein Company, USA/UK, 2014.
Victor/Victoria, Blake Edwards, MGM, USA, 1982.
Wall Street, Oliver Stone, Twentieth Century Fox, USA, 1987.
Warm Bodies, Jonathan Levine, Summit Entertainment, USA/Canada, 2013.
Wet Hot American Summer, David Wain, USA Films, USA, 2001.
What Not to Wear, BBC (2001–7); TLC (2003–13).
Whatever It Takes, David Raynr, Columbia Pictures, USA, 2000.

When Harry Met Sally, Rob Reiner, Castle Rock Entertainment, USA, 1989.
Wild in the Streets, Barry Shear, American International Pictures, USA, 1968.
The Wild One, László Benedek, Columbia Pictures, USA, 1953.
Working Girl, Mike Nichols, Twentieth Century Fox, USA, 1988.
X-Men, Bryan Singer, Marvel Studios, USA, 2000.
XOXO, Christopher Louie, Netflix, USA, 2016.
Zero Day, Ben Coccio, Avatar Films, USA, 2003.

INDEX

Actors Studio, 23, 53
adolescence, 3–5, 7–8, 12–15, 19, 24, 37, 69, 71, 90–2, 105, 143, 149–50, 156, 162, 172, 183, 186, 191
Altman, Rick, 16, 38–42, 48, 50, 131
American Graffiti (1973), 5, 14, 106, 108, 110–22, 132, 142, 144n7, 146, 187, 189
American International Pictures, 10–11, 20n4, 39, 150
Animal House (1978), 14–15
Augé, Marc, 79
Austin, J. L., 24–5

Babington, Bruce, 128
Backus, Jim, 29, 34
Bacon, Kevin, 58
Bakhtin, Mikhail, 48
Bande des Filles (2014), 3, 17
Baron, Cynthia, 22
Batman (1989), 53
Beach Boys, 115, 122
Beck, Bernard, 166
Benayoun, Robert, 18
Berger, John, 94
Bergstein, Eleanor, 123–5, 128–9
Bernstein, Jonathan, 69–70

Best, Amy, 65–6, 69, 72, 77, 82, 94, 103n2
Biltereyst, Daniel, 9
Bingham, Dennis, 52–3, 58
Blackboard Jungle (1955), 9–10, 112
Blair Witch Project, The (2001), 174
Bleach, Anthony C., 70
Bode, Lisa, 167
Bourdieu, Pierre, 66–7, 72, 75, 83, 86, 93
Braidotti, Rosi, 147–8, 161, 169, 171
Brando, Marlon, 23, 27, 40, 51–3, 132
Breakfast Club, The (1985), 3, 15, 64, 70, 133, 139–40, 153
Brickman, Barbara, 20n9
Brown, Jeffrey A., 149, 152, 164
Brown, William, 146, 150
Butler, Judith, 4–5, 23–9, 31, 33–5, 38–9, 42–4, 47, 49–50, 52–3, 55, 59, 61, 62, 67–9, 76, 84, 86, 88, 94–5, 99, 102, 147, 188; *see also* performative

Carnicke, Sharon, 22
Chronicle (2012), 4, 6, 149, 172–83, 187, 189

209

class, 3, 5, 17, 19, 27, 35, 38, 62, 66–7, 68, 69–77, 79–80, 85, 88, 90, 96–7, 100–2, 126, 129–30, 146–8, 186, 188
  working class, 66–74, 85, 88, 95, 96–7, 129, 153, 173, 188
  middle class, 4, 28, 30, 34, 64, 66, 68–9, 71, 73–4, 76, 84–5, 88, 91, 93, 95–8, 100, 124, 127, 134, 164, 188
  upper class, 55, 65, 70, 168
Clift, Montgomery, 23, 27
Clover, Carol, 164, 179
Clueless (1995), 3, 16, 80, 90, 134, 139
Cohan, Stephen, 25, 27, 39
Cohen, Jeffrey Jerome, 150
Cohn, Harry, 8
coming-of-age, 3, 16–18, 36–7, 65, 90, 106, 147, 162, 171, 177–8, 186, 188–9
Considine, David, 12–14, 18, 20n7
Constable, Catherine, 19
cool, 53–4, 59, 61, 93, 115, 154
Crazy, Stupid Love (2011), 109, 141
Creed, Barbara, 108, 177–8
Crick, Nicki, 95
Cripps, Thomas, 14
Crompton, Rosemary, 67
cyborg, 148–9, 161, 177, 179
cycle, 1, 4, 9, 10–11, 16, 51, 70, 95, 123, 150, 189; see also genre

Davis, Fred, 37, 106, 124
Dean, James, 5, 9–10, 21, 25, 26, 27, 28, 29, 31, 33–7, 51–2, 61, 114, 184n6
Deleuze, Gilles, 148, 161
delinquency, delinquent, 5, 9, 16, 21–2, 25–9, 32, 36, 40–1, 49, 51, 53–8, 60–1, 70, 113–15, 150
Denby, David, 153
Derrida, Jacques, 169–70
Deutch, Howard, 69, 72
De Vaney, Ann, 15, 69, 71
DeWitt, Jack, 110, 113
Diary of a Teenage Girl, The (2015), 18
Dika, Vera, 122
Dirty Dancing (1987), 6, 20n10, 106, 109, 122–32, 141–3, 189
Divergent (2014–), 17, 20n12, 190
Doherty, Thomas, 1, 8–11, 13–14, 18–19, 20n2, 115

Driscoll, Catherine, 1–3, 8, 10–13, 16, 18–19, 48
Dwyer, Michael D., 106, 110–11, 121–2
Dyer, Richard, 21–2, 35, 39, 43–4, 47, 107, 113, 126, 168, 185

Eastwood, Clint, 58, 187
Easy A (2010), 6, 106, 109, 132–43, 188
Eighties, 132–4, 138–9, 141, 143
Evans, Peter, 128
exploitation, 11–12

Falconer, Pete, 178–9
Fame (1980), 64, 123
Far From Heaven (2002), 113
Farrimond, Katherine, 138
feminine, femininity, 17, 24, 29, 31, 39, 42, 49, 58, 62, 66–9, 71–4, 77, 79, 82–8, 90, 91, 92, 93, 95–100, 102, 109, 117–18, 123, 127, 134, 136, 140, 154, 164–5, 167, 171, 178, 183, 188
feminism, feminist, 16–17, 49, 84, 89, 91, 108–9, 111, 116, 122–5, 127–9, 137, 139, 142, 165, 188
Ferris Bueller's Day Off (1986), 51, 139
Feuer, Jane, 3, 16, 20n10
Fey, Tina, 90–1, 93
Five Easy Pieces (1970), 52, 54, 111
Flanagan, Martin, 152–3, 156
Flashdance (1983), 15, 123–4
Footloose (1984), 15, 51, 58, 124
40-Year-Old Virgin, The (2005), 18
found-footage, 173, 175–6
Freeman, Hadley, 103n8, 110, 123, 133
Freeway (1995), 16–17, 95
Freud, Sigmund, 29–30
Fussell, Paul, 66

Garrett, Roberta, 133, 140
Gelder, Ken, 73
gender, 3–6, 17, 19, 23–33, 35, 38, 40, 42, 44–5, 49–50, 52–5, 59–62, 64–71, 73–9, 84, 88, 90, 95, 97–102, 107–11, 113, 116–19, 122–4, 126, 130, 133–5, 139–40, 142, 146–8, 154, 158, 162, 178–9, 186, 188, 190; see also feminine, masculine
genre, 1–4, 7–8, 10–16, 18–19, 43, 51, 54, 64–5, 69, 80, 91–2, 105–6, 147,

164, 172–3, 185–7, 189–90; *see also* cycle
Gibbs, John, 37
Gill, Rosalind, 108, 137, 140, 188
Gilligan, Sarah, 84, 87
Grainge, Paul, 14, 107, 140
Grant, Cary, 82
Grease (1978), 5, 21, 25, 37–50, 60–1, 64, 85, 137, 139, 186
Guattari, Félix, 148
Gunfighter, The (1950), 114

Hall, Stanley, G., 7–8, 12, 18
Halle, David, 66
Hangover, The (2009), 15
Haraway, Donna, 148, 169
Harry Potter (2001–11), 149–50, 161
Haskell, Molly, 14
Hassler-Forest, Dan, 148, 151–2, 159
Hayles, N. Katherine, 146, 172
Heathers (1989), 5, 16, 21, 25, 50–61, 90, 103n16, 187
Hebdige, Dick, 41, 73
Hegel, Georg, 25
heteronormative, heteronormativity, 3, 31–2, 35, 44, 47–8, 50, 60, 65–6, 70, 71–3, 77, 79–80, 82, 87, 91, 100–2, 158, 171, 188
High Plains Drifter (1973), 58
Hollinger, Hy, 11
homosocial, 32, 43, 56–7, 59, 62
Howard, Ron, 99, 113
Hughes, John, 3, 5, 15, 50–1, 64–5, 69–72, 92, 104n22, 110, 133–4, 139, 185
Hunger Games, The (2012–15), 17, 26, 100, 190
Hutcheon, Linda, 106–8, 112, 117, 142

interpellation, 66, 69, 79–80, 86

Jameson, Fredric, 14, 106–8, 110–11, 113, 118, 142
Jeffers McDonald, Tamar, 125, 136, 165
Jordan, Chris, 132
Jordan, Michael B., 4

Kael, Pauline, 70, 111
Kaplan, Richard, 160
Karlyn, Kathleen Rowe, 93
Kaveney, Roz, 4, 56, 60, 71, 79, 103n16
Kearney, Mary Celeste, 167

King, Barry, 23, 80
Klein, Amanda Ann, 9–10, 177
Klevan, Andrew, 21, 23

Lam, Celia, 174–6, 180–1
Lee, Christina, 110, 133
Let The Right One In (2008), 161
Lévi-Strauss, Claude, 66
Lewis, Jon, 32, 34–5
liminal, liminality, 2–5, 7, 18, 24, 28, 30, 39, 52, 71, 92–3, 125, 146–7, 149, 151, 161, 177, 179, 182, 186, 189
Lohan, Lindsay, 17, 92, 94–5, 98–9
Lovell, Terry, 67
Lucas, George, 5, 14, 110–11
Lyne, Charlie, 189

Mad Men (2007–15), 109, 116, 123
makeover, 5, 49, 66, 69, 81, 84–9, 96, 98, 102, 185–6
Mallory, George, 2
Manovich, Lev, 174
Martin, Adrian, 2, 14–16, 18, 19, 64, 104n19
masculine, masculinity, 5, 22, 24, 26–8, 30–46, 49, 54–5, 57, 61–2, 72, 74, 78, 84–5, 95, 113–14, 117–18, 120, 125, 140, 148, 153–4, 157, 159–61, 164, 168, 172, 186–7, 190
McCann, Graham, 26, 33–6
McKelly, James, 51
McRobbie, Angela, 17, 85–6, 89, 108–9, 128, 162
Mean Girls (2004), 5, 17, 66, 69, 90–102, 104n18, 164–5, 188
Method, the, 23, 28, 59, 186
Meyer, Stephanie, 161, 163, 169
Mineo, Sal, 21, 28, 33, 35–6
mise-en-scène, 2, 22, 33, 48, 118, 126, 156, 165
Moi, Toril, 67
Molloy, Claire, 123
moral panic, 9, 12, 90, 146, 189
Moseley, Rachel, 70, 73, 79, 103n14, 167
Mukherjea, Ananya, 162
musical, 15–16, 37–9, 42–4, 47–8, 50, 65, 123–31
  dual-focus narrative, 38–41, 48, 50
  utopia, 43, 60, 126, 128
Mustang (2015), 3, 17

Naremore, James, 21, 26–9
Negra, Diane, 96–7, 108, 139
Nicholson, Jack, 51–5, 187
nostalgia, nostalgic, 3, 5–6, 14, 38, 69, 76, 105–10, 113, 117, 120–8, 130, 132–4, 136–8, 140, 142–3n3, 151, 158
Not Another Teen Movie (2001), 185–6, 189–91

Orpen, Valerie, 27, 82

Paris is Burning (1990), 68
pastiche, 39, 107, 110, 113, 185
Peberdy, Donna, 22, 25
performance, 3, 5, 15, 19, 21–9, 31–8, 40–1, 45–6, 49–54, 56, 58, 61–2, 68, 70, 74, 84–5, 90, 99–100, 126, 131, 133–8, 187
performative, performativity, 5, 24–6, 61, 67, 188
Petersen, Anne-Helen, 165
Pitch Perfect (2012), 13, 15, 133
Pomerance, Murray, 32
postfeminism, postfeminist, 16–17, 20n11, 69, 89, 91, 96, 102, 107–9, 116, 122–3, 128, 133–40, 142, 162, 167, 188–9
posthuman, 3, 6, 143, 146, 148–52, 158–63, 166, 172–5, 179, 182–3, 189
Pountain, Dick, 53–4, 59, 115, 154
Presley, Elvis, 38, 44
Pretty in Pink (1986), 5, 66, 69–82, 90, 93, 96, 98, 101, 103n6, 136, 188
Pretty Woman (1990), 69, 88
Pride (2014), 106–7
Projansky, Sarah, 92, 100–1, 108
prom, 1, 4–5, 16, 60, 62, 65–6, 69–70, 72–4, 76–84, 87–9, 98, 100–2, 116–17, 136, 163–5, 170–2, 186, 188
Purse, Lisa, 150
Pygmalion, 1, 80–1

Radner, Hilary, 109, 122–3, 128
Ray, Nicholas, 5, 9, 26, 114, 172
Rebel Without a Cause (1955), 5, 9–10, 21, 25–37, 46, 50, 54, 55–6, 60–1, 82, 85, 114, 150, 172, 186
recognition, 25, 28, 59, 76, 95, 97, 147, 189

Redmayne, Eddie, 62n2
respectability, 28, 34, 73–4, 76, 88
Ringrose, Jessica, 17, 91, 95
Ringwald, Molly, 5, 70, 72–3, 99
River's Edge (1986), 51
Roberts, Kimberley, 16, 95
Robins, David, 53–4, 59, 115, 154
rock and roll, 9–11, 44, 112, 115, 127
'Rock Around the Clock', 112
Rock Around the Clock (1956), 10
Rottenberg, Catherine, 74

St. Elmo's Fire (1989), 13
Saturday Night Fever (1977), 14–15, 38, 40, 45, 49
Scarlet Letter, The, 132, 134, 139
Schatz, Thomas, 65, 187
Scheibel, Will, 21
Sedgwick, Eve Kosofsky, 32, 43, 56
Sender, Katherine, 98
Shane (1953), 114
Shary, Timothy, 1–2, 5–8, 10, 12–16, 18–19, 20n8, 25, 35, 48, 56, 63n12, 63n14, 65, 69–70, 103n9, 105, 108, 116, 149–50, 153–4, 173, 190
She's All That (1999), 1, 5, 66, 69, 80–90, 95–6, 98, 101–2, 146, 154, 170, 185
Shining, The (1980), 52
Shumway, David, 112, 120, 127–8, 132
Silverman, Kaja, 73
Simmons, Jerrold, 112
Sixteen Candles (1984), 70, 138–9
Skeggs, Beverley, 67–9, 71, 74, 91, 97, 102
Slater, Christian, 5, 21, 25, 51–4, 58, 187
Smith, Frances, 109–10, 134
Speed, Lesley, 37–8, 48, 105–6, 122
Spider-Man (2002), 6, 149, 151–63, 172, 182, 188–9
Spigel, Lynne, 109, 116, 123
Spooner, Catherine, 163
Spoto, Donald, 26, 33, 63n9
Sprengler, Christine, 125, 133, 143n5
Springer, Claudia, 26–7
Stand By Me (1987), 13, 105
Stanislavsky, Constantin, 23
Star Wars, 4, 111
Stewart, Kristen, 17, 149, 161, 164
Stewart, Susan, 107
Strasberg, Lee, 23
Studlar, Gaylyn, 99

subculture, 2, 41, 52, 73, 75, 114, 162
subgenre, 1, 4, 25–6, 54, 61, 65
Sullivan, Margaret, 98
Superbad (2007), 15
superhero, 133, 149, 151–3, 172–3

Tasker, Yvonne, 68–9, 88
Ten Things I Hate About You (1999), 16, 80
Thornton, Sarah, 75
Tincknell, Estella, 163
Travolta, John, 5, 15, 21, 25, 38, 40, 42, 44–6, 49, 186
Tropiano, Stephen, 6n4
Twilight (2008–12), 6, 17, 149, 161–72, 179, 182–3, 187, 189

Victor/Victoria (1982), 69
virginity, 16, 132, 135–6, 164, 177–9

Walderzak, Joseph, 158
Wall Street (1987), 74
Wexman, Virginia, 21, 26
whiteness, 4, 167–8
Wild One, The (1953), 9, 40, 51, 57
Williamson, Milly, 162
Wilson, George M., 37
Winston-Dixon, Wheeler, 10
Wiseman, Rosalind, 90–1, 93, 103n17
Wood, Natalie, 21, 28, 37
Wood, Robin, 2, 11–12, 80, 122, 185
Working Girl (1988), 69, 88
Wütherich, Rolf, 33

EU representative:
Easy Access System Europe
Mustamäe tee 50, 10621 Tallinn, Estonia
Gpsr.requests@easproject.com

www.ingramcontent.com/pod-product-compliance
Lightning Source LLC
Chambersburg PA
CBHW051058230426
43667CB00013B/2349